❯ Becoming an
ARCHITECT

Other Titles in the Series

Becoming a Digital Designer
Steven Heller and David Womack

Becoming a Graphic Designer, Third Edition
Steven Heller and Teresa Fernandes

Becoming an Interior Designer, Second Edition
Christine M. Piotrowski FASID, IIDA

Becoming Landscape Architect
Kelleann Foster

Becoming a Product Designer
Bruce Hannah

Becoming an Urban Planner
Michael Bayer, AICP, Nancy Frank, Ph.D., AICP, and Jason Valerius, AICP

SECOND EDITION

›Becoming an
ARCHITECT

A Guide to Careers in Design

Lee W. Waldrep, Ph.D.

WILEY

John Wiley & Sons, Inc.

Copyright ©2010 by John Wiley & Sons, Inc. All rights reserved.

Published by John Wiley & Sons, Inc., Hoboken, New Jersey

Published simultaneously in Canada

For general information about our other products and services, please contact our Customer Care Department within the United States at (800) 762-2974, outside the United States at (317) 572-3993 or fax (317) 572-4002.

Wiley also publishes its books in a variety of electronic formats. Some content that appears in print may not be available in electronic books. For more information about Wiley products, visit our web site at www.wiley.com.

Library of Congress Cataloging-in-Publication Data:

Waldrep, Lee W.
  Becoming an architect : a guide to careers in design / by Lee W. Waldrep. -- 2nd ed.
      p. cm.
  ISBN 978-0-470-37210-4 (pbk. : alk. paper)
  1. Architecture--Vocational guidance. I. Title. II. Title: Guide to careers in design.
  NA1995.W35 2010
  720.23--dc22
                                2009014021

Printed in the United States of America

10 9 8 7 6 5 4 3 2 1

To Cassidy, Karli, Anslie,
and my loving wife, Sherry

CONTENTS

❺ The Future of the Architecture Profession   283

FOREWORD

THE URGE TO MAKE AND DO is irresistible. It is the foundation of the desire to become an architect. Yet it is also an inner urge that is better described as a calling than a career choice. To become an architect implies a way of living and working that is not easily defined. Perhaps it is better understood as an exploratory journey that can have many variations from the responsibility to act as the principal orchestrator of a major building project to positions in government. But most of all, to become an architect is to form a way of thinking that influences the ability to see solutions that do not yet exist. This is the inherent power of the discipline of architecture, and it is what makes the study of architecture relevant in even the most difficult economic periods. To consider the study of architecture in this way is to understand that an architectural education is the foundation for many careers that relate not only to the traditional building industry but also to those that extend into a myriad of other choices. Among the choices that readily come to mind are the roles architects have assumed in real estate and business as well as in the entertainment industry and the fields of animation and information technology development. Clearly the choices and opportunities are broad, and the life of an individual who has studied architecture has been substantially enriched.

In this publication, Lee W. Waldrep has provided the insights to guide an individual through the many choices available in a career in architecture. Interviews with individuals who have undertaken this journey are useful not only as inspiration but also because the diversity of careers within the profession is well represented. A life in architecture is defined by opportunity and choice. It can be a journey made confusing by the number of curricular choices and the variety of institutional settings and career options. This publication sheds light on the path. Every potential student of architecture will benefit from the guidance on how to proceed with the selection of a place of study.

Perhaps what best characterizes the nature of this publication is that it represents the fact-finding that should precede an important life decision. The intense search is the beginning of the creative process. After all, the most important design problem the creative individual will ever confront is the design of his or her life.

MARVIN J. MALECHA, FAIA
2009 National President of the American Institute of Architects
Dean of the College of Design at North Carolina State University

PREFACE

IN SECOND GRADE, my ambition was to become a clown. Only later did I realize I wanted to become an architect. One of my older brothers first pursued architecture in college (he later switched to music). A ninth-grade drafting class was my first formal introduction to what I thought was the profession. At the same time, I had the opportunity to meet with an architect in my hometown. In high school, I interned in an architect's office, drafting and making models. All of these experiences helped me decide to pursue architecture in college.

After six years of college, two degrees at two universities, a year as national vice president of the American Institute of Architecture Students (AIAS), and three months working in a firm, I decided architecture was not a good fit for me. However, from my experiences in architecture, I realized that I wanted to help others in their pursuit of becoming an architect. Thus, the idea for this book has been over 20 years in development.

Becoming an Architect: A Guide to Careers in Design will help you navigate the process of becoming an architect. Its purpose is to provide you with an outline of the educational process: a National Architectural Accrediting Board (NAAB) accredited professional degree in architecture, the experience or internship component, and the Architect Registration Exam (ARE). Further, it will help you launch your professional career in architecture.

The first chapter, "The Definition of an Architect," introduces the professional's basic duties and tasks. After reading this chapter, you will be better able to decide if you are suited to become an architect. The chapter outlines the basic skills, characteristics, attitudes, motivations, and aptitudes of architects. Finally, it provides a profile of the architecture profession.

The second chapter, "The Education of an Architect," outlines the education necessary to becoming an architect. It emphasizes that the education of an architect is lifelong and does not end with the receipt of a formal degree.

The first of the chapter's three parts focuses on preparation—the courses you can take and the activities you can pursue to prepare for an architectural education.

The second part provides insight into selecting an appropriate program in architecture. It delineates the three routes to graduation with a professional degree program. Further, it outlines the attributes—individual, institution, and academic unit—to consider when selecting a program. It also lists resources to seek when making this crucial decision.

The third part of the chapter describes the typical architecture curriculum as outlined by the criteria and conditions set forth by the NAAB, the body that accredits degree programs in architecture.

As training is a required element of becoming an architect, the third chapter, "The Experience of an Architect," concentrates on gaining experience. First, it discusses strategies to gain experience while in school through part-time, summer, or cooperative education opportunities. It outlines programs at various universities that expose students to the real world of architecture. An additional portion uses the acronym A.R.C.H.I.T.E.C.T. in support of the search for positions that provide useful experience. The chapter also provides a basic overview of the Intern Development Program (IDP), a required program in almost all 50 states for documenting your experiences under the supervision of a licensed architect. It outlines the training requirements, the advisory system, and the recordkeeping system. Further, the chapter introduces the requirements and process of the ARE.

The fourth chapter, "The Careers of an Architect," outlines the career designing process (assessing, exploring, decision making, and planning) and the careers available to graduates of an architectural education—both traditional and nontraditional.

Finally, the fifth chapter, "The Future of the Architecture Profession," provides insight into the future of the profession of architecture. Terms associated with the future of the profession are outlined and, along with those focused on throughout the book, answer the question, "What do you see as the future for the architecture profession?"

Career profiles of architecture students, interns, educators, and practitioners appear throughout the book and are a wonderful resource for personal stories. Some profiles highlight the traditional path of an architect within a private architecture firm, while others describe related settings in which an architect might work—corporations, government agencies, and education and research. A series of pointed questions related to the profession and the responses of those individuals profiled are also distributed throughout.

The first of three appendixes lists resources for further information. Note especially the first five associations listed: the American Institute of Architects (AIA), AIAS, Association of Collegiate Schools of Architecture (ACSA), NAAB, and National Council of Architectural Registration Boards (NCARB). Also included are career-related associations and other useful resources, including websites, and recommended reading.

The second appendix lists institutions offering NAAB/Canadian Architectural Certification Board (CACB-CCCA) accredited programs in the United States and Canada. The third appendix lists those students, interns, and professionals profiled in the book.

As you will soon discover, becoming an architect is a satisfying and worthwhile endeavor. Enjoy the process of becoming and being an architect, as it will provide a long and meaningful career path for your life.

LEE W. WALDREP, Ph.D.

(ACKNOWLEDGMENTS)

WHEN I COMPLETED my doctoral dissertation in 1993, I stated that authoring it was the closest I would ever come to designing architecture. This statement remains true, but in terms of work, authoring this book far exceeds writing my dissertation. I still may never design a residence or a skyscraper, but I hope this book helps future architects design their careers.

First and foremost, I would like to acknowledge the support of my family—Sherry, my wife, and my triplet daughters, Cassidy, Karli, and Anslie. Without their willingness to let me escape from family obligations, I would not have completed this project. Now that the book is complete, I am ready to play Monopoly.

As well, I wish to express my appreciation to the students, interns, educators, and architects profiled throughout this book, many of whom I have known throughout my career (see Appendix C). Without exception, all were more than willing participants to this project and are as much the authors of this book as I am. Thanks are also due to Brian P. Kelly, associate professor in the Architecture Program of the School of Architecture, Planning, and Preservation at the University of Maryland, along with its faculty, staff, and students. Additional thanks are extended to my colleagues, Andrea Rutledge, NAAB executive director, and the staff and board of NAAB.

Special kudos to the following individuals: Jenny Castronuovo, who more than assisted me with the collection of images for the book; Margaret DeLeeuw, Shawna Grant, Allison Wilson, Michelle Rinehart, and Deana Moore, who provided insight as the manuscript was being written; and Michal Seltzer, for mocking up the cover for daily inspiration. Also, I wish to express my appreciation to Dr. Kathryn H. Anthony, a special friend who knows all too well the struggles and joys of authoring a book. My appreciation is also extended to Grace H. Kim, AIA, a friend who first recommended to John Wiley & Sons that I would be a good author for this project. She was also instrumental in providing images.

I wish to express my appreciation to John Czarnecki, my editor at Wiley, for first contacting me about the idea for the book and guiding me throughout the process. My thanks are also extended to the others with whom I worked at Wiley.

Finally, I extend appreciation and love to my parents, Carl E. and Marsha L. Waldrep, who will never see the results of my labor but certainly were an inspiration to me.

1 The Definition of an Architect

He looked at the granite. To be cut, he thought, and made into walls. He looked at a tree. To be split and made into rafters. He looked at a streak of rust on the stone and thought of iron ore under the ground. To be melted and to emerge as girders against the sky. These rocks, he thought, are here for me; waiting for the drill, the dynamite and my voice; waiting to be split, ripped, pounded, reborn, waiting for the shape of my hands will give to them.

AYN RAND, The Fountainhead[1]

AFTER READING THE PRECEDING TEXT from *The Fountainhead* by Ayn Rand, what are your thoughts and feelings? Can you relate to the main character, Howard Roark, in this passage? Are you overcome with the possibilities of creating with the materials around you?

Do you want to be an architect? Do you wish to study architecture? If your answer is "Yes" to any of these questions, this book is for you.

What is the definition of an architect? *The American Heritage Dictionary*[2] defines *architect* as:

1. One who designs and supervises the construction of buildings or other structures. *är-ki-tekt*, n. [MF architecte, fr. L architectus, fr. Gk architekton master builder, fr. Archi- + tekton builder]

Of course, this definition simply scratches the surface. Becoming and being an architect are much more.

◀ Newseum, Washington, DC. Architect: Polshek Partnership Architects LLP.
PHOTOGRAPHER: LEE W. WALDREP, Ph.D.

What Do Architects Do?

People need places in which to live, work, play, learn, worship, meet, govern, shop, eat—private and public spaces, indoors and out; rooms, buildings, and complexes; neighborhoods and towns; suburbs and cities. Architects, professionals trained in the art and science of building design and licensed to protect public health, safety, and welfare, transform these needs into concepts and then develop the concepts into building images that can be constructed by others.

In designing buildings, architects communicate with and assist those who have needs—clients, users, and the public as a whole—and those who will make the spaces that satisfy those needs—builders and contractors, plumbers and painters, carpenters, and air conditioning mechanics.

Whether the project is a room or a city, a new building or the renovation of an old one, architects provide the professional services—ideas and insights, design and technical knowledge, drawings and specifications, administration, coordination, and informed decision making—whereby an extraordinary range of functional, aesthetic, technological, economic, human, environmental, and safety factors are melded into a coherent and appropriate solution to the problems at hand.

This is what architects are, conceivers of buildings. What they do is to design, that is, supply concrete images for a new structure so that it can be put up. The primary task of the architect, then as now, is to communicate what proposed buildings should be and look like. . . . The architect's role is that of mediator between the client or patron, that is, the person who decides to build, and the work force with its overseers, which we might collectively refer to as the builder.

SPIRO KOSTOF[3]

Parthenon, Athens, Greece. PHOTOGRAPHER: R. LINDLEY VANN.

But how does an architect truly design? It begins with a client with the need for a building, a project. To design and build this project, an architect follows the architectural design process. This process begins with the schematic design phase, with the architect first gaining an understanding of the scope of the project to be built from the client. With the program determined, the architect develops preliminary concepts and ideas for the project and presents these to the client for approval or revision. In addition, the architect researches zoning or other restrictions. Next is the design development phase.

In design development, the initial concepts and ideas are further refined. The architect begins to determine the building materials of the project as well as detailing the mechanical, electrical, plumbing, and structural aspects of the project. The architect will formally present the project, at this stage of development, to the client for approval. Next is the construction document phase.

During construction document phase, the architect produces detailed drawings and specifications of the project to be used for construction. These construction documents include all pertinent information necessary for construction. Once completed, the construction documents (CDs) are sent to potential contractors for bidding. Next is the bid or negotiation phase.

In preparation for actual construction, the architect prepares the bid documents. The bid documents include a number of documents for potential contractors to use in preparing a bid (cost estimate) to construct the project. Once bids are received from contractors, the architect will assist the client in evaluating and selecting the winning proposal. In the end, a contract is awarded to the selected bidder, which allows construction to begin. Next is the construction phase.

During construction, the architect's responsibilities will vary depending on the agreement with the client, but most commonly the architect will assist the contractor to construct the project as specified in the construction documents. As questions or issues arise on the construction site, the architect is there to address them. Depending on the issue, the architect may be required to issue additional drawings.

Thus, an architect must be equipped with a number of talents and skills to take a project from its initial idea to final construction. In the profession, almost all projects are undertaken by an architectural firm consisting of teams of architects, related professionals, and consultants, although there may be some smaller projects, usually residential, that might be led by a sole architect.

Why Architecture?

Why do you desire to become an architect? Have you been building with Legos since you were two? Did a counselor suggest architecture to you because of a strong interest and skills in mathematics and art? Or are there other reasons? Aspiring architects cite a love of drawing, creating, and designing; a desire to make a difference in the community; an aptitude for mathematics and science; or a connection to a family member in the profession. Whatever your reason, are you suited to become an architect?

Is Architecture for You?

How do you know if the pursuit of architecture is right for you? Those within the profession suggest that if you are creative or artistic and good in mathematics and science, you may have what it takes to be a successful architect. However, Dana Cuff, author of *Architecture: The Story of Practice,* suggests it takes more:

> There are two qualities that neither employers nor educators can instill and without which, it is assumed, one cannot become a "good" architect: dedication and talent.
>
> DANA CUFF[4]

Because of the breadth of skills and talents necessary to be an architect, you may be able to find your niche within the profession regardless. It takes three attributes to be a successful architecture student—intelligence, creativity, and dedication—and you need any two of the three. Also, your education will develop your knowledge base and design talents.

Unfortunately, there is no magic test to determine if becoming an architect is for you. Perhaps the most effective way to determine if you should consider becoming an architect is to experience the profession firsthand. Ask lots of questions and recognize that many related career fields might also be appropriate for you.

For the architect must, on the one hand, be a person who is fascinated by how things work and how he can make them work, not in the sense of inventing or repairing machinery, but rather in the organization of time–space elements to produce the desired results; on the other hand, he must have an above average feeling for aesthetics and quite some ability at drawing, painting, and the visual arts in general.

EUGENE RASKIN[5]

What is architecture?

❯ The creation of space.

John W. Myefski, AIA, Principal, Myefski Cook Architects, Inc.

❯ Architecture is the physical and spiritual transformation of chaos into order, darkness into light, and space into place.

Nathan Kipnis, AIA, Principal, Nathan Kipnis Architects, Inc.

❯ As a creative science, architecture is the marriage of art and science.

Lisa A. Swan, Residential Designer, Design Forward

❯ Architecture is the design and manipulation of the built environment to create a sense of place. It is a confluence of science and art that addresses programmatic and aesthetic requirements within the constraints of budget, schedule, life safety, and social responsibility.

Robert D. Roubik, AIA, LEED AP, Project Architect, Antunovich Associates Architects and Planners

❯ To me, architecture is anything that can be designed— a chair, a light fixture, a website, a logo, a building, or a city.

William J. Carpenter, Ph.D., FAIA, Associate Professor, Southern Polytechnic State University; President, Lightroom

❯ Architecture is an attempt to consciously control the built environment through the balanced application of art and science. Those of us who practice architecture orchestrate economics, politics, art, and technology exclusively to create objects that impact the physical world we inhabit.

W. Stephen Saunders, AIA, Principal, Eckenhoff Saunders Architects, Inc.

❯ Architecture is the design and construction of forms to create space.

Margaret DeLeeuw, Marketing Director, Celli-Flynn Brennan Architects & Planners

What is architecture? (Continued)

❯ Architecture is the result of all that is conceived, planned, and created by an architect. It involves taking leadership in the process of working with a client, societal, or business challenge, identifying and defining the specific problems and opportunities for that challenge, and then synthesizing them into the most basic components and developing solution alternatives. Architecture is the result of using this process under the direction of a technically knowledgeable professional.

Randall J. Tharp, RA, Senior Vice-President, A. Epstein and Sons International, Inc.

❯ Architecture is the built environments that shape the daily lives of people.

Grace H. Kim, AIA, Principal, Schemata Workshop, Inc.

❯ Architecture is a passion, a vocation, a calling. It has been described as a social art and an artful science. Architecture creates space and formalizes relationships in the built environment. Architecture enriches and affects lives; it is both personal and public. Architecture provides great opportunity yet requires extreme discipline, restraint, and skill. Creativity, problem solving, a deep understanding of the objectives and underlying issues, and sensitivity to the effected environments (physical, social, economic) are key traits. Architecture creates form and inspires the future.

Catherine McNeel Florreich, Associate AIA, Architectural Intern, Eley Guild Hardy Architects, PA

❯ Architecture is the special place, the extraordinary space that enriches our lives.

Diane Blair Black, AIA, Vice-President, RTKL Associates, Inc.

❯ Architecture is the forming of space and program into an aesthetic system.

Douglas Garofalo, FAIA, Professor, University of Illinois at Chicago; President, Garofalo Architects

❯ Architecture is a collaborative process, the result of which is a building, a series of buildings, or interventions in the landscape that enrich the environment.

Lynsey Jane Gemmell, AIA, Project Manager/Associate, Holabird & Root

❯ Architecture is construction that embraces the aesthetic, symbolic, tectonic, and cultural characteristics that best describe a particular place, people, and epoch.

Robert M. Beckley, FAIA, Professor and Dean Emeritus, University of Michigan

❯ Architecture is the shelter for human existence. The process of architecture is the blend of art and science.

Patricia Saldana Natke, AIA, Principal and President, Urban Works, Ltd.

❯ Architecture is the art of designing buildings and spaces within a given set of parameters. Those parameters may include the programmatic needs of the project, the client's budget, building code regulations, and the inherent properties of the materials being used. Great architecture finds the best solution to a design problem by using both creativity and practicality. Part sculpture, part environmental psychology, part construction technology, architecture is the combination of many separate forces into a harmonic whole.

Carolyn G. Jones, AIA, Director, Callison

❯ Architecture is a blend of art and science for the creation of spaces and places that elevate the human spirit.

Kathryn H. Anthony, Ph.D., Professor, University of Illinois at Urbana-Champaign

❯ Architecture is the synthesis of art and science utilized to develop a solution to a challenge in the built environment.

Elizabeth Kalin, Architectural Intern, Studio Gang Architects

New York City, View from Empire State Building.
PHOTOGRAPHER: MICHAEL R. MARIANO, AIA.

❯ Architecture is a method to solve issues relevant to a progressing contemporary culture.

Brad Zuger, Architectural Designer, Shanghai MADA, S.P.A.M.

❯ More than a building, architecture is beauty and function in form.

Christopher J. Gribbs, Associate AIA; Senior Director, American Institute of Architects

❯ Architecture is everything. It is the house in which one lives; it is the office in which one works. Architecture is the hospital in which one watches loved ones die or recover. It is the church in which people marry the people they love. Architecture is the movie theater where you had your first date. Architecture is the room you grew up in, on that quiet street in the country. It is the apartment building you lived in with your first college roommate. It is the playground where you first encountered the merry-go-round.

Architecture is in every memory you will ever have, because it is everything and everywhere. One might dare to ask, "What is *not* architecture?" At its purest, architecture is the form that follows the function.

Ahkilah Z. Johnson, Chief of Staff Investment Services, Cherokee Northeast, LLC

❯ Architecture is that form of building and place-making that elevates and illuminates the meaning of being human.

Joseph Bilello, Ph.D., AIA, Professor and Former Dean, Ball State University

❯ As the Greek origin of the word defines it, architecture is both art and science. It is the practice of bringing these two objectives together in a manner of achieving "form, function, and design."

Kathy Denise Dixon, AIA, NOMA, Associate Principal, Arel Architects, Inc.

❯ Architecture is the thoughtful and expert integration of aesthetics, function, and usability in buildings and facilities.

Lois Thibault, RA, Coordinator of Research, U.S. Architectural and Transportation Barriers Compliance Board (Access Board)

❯ Architecture is the art and science of planning and designing structures and environments to house the activities of humans.

H. Alan Brangman, AIA, University Architect, Georgetown University

What is architecture? (Continued)

❭ Grounded by a broad understanding, architecture is the conscious shaping of the mental and physical forces and relations within a specific environment to sustain and celebrate life. When entering an exemplary piece of architecture, our senses are heightened, we slow, pause, and upon reflection we are fundamentally changed.

Max Underwood, AIA, Professor, Arizona State University

❭ Architecture is the structuring of the built environment for the people who use it to solve their problems and needs including but not limited to the need for organization, association, separation, and shelter in a way that is inspirational, pleasing to the eye, generally is responsibly built (on budget and schedule), is sensitive to the environment in which it is found, (community and nature), is built to withstand the test of time, and improves their quality of life.

Ambassador Richard N. Swett (r), FAIA, President, Swett Associates, Inc.

❭ Architecture is the design of the built environment through the programming of needs, three-dimensional design, and the application of appropriate building technologies.

Eric Taylor, Associate AIA, Photographer, Taylor Design & Photography, Inc.

❭ Architecture is the art of building. Simply put, architecture is those buildings or places that inspire us. Architecture is also about the act of place-making, or making one feel comfortable. Architecture is not a slave to fads or trends. It is timeless and ages gracefully. God created a beautiful earth. Man has been charged with the stewardship of the earth. Good architecture enhances God's creation.

Edward J. Shannon, AIA, Director of Design, Benvenuti & Stein Design, Inc.

❭ Architecture is the immediate interface between people's lives and the societal frameworks in which

Interior, Johnson Wax Building, Racine, Wisconsin. Architect: Frank Lloyd Wright. PHOTOGRAPHER: R. LINDLEY VANN.

they operate. It can facilitate opportunity, be used as a tool of oppression or reside in an arbitrary and benign middle ground.

Wayne A. Mortensen, Associate AIA, NASW, Project Manager/Urban Designer, H3 Studio; Lecturer, Washington University

❭ Architecture is the creation of habitable space where social interactions and individual functions can take place.

Michelle Hunter, Lead Designer, Mark Gould Architect

❭ Architecture makes a difference in the lives of people.

Lynn N. Simon, AIA, LEED AP, President, Simon & Associates, Inc.

❭ Architecture is about the creative process of making and involves the many disciplines of craft and design. It touches all of us, informing and shaping the experiences of our lives in rich and meaningful ways. We cannot underestimate the human experience as part of the designed world we live in.

Barbara Crisp, Principal, bcrisp llc

❭ Architecture is the creation and communication of ideas. It is the creative and technical process for the design, management and construction of the built environment. It represents a collaboration and coordination with a broad range of experts to get a building built.

Robert D. Fox, AIA, IIDA, Principal, FOX Architects

❭ Architecture is the combination of art and science to design spaces, whether enclosed or open to the elements, for the protection, use, and enjoyment of others.

F. Michael Ayles, AIA, Principal, Business Development, Antinozzi Associates

❭ Architecture is many different things to people. To the vast majority of the population, architecture is that which allows their lives to take place in comfort and is, for the most part, unknowingly experienced. To those who are educated in architecture,

it's an eclectic field that brings together aesthetics, engineering, and culture.

Allison Wilson, Bachelor of Science Graduate, University of Maryland

❭ Beyond buildings, architecture is about the relationships between materials and among things more than it is about the things themselves. As such, architecture is primarily about prepositions: above, below, between, within, among, through, under, etc. This is partly why Renaissance painters made such good architects, but it is also what I think the contemporary painter/architect Sam Mockbee was talking about when he said, "Architecture has to be about more than just architecture." Being based on relationships, architecture is also fundamentally about human interaction.

Casius Pealer, J.D., Assistant General Counsel (Real Estate), District of Columbia Housing Authority; Cofounder, ARCHVoices

❭ Space, whether physical or virtual, that can support a thought.

Amy Yurko, AIA, Founder/Director, BrainSpaces

❭ From my perspective, the process of creating architecture is puzzle solving on a majestic scale. This translates into the critical thinking and problem-solving aspects of the profession that architecture programs are so good at teaching and that our clients rely on us for as we help them accomplish their goals.

The architecture project/puzzle contains an infinite number of variables. Some are static; some are dynamic. The attributes of some are known and universally understood; for others, the attributes are unique to the person investigating them or experiencing them. The puzzle is constantly evolving, and no one has control over it! Most interesting of all, the result of the architecture project/puzzle is never complete, and no one ever sees it the same as someone else or even experiences it themselves in the same way.

Kathryn T. Prigmore, FAIA, Senior Project Manager, HDR Architecture, Inc.

What is architecture? (Continued)

❭ Architecture is the fully imagined design and the realization that comes to be.

Jennifer Jaramillo, Architectural Intern, Dekker/Perich/ Sabatini, LLC

❭ Architecture is the process of creating useful, efficient, and attractive structures.

David R. Groff, Master of Architecture Candidate, Virginia Tech

❭ Architecture is the shaping of environments, real or imagined, that affect the way people think, feel, act, or respond to their surroundings. In this context, architecture can be both a noun and a verb; in other words, it can be the painting itself, or the act of painting.

Architecture appeals to the senses. It can comfort us or intimidate us. It can make us feel welcome and home, or alone and cold. Architecture can be as much about the intended desires of the designer's imagination or the unintended consequences delivered when architecture is not considered more fully in its proper context. Real or imagined, the environment we live, work, and play in is directly influenced by the architecture that surrounds us. In essence, architecture is humanity.

Shannon Kraus, AIA, MBA, Vice-President, HKS Architects

❭ Practical and artistic development of our environment. Winston Churchill once said, to paraphrase, what we build in stone we remember, so at some level architecture is about the creation of the making of memories and developing a sense of place.

Mary Katherine Lanzillotta, FAIA, Partner, Hartman-Cox Architects

❭ The development of architecture is as much a design process as it is a simulation of inhabitable space(s) and building vocabularies. I will go as far to say that architecture is not architecture unless it was developed by means of an analytical process.

Thomas Fowler, IV, AIA, Professor and Director, Collaborative Integrative-Interdisciplinary Digital-Design Studio (CIDS), California Polytechnic State University—San Luis Obispo

❭ Architecture is both a process and a physical construct. As a process it is the translation of the intangible (the vision or dreams of the client, the building program, etc.) into the tangible (functional space). As a physical construct it can manifest as the molding of space to meet the practical needs of shelter. However, architecture is more than this definition suggests. As John Ruskin once proposed, "the study of architecture is the study of all things; architecture is everything."

Margaret R. Tarampi, Associate AIA, Doctor of Philosophy Candidate, University of Utah

▼ Stonehenge, England. PHOTOGRAPHER: KARL DU PUY.

Past Is Prologue

MARY KATHERINE LANZILLOTTA, FAIA

Partner, Hartman-Cox Architects

Washington, DC

Why and how did you become an architect?

❯ Having an idea develop into drawings and then a building where one lives or works is thrilling. My parents added onto our home and then built a new home when I was a child. The reality of this experience and living through the construction was very exciting. I knew by the time I was a teenager I wanted to find some way to be involved in the building process.

Why and how did you decide on which school to attend for your architecture degree? What degree(s) do you possess?

❯ As I was trying to decide whether to pursue engineering or architecture, the University of Virginia (UVA) offered a summer program for high school students on the "grounds" in Charlottesville. My parents agreed to let me attend the program to determine if architecture was a good fit for me. As part of the program, I attended morning lectures on history, visited job sites and then had a "studio" program in the afternoon. The experience was very positive, and I knew I wanted to pursue the bachelor of science in architecture at UVA.

After four years and a dozen or so architectural history courses at UVA, I knew I wanted to be more involved with the preserving the built environment. For graduate school, I only applied to programs that offered a combination of architecture and preservation; I completed a Master of Architecture

Lincoln Gallery, Smithsonian Donald W. Reynolds Center for American Art and Portraiture. Smithsonian Institution, Washington, DC. Architect: Hartman-Cox Architects. PHOTOGRAPHER: BRYAN BECKER.

at the University of Pennsylvania and a Certificate in Historic Preservation.

What has been your greatest challenge as an architect?

❯ Reminding myself to stay focused on the big picture and not to get bogged down in the details. To do this often requires me to step back and think creatively about how to solve the challenge in a different way.

As a partner at Hartman-Cox Architects, what are your primary responsibilities and duties?

❯ One primary responsibility is to pursue, secure, and execute good work. As one who is interested in preservation, I tend to look for more work in this same area but am also open to exploring new opportunities. My other duties are "as assigned" as we do not have rigidly set roles but look to see what is needed and where.

A handful of Hartman-Cox Architects projects relate to historic preservation, adaptive reuse, and rehabilitation. How and why are these issues important to architecture?

❯ Most of the Hartman-Cox projects relate to providing a continuity of the sense of place. This can be achieved by preserving existing buildings, adding onto existing buildings in a sensitive and appropriate manner, or by building a new building which respects its neighbors and reinterprets the sense of place. Our firm believes in building timeless buildings of their place. The continuity of history is important culturally as there are specific reasons why particular materials are used in some locations and not in others and, in the process, they leave us with a lesson about the use of local materials and technology. In the case of the Old Patent Office building, now the Smithsonian Donald W. Reynolds Center for American Art and Portraiture,

▼ Smithsonian Donald W. Reynolds Center for American Art and Portraiture. Smithsonian Institution, Washington, DC. Architect: Hartman-Cox Architects. PHOTOGRAPHER: BRYAN BECKER.

Luce Foundation Center for American Art. Smithsonian Donald W. Reynolds Center for American Art and Portraiture. Smithsonian Institution, Washington, DC. Architect: Hartman-Cox Architects. PHOTOGRAPHER: BRYAN BECKER.

we can see the evolution of much of the nineteenth century technology and architectural history from the restraint and classicism of Robert Mills with the solid masonry vaults to the exuberance and mannerism of Adolph Cluss as seen in the Luce Foundation Center. Buildings also share the cultural memories of place from the soldier's carving his initials in the shutter of a window to the inaugural ball of President Lincoln.

Buildings also embody an enormous amount of energy, and to reuse or renovate buildings appropriately to keep them in use is a respon-

sible approach. In 1958, the General Services Administration considered tearing down the Old Patent Office Building that occupies two city blocks and turning the site into a parking lot. The amount of wasted materials would have been vast and the history would have been lost.

What is the most/least satisfying part of your career as an architect?

❯ The most satisfying experiences are watching people in the buildings and see how they are enjoying the building and see if they are experiencing it in the manner we expected. Of course, if when you find the public is not as pleased with some aspect, these are the most instructive moments. All architects should visit their own buildings to see what works and what does not so they can improve upon their experience.

Can you provide details on Architecture in the Schools and why it is important for you to serve the profession in this way?

❯ A program of the Washington Architectural Foundation, Architecture in the Schools (AIS) teams volunteer architects with pre-K to twelfth grade classroom teachers to use architecture and design concepts to reinforce learning standards across the curriculum. Established in 1992, the Architecture in the Schools program originated in the District of Columbia and expanded to the greater Washington metropolitan area in 2002.

Students in the program (1) learn problem-solving techniques, (2) explore different ways to express their ideas, (3) examine their environment through the classroom projects they design, (4) apply abstract concepts to real-life scenarios, (5) develop a cross-curricular understanding of subject matter, and (6) cultivate civic awareness of how the children can influence their environment.

Load Testing Columns, Oyster Elementary School Third Grade, Washington, DC. Washington Architectural Foundation, Architecture in the Schools. COURTESY OF THE WASHINGTON ARCHITECTURAL FOUNDATION.

Since its inception over 320 schools and over 8,400 students have participated in the program. The Architecture in the Schools program has expanded to include professional development programs for teachers to learn more about how to integrate design and architecture into their curriculums and a series of architectural walking tours for children in Washington, DC neighborhoods.

The experience of opening the eyes of children to the world around them and having them think critically about choices in their neighborhoods has had a profound impact on me. The opportunity to share my understanding of design and architecture with these students has forced me to learn to speak about architecture in a readily understandable way. The students' questions helped me to think critically about how to present ideas in a new approachable manner. Further, these students will grow up and become homeowners or members of a citizen's advisory committee. When this next generation has to think critically

about a design issue that may impact or influence their communities, I hope they will have some frame of reference on which to base their decisions.

Who or what experience(s) has been a major influence on your career?

❯ Without setting out to do so, I have found myself gravitating toward projects that have an educational theme. The preservation projects are educational in what and how the buildings are preserved and the missions of the organizations themselves whether it is preserving the Lincoln or Jefferson Memorials or renovating the UNC Morehead Planetarium Building. The Architecture in the Schools program is more directly educational, but the program attempts to encourage children to look at their world and think critically about it while they are still open minded.

My current partners, Warren J. Cox, Lee Becker, and Graham Davidson, and emeritus partner,

George Hartman and all of the members of the Hartman-Cox team over the years particularly those who took the time to help me understand what was required and patiently answered all of my questions.

My parents encouraged me to explore architecture both as a young child by building and, then, as a student when I wanted to pursue architecture as a career. My parents also were role models for getting involved in and giving back to the community through their own service.

The hundreds of Architecture in the Schools volunteers who have given so freely of their time to share their knowledge of architecture and the built environment with the schoolchildren in DC and the metropolitan area to bring AIS program to life in the schools.

Rolaine Copeland, Hon. AIA, was the Architecture in Education program director at the Foundation for Architecture in Philadelphia and who encouraged me to start the Architecture in the Schools program in DC.

Daring to Lead

SHANNON KRAUS, AIA, MBA

Vice-President

HKS Architects

Dallas, Texas

Why and how did you become an architect?

❭ I became an architect simply because it was a lifelong goal. A life's goal achieved. A passion delivered. It was something I set my mind on from the time I was in fourth grade when the only class I had true interest in was art; my mother had the vision to open my mind to architecture as an occupation that would fit my interests.

It was through art and imagination that I could express myself. I did this through the pictures I would draw, the models I would build, and the forts I would enlist the neighborhood kids to help construct. From there, becoming an architect simply felt right.

However, in the end I did become an architect to make a difference. While I pursued architecture because that is where I could express myself, I have found that what I enjoy most about this amazing profession is having the ability to work with diverse groups of people to solve complex problems so that others can fulfill their dreams—thus really making a difference by turning vision to reality.

From my first day on campus at Southern Illinois University (SIU) to gaining registration as an architect in the state of Texas, my journey took approximately 12 years—four years of undergraduate work, one year as American Institute of Architecture Students (AIAS) vice president, three years in graduate school for the Master of Business Administration (M.B.A.) and Master of Architecture, and four years of internship at RTKL finished concurrently with the nine exams spread over 18 months.

Ahuja Medical Center, Beachwood, Ohio. Architects: HKS Architects and Array Healthcare Facilities Solutions. PHOTOGRAPHER: SHANNON KRAUS, AIA, MBA.

Why and how did you decide on which school to attend for your architecture degree? What degree(s) do you possess?

❯ Coming out of McArthur High School in the central Illinois town of Decatur, with the ambition to pursue architecture, I found myself at a small, but terrific undergraduate program at Southern Illinois University at Carbondale. How I ended up there was primarily the result of not enough information, and economics. They had a four-year architecture program, and it was less expensive than most any other school in the area. What I did not know was that the reason it was less expensive was because their architecture program was not accredited. In the end, this turned to be a blessing—SIU was one of the best, if not luckiest, decisions I made.

Through SIU I learned the art of architecture. I learned to think, draw, paint, sketch, and resolve complex variables into rational solutions. While not known for design, the school was heavily based in the fundamentals, including learning how buildings go together—more so than most schools cover. My education at SIU provided me with the best foundation for becoming an architect I could have asked for.

For graduate school I ultimately chose the University of Illinois at Urbana-Champaign. Having just completed my term as national vice president of the American Institute of Architecture Students, a full-time job in DC following my undergraduate studies, I came to realize that the single biggest gap in the amazingly rich and diverse education that architecture provides is business.

As such, I chose to apply to universities where I could also attend business school—a decision that ultimately led into my acceptance into the school of architecture and the school of business at the University of Illinois, where I graduated summa cum laude with a Master in Business Administration, and a Master in Architecture. Where the M.B.A. equipped me to think more holistically about business, and refined my communications skills, the M.Arch. filled in the remaining gaps with a curriculum more focused on design and design theory.

Reflecting back on how I chose the schools I did, I do believe that the profession does not have an adequate guidance system for assisting students interested in architecture. I say this because in many ways the school you choose will ultimately go a long way towards determining the type of professional you become.

What has been your greatest challenge as an architect?

❯ As an architect, I would have to say my greatest challenge would be one of my current projects that is for Hadassah in Jerusalem, Israel. Not only has it been a challenging project in terms of healthcare planning, but it also has been a challenging design problem due to the numerous site variables (it is located at the top of a mountain in Ein Karem, overlooking the birth site of John the Baptist), the diverse culture, and the rich context. Our goal is to provide a modern, state-of-the-art facility that can respond to the needs of the region, while embracing the historical significance of the surrounding area. Like most projects, this will be a collaborative effort, where we can draw from the combined strengths of the design team and our consultants to deliver a project that exceeds the client's needs.

Hadassah Medical Center Bed Tower, Jerusalem, Israel. Architect: HKS Architects. ARTIST: MICHAEL LUNGREN.

Why did you pursue two graduate degrees— Master of Architecture and Master of Business Administration—during your graduate studies?

❯ I believe in the notion that an architect is a generalist. The architectural education is extremely comprehensive and provides the foundation suitable for many careers; however, business seemed to be the one missing ingredient.

After serving as AIAS national vice president, I quickly came to realize that architecture is a business and that there was much more to learn—so I decided to go back to school and round out my education by earning an M.B.A. in addition to the Master of Architecture. After speaking with others, I also knew that if I were to ever pursue the M.B.A., the time to do it was then—as there were no guarantees that such an opportunity would be available later in life.

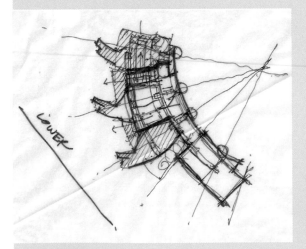

Ahuja Medical Center, Beachwood, Ohio. Architect: HKS Architects and Array Healthcare Facilities Solutions. RENDERING: SHANNON KRAUS, AIA, MBA.

Ultimately I felt the M.B.A. would help me simply by providing additional tools for me to draw upon. However, in addition to the business skills, the M.B.A. had many other benefits that I did not anticipate. The program I went through proved valuable in helping me to hone my communication skills, problem-solving ability, and leadership skills. In many ways, the business degree was not as much about accounting or finance as it was about maximizing resources and leadership.

As one of the youngest vice presidents in the history of the AIA, what would you say was your most significant achievement?

❯ During my tenure as AIA Vice President I had the fortune of being involved in several meaningful things that I feel truly help the profession. One of the most significant was working with my fellow executive committee members to help the AIA craft and adopt a policy supporting the 2030 Challenge. Other milestones include the development of a national ARE scholarship, as well as the creation of a National Research fund for evidence-based design. In each case, I was able to help facilitate the continued growth and development of the AIAS's transformation into a knowledge-based organization. My goal as vice president was simply to have made a difference—to have a positive impact on the evolution of the institute, no matter how small. In doing this, it's now my hope that others are as passionate about the profession as I am will be similarly encouraged to get engaged and get involved.

As a relatively young architect in a large firm, what are your primary responsibilities and duties?

❯ Currently I am a studio leader for a 35-person healthcare studio. My official role is director of

Flower Mound Hospital, Flower Mound, Texas. Architect: HKS, Inc. RENDERING: SHANNON KRAUS, AIA, MBA.

design. This would include serving as the senior design lead on multiple projects, cultivating new work, working with clients to deliver on their expectations, and working with the team to adequately staff projects, develop talent, and nurture new leaders.

Some of my recent projects include Ahuja Medical Center in Cleveland, Ohio; Flower Mound Hospital in Flower Mound, Texas; and Enze Medical Center in China. In all of these projects, regardless of my role, my goal is to understand the clients' needs, listen to their dreams, and work with them to identify innovative design solutions that they can implement on time and on budget.

What is the most satisfying part of your career as an architect?

❱ Seeing projects you pour your heart and soul into get built. When you are pursuing something you love and look forward to, there isn't a greater feeling in the world than to see not only your vision realized but that of your team and client. I work for one of the best firms in the world, and it is great knowing that through a team effort, where you draw from each other's strengths and weaknesses, that truly great architecture can be realized.

What is the most important quality or skill of a healthcare designer?

❱ Patience, communication, and knowledge are the most important skill sets of a designer in healthcare, or any area for that matter. As a programmer and designer in healthcare, we work directly with clients, physicians, nurses, equipment specialist, contractors, builders, project managers, and business leaders. In each case, the architect must be knowledgeable enough of the subject matter being programmed to effectively communicate in the language of the particular user being met with. Most issues and challenges are the result of poor communication, so having the patience to work through misconceptions and differences of opinions is key to resolving issues as you develop a program or a project design solution. The knowledge of healthcare facilities comes through trial and error, is learned more on the job than in school. You have to be "heads-up" in the office, seek out every opportunity to participate in a meeting or go on a tour.

Who has been a major influence on your career?

❯ There have been many great influences on my career, but none greater than my parents and my wife. While I have benefited from many great mentors, and try to learn from all of those around me, it is my parents who helped shape me into the man I am today, teaching me to believe that I could do anything I put my mind to. And it is my wife who helps keep me focused, motivated, and on track with an even-keeled perspective that brings with it humility and grace. Without a doubt I am blessed to have them as positive influences in my life and I know that I would not be where I am today if not for them.

What has been your most rewarding endeavor as a professional?

❯ Without hesitation it would be the planning, design, and construction of a clubhouse for a Make-A-Wish child named Giovanna. At the age of 13, Giovanna, who was challenged with a potential life-threatening illness, was given the opportunity by the Make-A-Wish Foundation of North Texas to have one of her wishes come true. While she could wish for just about anything, her wish was to have a clubhouse—a place that she could have as her own, and a place she could have friends over for a slumber party.

The result was a 400-square-foot clubhouse with a loft, fire pole, and screen porch, inspired by Giovanna's own vision. Interns designed the project with Giovanna as the client. She was given schematic designs, models, and material boards. Without a doubt it was a very rewarding experience. Knowing that we were able to utilize our design skills to make her vision—her wish—a reality, was very rewarding.

Architecture as a New Media

WILLIAM J. CARPENTER, Ph.D., FAIA

Associate Professor

School of Architecture, Civil Engineering Technology and Construction

Southern Polytechnic State University

Marietta, Georgia

President, Lightroom

Decatur, Georgia

Why and how did you become an architect?

❯ I grew up in New York. I became an architect because of my sixth grade teacher, Robert Fisher.

I was his first student to go to architecture school and I could not have done it without him. He invented classes for me, such as eco-tecture, that emphasized sustainable design before it was in vogue. He collected donations from many of the businesses in our town to create a scholarship for me that he gave me at high school graduation. This summer I went to visit him and he had all of the drawings and books I had sent him displayed in his library. I would not have known what architecture was without him.

I was able then to apprentice for two great architects: first, Norman Jaffe, FAIA, in New York and then Samuel Mockbee, FAIA, in Mississippi. Mockbee later received the America Institute of Architects (AIA) Gold Medal.

The Breen Residence, Atlanta, Georgia. Architect: William J. Carpenter, FAIA, Ph.D. PHOTOGRAPHER: KEVIN BRYD.

Why and how did you decide on which schools to attend for your architecture degree? What degree(s) do you possess?

❯ Bachelor of architecture, master of architecture, and Ph.D. in architecture. I went to Mississippi State for my undergraduate studies because I asked Richard Meier at a career day what school he would attend and he said he had just returned from there and something interesting was happening there. At 17, I packed my bags and arrived from New York. He was so right—I was able to study with Robert Ford, Christopher Risher, and Merrill Elam.

I chose Virginia Tech for graduate studies because of its emphasis on urbanism and tectonics. No school in the world offers a better balance of these pedagogical intents—of course, I *am* an alumnus. Jaan Holt and Gregory Hunt were amazing professors and left an indelible imprint on me.

For my doctorate I wanted to go to England. There I was able to study with Professor Thomas Muir before he retired. I studied at the University of Central England at Birmingham Polytechnic which is one of the oldest programs in the United Kingdom. Muir, Alan Green, and Denys Hinton gave me an appreciation for Europe, how to live and where to find the best pubs. I have never met anyone with a deeper commitment to architectural education and learning.

What has been your greatest challenge as an architect?

❯ The greatest challenge I have is balancing my time. I have two wonderful daughters and desire to be an integral part of their lives. I have amazing students to teach, and I work for great clients on architectural commissions. I have been blessed.

The biggest challenge is getting all it done well. One of the ways I keep it all together is to keep a journal/sketchbook, in which I try to keep new ideas or work on existing ideas at many different scales.

How does your work as a faculty member inform your architectural practice and vice versa?

❯ My students constantly inspire me and help me see things in new ways. I always invite them to my studio and to see new projects. I try to be involved in their lives during and after school. They are why I teach and I owe them a lot. I also try to involve students in actual projects such as our community outreach in Reynoldstown (in downtown Atlanta).

What are your primary responsibilities and duties as an architect and a faculty member?

❯ I am president of Lightroom, an architecture and new media firm in Decatur, Georgia. In the past few years we have won awards in a number of different disciplines, including being on the team who won the international 48-hour film festival, being on the team that had a short film accepted to Cannes, and two major awards of excellence from the AIA and from *Print Magazine*. I do not think awards define you, but I appreciate that they are from very diverse organizations, all for excellent design.

I am also director of the evening professional program in Architecture, where I teach the thesis studio, which is very enjoyable. I like teaching at the fifth-year level. I am currently working on a very exciting documentary film with my students on the history of the Virgin Mary's home in Ephesus, Turkey.

 ▶ Lightroom Studios, Decatur, Georgia. Architect: William J. Carpenter, FAIA, Ph.D. PHOTOGRAPHER: KEVIN BRYD

▼ Lightcatcher, Decatur, Georgia. Architect: William J. Carpenter, FAIA, Ph.D. PHOTOGRAPHER: KEVIN BRYD.

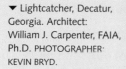

You authored the book **Modern Sustainable Residential Design: A Guide for Design Professionals** *(Wiley, 2009). What is sustainable design and why is it important for design professionals?*

❯ Sustainable architecture is designing efficient buildings that can produce their own energy and allow for the least damage to the earth possible—such as using recycled buildings or materials. It is important for design professionals because economy (part of the Vitruvian triad) is an essential element of great design.

About two years ago the editor of *Dwell* magazine contacted me to write their first book. I have always been impressed with how they humanized modernism with pictures of people and looking comfortable in their homes. Sustainability is often seen as a fad amongst architects and the public. I believe it is an integral part of architecture and the best modern buildings I know—such as the Second Jacobs house by Frank Lloyd Wright and his Rosenbaum House—are great examples of sustainable modern buildings. I am concerned today about sustainable buildings that look modern-"ish" and not "modernist." This is the difference between style and commitment and authenticity. In the future I believe that sustainable architecture will produce power for us—whether it is a house or an entire city. An important sustainable principle that students need to remember is that the adaptive reuse of buildings can be one of the most sensitive moves an architect can make.

Enhancing Business Through Design

ROBERT D. FOX, AIA, IIDA

Principal, FOX Architects

McLean, Virginia/Washington, DC

Why and how did you become an architect?

❯ My father was an architect, and I grew up in the offices of Louis Kahn and Romaldo Giurgola when I was a kid. When I was faced with having to get serious about what I wanted to do, architecture was where I felt most comfortable.

Why and how did you decide on attending Temple University for your architecture degree? What degree(s) do you possess?

❯ I have a bachelor of architecture from Temple University. Because my father taught there so I received the family discount making the decision easy.

What has been your greatest challenge as an architect?

❯ Design is something of incredible beauty and value; the spaces we create add significantly to the health, beauty, and economics of place, but architects are the last ones to realize that and, in fact, architects tend to devalue the real value of design.

One of the greatest challenges is keeping up with the rapidly changing information about the profession. I could not imagine being a single practitioner; you would just be falling further and further behind.

Earlier in your career, you specialized in corporate interiors. How does interior architecture differ from architecture?

❯ Interior architecture is much closer to the individuals who use the space, and I get to see much more closely the impact of the design. I also enjoy learning about other businesses and people.

U.S. Pharmacopoeia Master Development Plan, Rockville, Maryland. Architect: FOX Architects.

As a principal of a firm, what are your primary responsibilities and duties?

❯ There are the basics of the financials, marketing, human resources, legal, insurance, real estate, IT, software, contracts, etc., that I did not learn in school.

More importantly, I enable design. I am responsible for listening, and then I am responsible for developing and communicating the direction of the firm in a clear and concise manner, and building consensus. I need to find the strengths in others and enable them to perform at very high levels, to offer my experience and expertise. Then I need to stay out of the way to let it all happen.

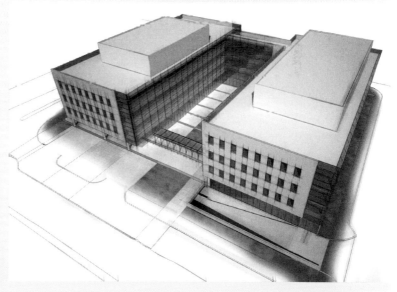

U.S. Pharmacopoeia Master Development Plan, Rockville, Maryland. Architect: FOX Architects.

U.S. Pharmacopoeia Master Development Plan, Rockville, Maryland. Architect: FOX Architects.

FOX Architects specializes in architecture, interior design, graphic design, multimedia design, and signage. How do these different design disciplines interact within your work?

❯ The reason that we have a multidisciplinary design practice is to expand and engage the dialogue of our work. We cannot get breakthrough ideas if we are talking only to ourselves; we need different ideas and perspectives to stay fresh and develop really new ideas.

What is the most/least satisfying part of your career as an architect?

❯ The most satisfying part is seeing others get it and realize their potential—that is really exciting. I also enjoy learning about other businesses and seeing different business models.

Feeling like I am one of a very few that realize the value of design and trying to get what we deserve is the least satisfying. We carry so much liability for what we do, few professionals really understand the risks that they take on—they just want to design, and while that may be fun, you cannot achieve the kind of goals to do better and better work, more research, seek better projects unless you are making a decent profit. Architects limit themselves.

Who or what experience has been a major influence on your career?

❯ First, my dad has been a big influence. In addition, I have been influenced by a number of the developers with whom we work and seeing what it really takes to put a building together—the debt and financing, operation, management, sales, and leasing.

A Teacher's View

THOMAS FOWLER, IV, AIA

Professor and Director

Collaborative Integrative-Interdisciplinary Digital-Design Studio (CIDS)

California Polytechnic State University–San Luis Obispo

San Luis Obispo, California

Why and how did you become an architect?

❯ My primary motivation for pursuing architecture began with an interest at a very young age and a desire to understand how everything worked by taking things apart and sometimes getting them back together (not always). I did not know of another profession at the time that would give me a global sense of how things worked and how to document discoveries of what I found through drawings. I had very naïve but romantic notions of what architects supposedly did—but this was just the vehicle that propelled me into going to school to learn about more about architecture.

Why and how did you decide on which school to attend for your architecture degree? What degree(s) do you possess?

❯ I possess a bachelor of architecture from New York Institute of Technology/Old Westbury and a master of architecture from Cornell University. My decision for selecting my undergraduate institution was based on what I could afford to pay, the location, and which schools would admit me. Selecting the graduate program was because of an opportu-

Lumeire Ghosting Portable Theater Project, CIDS Project at California Polytechnic State University–San Luis Obispo, CA. Faculty: Thomas Fowler, IV, AIA.

nity to work as an administrator and do graduate work at the same time. The reason for pursuing graduate work was to obtain additional design theory and to explore the possibilities of teaching.

What is the greatest challenge facing the future of the profession?

❯ The greatest challenge is the lack of accessible and visible role models in the profession and in the academic environments for aspiring ethnic minority and women students interested in pursuing this field.

From my own experience, I was fortunate to have a cousin that practiced architecture in New York City who allowed me to work in his office from high school through my undergraduate studies. This was the component of my education that actually kept me in school, since my challenge was to see the relevancy of my schooling to the eventual practice of architecture. For all students, some linkage to role models is helpful when things do get tough to sort out while in school.

From my undergraduate education and beyond, I have always been very fortunate to find role models to keep me on track and to expose me to opportunities that I would not had known about otherwise. I think it is important to have a strong sense of your destination but have some flexibility as to what the path might be to achieve this goal. Ultimately, stay agile in your ability to modify your future goals as they relate to experiences acquired on your path of learning.

How does your work as a faculty member inform your architectural practice and vice versa?

❯ Being constantly surrounded by the same age group of bright minds, always made up of a diverse

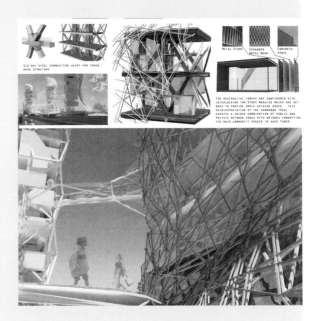

"Urban Filtration" Housing Project, Students: Architecture: Rachel Glabe and Megan West. Structural Engineering: Caitlin Potter and Leigh Guggemos. Faculty: Thomas Fowler, IV, AIA; James Doerfler, AIA; Mark Cabrinha; Kevin Dong, SE.

range of individuals, who are able to generate a collective range of other ways of seeing a problem is a valuable learning experience to the teacher. Teachers learn at an accelerated rate from their students. Students will always challenge the conventions on how things go to together.

As an academic whose practice of architecture is embedded in working with students in the design and construction of a range of building mockups and prototypical structures, this form of practice has been helpful in acquiring examples to show students regarding the intimate process of how design and the construction process works at a smaller scale. The academic involved in practice always has a voice in the back of his/her mind asking the question "how can I capture this process in such a way as to explain it to students so they will be able to learn from it."

What are your primary responsibilities and duties as an architect and as a faculty member?

❯ I think some practitioners want to see faculty as practicing architects first and as academicians second—since it seems to be a logical way to ensure that students will be learning the skills that they need to become architects. From my experience being a practitioner first does not ensure this linkage to practice, but this depends more on what teaching strategies that are developed to provide students with the tools for understanding these connections.

Practitioners need to understand that they play an important role in the education of architects too. There is also talk about needing students to deal with more of a complexity of design issues while in school, but I would argue issues have to be simplified so students can develop ideas beyond the planning stages of a project into constructible architectural vocabularies. Acceptable levels of design development are lacking in many studios since too much time is spent on thinking about the complexities.

How does teaching differ from practicing architecture?

❯ What a teacher does is very much a mystery to those who do not teach, which I think is more of a problem for universities to solve regarding how to decode the process for what academics do as opposed to non-academics. I often hear that the role of an architecture professor is to teach students the skills to build buildings. I would argue the role of an architecture professor is far greater than just this. Teaching is more of a modeling of future citi-

Tobacco Barn Collage, Horry County, South Carolina. Architect: Thomas Fowler, IV, AIA.

zens who will make great contributions to society as upstanding citizens in addition to also having the knowledge to create architecture. Good teaching is where both the student and teacher learn from the interaction. This is why most are attracted to teaching—since this role provides a continuous mechanism to learn.

During your career, you have been a member of more than one of the national boards of the collateral organizations. What has that involvement meant for your career?

❯ It is often the perception that individuals who become involved as volunteers with associations have limited interest in the broader issues that affect the profession (i.e., design, etc.). I actually have the opposite view that active involvement with the collaterals has given me a broader view and appreciation for the profession. Navigating association work is the ultimate design prob- lem for consensus as you move through a bu- reaucracy. I served as national president of the AIAS (1984–1985), and served as Association of Collegiate Schools of Architecture (ACSA) faculty advisor (2001–2003), served as secretary for the ACSA (2004–2006), and board member for National Architectural Accrediting Board (NAAB) (2006–2008) and secretary (2007–2008). Involvement in association work allows you to establish a macro view of the profession through a variety of networks that over time disperse and expand as people move on to different things.

A Gentle Woman's Profession

KATHY DENISE DIXON, AIA, NOMA

Associate Principal

Arel Architects, Inc.

Clinton, Maryland

Why and how did you become an architect?

❯ My becoming an architect is the result of several influences during my childhood, not the least of which is the fact that my father was an architect for the Army Corps of Engineers. In a sense, I think I inherited the desire to be an architect. But more- over, the fact that I had a creative nature, drawing ability, and good math skills also led me to pursue architecture.

Randle Highlands Elementary School, District of Columbia Public Schools, Washington, DC. Architect: Jacobs Engineering. PHOTOGRAPHER: KATHY DENISE DIXON, AIA, NOMA.

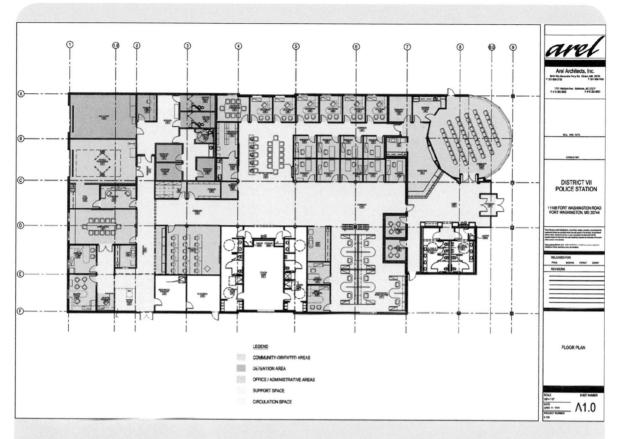

District VII Police Station, Prince George's County, Fort Washington, Maryland Architect: Arel Architects, Inc. DRAWING: RONALD D. LIPFORD, AIA, NOMA.

Why and how did you decide on which school to attend for your architecture degree? What degree(s) do you possess?

❯ It was a fairly easy choice to decide to pursue architecture at Howard University due to the fact that they were the only institution that offered me a five-year scholarship. After my bachelor of architecture, I also pursued a master of arts in urban planning at University of California at Los Angeles (UCLA) with a focus was housing and community development.

Why did you pursue the additional degree— Master of Arts Urban Planning from UCLA?

❯ I felt that pursuing a degree in planning would enhance my perspective as an architect. Even the best architecture has to respond to context. On a broader scale, understanding context, community, environment, and our society is essential for a well-rounded architect. I believe all architects should learn more about urban planning, planning policy, and urban design so we are not designing in a vacuum.

What has been your greatest challenge as an architect?

❯ Personally, my greatest challenge has probably been gathering up the personal confidence to do well in the profession. I was licensed at 29 years of age and had two professional degrees, plus I had obtained additional certifications. However, with all the education and achievements, I was not confident that I could make the decisions and lead the design process and team on my own. I remember having a talk about the lack of confidence with a colleague who had recently started his own consulting business. He told me that I just had to believe in myself and be confident that I can make the decisions and do what is required. He suggested that everyone has this challenge and he had to deal with the same issues in starting his business. It still took more years of experience before I felt I could lead a design team, but I have overcome that personal and internal self-challenge.

What are your primary responsibilities and duties?

❯ As associate principal, I work on a variety of tasks from traditional architecture to marketing the firm. I am currently responsible for a variety of municipal projects for the local county government. The firm has only recently begun working heavily with the local government and has resulted in a number of civic architecture projects including, fire stations, schools, police stations, and other building types.

With respect to marketing, I share the responsibility of seeking new work and responding to requests for proposals with the principal of the firm. This requires time to review bid lists, write qualifications statements, and partner with various firms to ob-

tain new projects. Attending pre-bid meetings and networking with engineers and other architects is an important aspect of putting together a project team.

What is the most/least satisfying part of your career as an architect?

❯ Seeing the finished product of your labor is probably the most satisfying of any career one can choose. To visit, experience, and reflect over the completed structure and the decisions that went into its creation is a satisfaction that few others will experience.

Probably one of the least satisfying aspects of being an architect is the length of time it takes to see your work come to fruition. Other careers generally have immediate results. However, the length of time to design and construct a building can be 18 months or longer. It is challenging, especially as a young architect, to have to wait so long to see the realization of what you have been working on.

During your career, you have been involved with the National Organization of Minority Architects (NOMA). What is the NOMA and how has your involvement benefited your professional career?

❯ The NOMA is a professional networking organization founded in 1971 to assist minority architects in their career development. Although the number of minority architects is increasing, there are currently only +/– 220 licensed African American women architects in the country. This presents challenges for individuals pursuing the field of architecture and requires a great deal of mentoring. Prior to deciding to pursue a career in architecture, I did not know a single African American woman architect. I only met a couple during my college studies. Although I became licensed on my own, it would have been very beneficial for me to have known and

Potomac Consolidated TRACON, Federal Aviation Administration, Warrenton, Virginia. Architect: Jacobs Engineering. PHOTOGRAPHERS: KATHY DENISE DIXON/ YUYAN ZHOU.

potentially been mentored by a woman architect. As a result, I am involved with the NOMA and have a particular interest in mentoring young African American women in the field of architecture.

Professionally, through the NOMA, I have become acquainted with owners and principals of African American–owned firms around the country. This familiarity leads to partnering for potential projects and even opportunities for employment changes.

Who or what experience has been a major influence on your career?

❯ Of course, my father was a major influence in my decision to become an architect. I am very much like my father in character and interests. I was also fortunate to have Barry Washington, an interior designer, serve as a role model early on in my career. On my first job working as a CADD operator for the U.S. Department of Justice, I worked with Mr. Washington on various facility management projects. Barry required a high level of professionalism and quality of work during my three-year internship. His expectation for design excellence has remained with me throughout my career.

From Verbal Concept to Fabrication

DOUGLAS GAROFALO, FAIA

Professor, School of Architecture

University of Illinois at Chicago

Chicago, Illinois

President

Garofalo Architects, Inc.

Chicago, Illinois

Why and how did you become an architect?

❯ Initially, I wanted to become an architect because it seemed to combine my interests in making, building, and the arts; I became an architect by attending a five-year bachelor of architecture degree program, working a few years in an office, studying for and passing the Architect Registration Exam (ARE), and then attending graduate school. I consider all four of these steps equally important.

Why and how did you decide on which school to attend for your architecture degree? What degree(s) do you possess?

❯ I decided on Notre Dame for undergraduate school because it had one year entirely in Rome, Italy. I went to Yale for graduate school based on the strength of both the art and architecture schools.

What has been your greatest challenge as an architect?

❯ Perhaps it is the necessity of protecting design concepts throughout the life of a project. That this integrity is maintained is not a given—quite the opposite in many cases. Also the general resistance to contemporary projects in the United States; we have much success, but it is usually not easy.

Nothstine Residence, Green Bay, Wisconsin. Architect: Garofalo Architects. PHOTOGRAPHER: GAROFALO ARCHITECTS.

Hyde Park Art Center, Chicago.
Architect: Garofalo Architects.

How do you balance the challenging demands of both an architectural practice and teaching within a program in architecture?

❭ I would not refer to this situation as a balance, but a competition for time; it is something that continues to evolve as the work in the office changes. The one does feed the other though, and I feel that sometimes I get as much from the students as they from me.

You were involved with the award-winning Korean Presbyterian Church of New York, the first building truly conceived and executed with digital media. Please provide more insight on the experience of designing by digital media.

❭ We were able to exploit these relatively new digital tools from email file transfer to complex manipulations of form and program over the Internet to form a truly unique collaboration. Also, and perhaps more relevant to our current work, the use of multiple software programs (as opposed to one or two), enhances our interests in the software program over time, complex geometries, patterned space and surface, repetitive structure, and many other concepts. Increasingly, digital technology allows us to be more involved in fabrication and building as well.

What are your primary responsibilities and duties as an architect?

❭ My office is organized to run as a studio in the truest sense of the word, or at least my definition of it; everyone does everything insofar as it is possible, meaning everyone acts as a designer and everyone runs projects. This makes me a sort of director, overseeing and collaborating.

What is the most satisfying part of your job?

❭ It may sound simple, but the seemingly simple verbal banter and exchanges in the office result in some very interesting concepts. We then develop these in a sophisticated way. The act of making, from verbal concept all the way through to fabrication is most satisfying. And of course, seeing the structure built and inhabited.

What is the least satisfying part of your job?

❭ The amount of so-called justification to complete a building is astounding; most of it is necessary and good, but some of it is absurd. A good example of this is how hard it is to obtain a building permit.

▲ Spring Prairie Residence, Spring Prairie, Wisconsin. Architect: Garofalo Architects. PHOTOGRAPHER: NATHAN KIRKMAN.

◀ IN.FORMant.system – Museum of Contemporary Art, Chicago. Architect: Garofalo Architects. PHOTOGRAPHER: GAROFALO ARCHITECTS.

Another unique project during your career was the full-scale prototype newsstand at the Museum of Contemporary Art in Chicago. Please describe this project and its uniqueness.

❯ The IN.FOrmant.system was a built response to a set of questions raised by the Museum of Contemporary Art in Chicago for the exhibit "Material Evidence: Chicago Architecture @ 2000." We were asked to consider issues of materiality in relation to the program of a newsstand, which was constructed full-scale and installed at the museum. The IN.FOrmant.system refers to a future micro-urbanism of many structures in the city dispensing information in variable ways.

The prototype as constructed at the museum demonstrated three ideas relative to materiality: first, that the interaction of even a small palette of materials, both conventional and new, can be treated as a flow of matter; second, that this performance is conceived and constructed using parametric modeling techniques inherent to animation software; and finally, that the material and spatial effects produced by these two ideas may collaborate with and expand the given program of a newsstand.

Who or what experience has been a major influence on your career?

❭ I have had the benefit of many amazing teachers, so it would be hard to single out even a few. Other influences include having the opportunity to travel as a student in Italy and as a Skidmore, Owings & Merrill (SOM) Traveling Fellowship recipient through India and Asia.

Profile of the Profession

According to the Bureau of Labor Statistics, U.S. Department of Labor,[6] 132,000 architects were practicing in the United States in 2006, the last year for which statistics are available. Employment projections for the occupation of architect are expected to grow by 23,000 (18 percent) between 2006 and 2016. The employment of architects is projected to grow faster than average for all occupations through 2016, and additional job openings will stem from the need to replace architects who retire, transfer to new occupations, or leave the labor force permanently for other reasons. Growth in construction, particularly of such nonresidential structures as office buildings, shopping centers, schools, and health care facilities, is expected to spur employment.

With this projected growth of the profession, should you consider architecture? Before you answer, consider the following. According to the National Architectural Accrediting Board (NAAB),[7] 29,133 students were studying architecture in professional degree programs in the United States during the 2007–2008 academic year. Further, 5,781 students graduated with the NAAB-accredited degree. If you assume that the number of graduates with the accredited degree remains the same for 2006–2016, the projected time frame, 57,810 individuals with an NAAB-accredited degree may be competing for the projected 23,000 openings. Clearly, based on employment projections, the competition for architectural positions will be keen over the next decade. Take solace, though, because graduates with an architectural education may enter many career fields other than architecture; see Chapter 4, "The Careers of an Architect."

In its 2008 survey of registered architects, the National Council of Architectural Registration Boards[8] (NCARB) reports 104,126 registered architects living in the 55 reporting jurisdictions, including all 50 states, the District of Columbia, Guam, the Northern Mariana Islands, Puerto Rico, and the Virgin Islands. This total is an approximate 7 percent decrease from the previous year's survey.

While the AIA[9] does not represent the entire profession, its membership does constitute a majority. Therefore, it is worth reporting its facts and figures. Of the nearly 83,000 members of the AIA, 68 percent (56,440) are licensed architects. The remaining ones are associate or allied members.

Of all AIA architect members, 81 percent practice in architecture firms, 2 percent practice in the corporate sector, and 2 percent practice in government, while the remaining ones practice at design firms, universities or schools, contractors' or builder firms, and engineering firms.

SALARY

According to the Bureau of Labor Statistics, U.S. Department of Labor,[10] the 2007 median annual earnings of wage and salary architects were $64,150. The middle 50 percent earned between $49,780 and $83,450. The lowest 10 percent earned less than $39,420, and the highest 10 percent earned more than $104,970. Salaries fluctuate, depending on the region of the country, the amount of experience an individual has, and even the type of employer.

Further data on the salaries of architects is provided by the 2009 Compensation and Benefits Survey published by Design Intelligence.[11] According to this survey from 460 professional practice locations, interns with one year's experience earn a mean salary of $39,680 and those with three years experience earn $47,043. Licensed architects with five to nine years of experience earn a mean salary of $60,825, and those who have over 20 years of experience earn $100,723. Individuals in leadership positions, associate principals, earn a mean salary of $106,333, while principals earn $147,452.

Finally, data from the 2008 AIA Compensation Survey[12] reports the following salaries: senior design/project management staff, $98,800; architect/designer, $71,600; and interns, $45,400. These salaries represent a 6 percent increase from the previous survey in 2005. Of course, these salaries were also collected prior to the economic downturn in the latter part of 2008 and early 2009.

DIVERSITY

What is diversity, and why is it important? The following answer is from *Designing for Diversity,* by Kathryn H. Anthony, Ph.D.:

> Diversity is a set of human traits that have an impact on individuals' values, opportunities, and perceptions of self and others at work. At minimum, it includes six core dimensions: age, ethnicity, gender, mental or physical abilities, race, and sexual orientation.[13]

In the context of the architectural profession, diversity is extremely important because, for many years, the profession has been known as a white man's profession. This label is no longer appropriate, as the profession is beginning to make strides, but consider the representation of women and individuals of color. Again, the AIA is the most reliable source for estimates.

According to the AIA, 10 percent (about 7,500) of full members are women, and eight percent (about 6,000) are individuals of color. Within the schools, the numbers are dramatically better. According to the NAAB, the percentage of female students pursuing architecture in accredited professional degree programs is 41 percent (11,985). Twenty-nine percent of students (8,446) are individuals of color.

What are the most important skills an architect needs to be successful?

> Self-awareness: a well-rounded experience is good, but focus on your specific talents and skills that you enjoy.

Amy Yurko, AIA, Founder/Director, BrainSpaces

> To be successful, you must be able to adapt to your surroundings. You must be a good communicator and, more importantly, a good listener. You must be open to taking risks and looking at things in a different way.

H. Alan Brangman, AIA, University Architect, Georgetown University

> To be successful professionally and personally as an architect, passion, the courage to create, the ability to listen, communication, collaborative spirit, and perseverance are all essential.

Diane Blair Black, AIA, Vice-President, RTKL Associates, Inc.

> Creativity, design, technical skills, management, communication and excellent leadership skills are required. It requires a very high level of maturity.

Robert D. Fox, AIA, IIDA, Principal, FOX Architects

> Architects must have the following skills (the order depends on the individual): (a) excellent communication skills (e.g., writing, speaking, and traditional and digital drawing ability); (b) tolerance for ambiguity; (c) agility; (d) an analytical mind; (e) attention to both the macro and the micro; (f) humility; and (g) graphical diagramming.

Thomas Fowler, IV, AIA, Professor and Director, Collaborative Integrative-Interdisciplinary Digital-Design Studio (CIDS), California Polytechnic State University–San Luis Obispo

> Learning to communicate both visually and verbally is critical. Design work must be able to speak for itself, with no verbal explanation. In addition, however, architects must learn effective oral communication skills. They must practice their presentations over and over again, and they must learn from their mistakes. They also must learn how to be attentive listeners, as understanding the needs of clients and users is critical to a successful practice with repeat clients.

Kathryn H. Anthony, Ph.D., Professor, University of Illinois at Urbana-Champaign

> Communication is the most important skill. An architect must be able to communicate with clients differently than with contractors. An architect must be able to present in front of a 12-person board of directors or a married couple. An architect must create written proposals and reports in the morning, then must turn around and create a massing diagram sketch or stair detail later in the day. An architect must be able to explain a technical aspect of a project in a project meeting just as well as attempt to convince a client of an aesthetic idea in a design.

F. Michael Ayles, AIA, Principal, Business Development, Antinozzi Associates

> Every architect must have two attributes. First is the ability to deal with ambiguous problems. Architectural problems, while often complex, cannot, for the most part, be reduced to a single optimized answer. Typically, architectural problems have many possible solutions. The answer often lies not in finding the *right* solution but in finding the *best* solution. Le Corbusier, one of the twentieth century's greatest architects, described finding architectural solutions "as a patient search."

The second attribute is curiosity. Architecture is not a static profession. What you learn in a formal education is just the beginning. To be a successful architect, especially in this age of rapid change, you must acquire new knowledge and skills nearly every day. To do this, you need insatiable curiosity that drives you to know more and to continue a process of lifelong learning.

What are the most important skills an architect needs to be successful?(Continued)

Notice I have talked about attributes rather than skills. I believe these personal attributes are more important than learned skills. I do not mean to skip the skills issue. The necessary skills are basic—reading, writing, and arithmetic in all their current manifestations—plus communication skills, leadership skills, cognitive skills, and—I think the most important skill of all—the skill to imagine unbuilt worlds.

Robert M. Beckley, FAIA, Professor and Dean Emeritus, University of Michigan

Cosmonaut Museum, Moscow, Russia. PHOTOGRAPHER: TED SHELTON, AIA.

❭ Patience, willingness to listen, good personal skills in dealing with clients, and last but not least, ability to design.

John W. Myefski, AIA, Principal, Myefski Cook Architects, Inc.

❭ Self-knowledge. Exercise your capacity for self-learning as soon as you can—understand how deeply you want to be an architect and reflect on it throughout your decision-making [sic]. For some, the want is a passion or obsession; for others, it is a curiosity that grows over time. These people require alternate paths.

Travel. Observe and talk to people. Travel may be the greatest teacher.

Do not worry about failure. Follow the maxim of IBM's Thomas Watson Jr.: "Want to succeed faster? Accelerate your rate of failure!" Have the courage to take that risk!

Joseph Bilello, Ph.D., AIA, Professor and Former Dean, Ball State University

The most important skill is listening. I find that too many architects do not listen well; it takes practice.

William J. Carpenter, Ph.D., FAIA, Associate Professor, Southern Polytechnic State University; President, Lightroom

❭ To observe and to listen, and translate the information gained into a meaningful medium that can be understood by clients. Architecture is not about you and what you want; it is about your clients and working as a team to achieve their goals. You can educate them, which is critical, but you must step back from your own ego-based agenda and serve them. This does not mean the design is compromised; it just means you know and honor the constraints.

Barbara Crisp, Principal, bcrisp, llc

> The two most important skills for success in architecture are critical thinking and problem solving. I used to think creativity was the most vital skill for an architect to possess; however, I have come to realize that creativity alone does not produce substance. A rational thinker who knows architectural history and has a strong design process will make good architecture.

Margaret DeLeeuw, Marketing Director, Celli-Flynn Brennan Architects & Planners

> A creative sensibility, the ability to solve complex issues without precedents to follow, and a commitment to the discipline.

Douglas Garofalo, FAIA, Professor, University of Illinois at Chicago, President, Garofalo Architects, Inc.

> Good communication skills. Architecture is a collaborative process and requires that architects be good team players as well as leaders.

Lynsey Jane Gemmell, AIA, Project Manager/Associate, Holabird & Root

> Be both patient and persistent. Often the work of the architect is a series of compromises.

Christopher J. Gribbs, Associate AIA, Senior Director, American Institute of Architects

> An architect must be open-minded and able to constantly evaluate and reevaluate every decision. Also—this isn't really a skill—an architect must realize you do not need to reinvent the wheel with every design; they don't teach you this in school. So many beautiful and efficient structures already exist; we need not create something unique every day. We can be creative, but we must learn from the past and try to make it better.

David R. Groff, Master of Architecture Candidate, Virginia Tech–Washington Alexandria Architecture Center

> Patience, diligence—because architectural education is so rigorous, diligence is a must—attention to detail, and passion. I know I still want to be an architect because my passion for creating is undiminished.

Michelle Hunter, Lead Designer, Mark Gould Architect

Chicago Townhomes, Chicago. PHOTOGRAPHER: ISABELLE GOURNAY.

What are the most important skills an architect needs to be successful?(Continued)

❯ Sensitivity. Architects must understand what the environment and the end user need and want. Architects cannot properly respond to the needs of the end user if they are not sensitive to the need. The need may be structural, environmental, aesthetic, climatic, religious, or a combination of these elements—or others.

Ahkilah J. Johnson, Chief of Staff Investment Services, Cherokee Northeast, LLC

❯ Collaboration, teamwork, and people skills are probably the most important and most undervalued skills an architect needs in today's professional practice. But perhaps most importantly, the ability to work collaboratively with clients, to lead them through the project process, can make the difference between a good project and a great one.

Carolyn G. Jones, AIA, Director, Callison

❯ Patience, an ability to see things in a positive way, an ability to listen, and a creative spirit.

Courtney Miller-Bellairs, Assistant Director/Senior Lecturer, Architecture Program, University of Maryland

❯ Having a good eye is one of the most important attributes of a successful architect, but "a good eye" is difficult to describe in words. It affects your projects, your presentations to clients, your marketing efforts to obtain new projects—everything.

Being good with your hands is important, especially in building models but also to get a tactile feel for materials and how they are put together in the field.

Strong writing is also important for architects. Writing is critical to obtaining jobs or awards, preparing contracts, and developing complete and accurate specifications for a particular project.

Enjoying the social aspects and challenges of working with people is very important. Every real-world project involves teamwork. Often, multiple consultants are involved, sometimes multiple clients, always many people who do not always naturally communicate well with each other! It is always the architect's job to keep the lines of communication open via drawings, meetings, conference calls, and so on.

Elizabeth Kalin, Architectural Intern, Studio Gang Architects

❯ Observation; graphic and verbal communication skills; tenacity, perseverance, and fortitude.

Mary Kay Lanzillotta, FAIA, Partner, Hartman-Cox Architects

❯ Communication; positive attitude; critical thinking; and flexibility.

Lynn N. Simon, AIA, LEED AP, President, Simon & Associates, Inc.

❯ Leadership is the most important skill an architect can possess. As the client's advocate and the head of the consultant team, the architect must maintain an overview of the project and provide consistent guidance to ensure its success as well as the long-lasting relationships developed during its course. A great leader is a skilled at listening, showing empathy, and creating a vision.

Grace H. Kim, AIA, Principal, Schemata Workshop, Inc.

❯ Passion and compassion, critical reasoning and problem solving, leadership and collaboration, communication and patience, and determination and faith. It is the careful balance of these relationships that lead to success in architecture.

Margaret R. Tarampi, Associate AIA, Doctor of Philosophy Candidate, University of Utah

❯ I have found that people who like to solve puzzles can do well in architecture. Getting a building designed and through construction takes a tremendous amount of patience and keeping your eye on

Rotunda, University of Virginia, Charlottesville, Virginia. Architect: Thomas Jefferson. PHOTOGRAPHER: R. LINDLEY VANN.

the big picture. In my opinion, the design of the building is the easy part. Turning that design into something the owner approves, figuring out the detailing, coming in on budget, getting approved by the local community, and working within applicable building and zoning codes requires tremendous focus.

Playing psychiatrist to clients is another critical quality. Balancing various client representatives' demands, whether for a couple or a board of directors, requires listening carefully to them and coming up with solutions that satisfy all of their important criteria. They may have other agendas in getting design solutions to go their way, so I find I have to handle their requests carefully.

Excellent design skills are a given to being an architectural designer. However, being an architect does not necessarily mean being a great designer. Few people involved in the profession of architecture are designers. Many are office managers, specification writers, marketing personnel, architectural critics who write for newspapers or magazines, people who work at banks and for developers to review projects, and so on.

Nathan Kipnis, AIA, Principal, Nathan Kipnis Architects, Inc.

❯ The most important skills are communication, imagination, communication, problem solving, and communication. Architects must have the imagination to dream up the vision of clients, the communication skills to articulate that vision so the client can understand it, and the ability to resolve complex variables in order to make that vision a reality. The fundamentals of math, science, and art are relevant, but they are tools that support imagination, communication, and problem solving.

Shannon Kraus, AIA, MBA, Vice-President, HKS

❯ Verbal, written, and graphic communication skills are the most important needed to be a successful architect. Since there are many players involved in a building being designed and built, clear communication is imperative to convey your ideas to others.

Robert D. Roubik, AIA, LEED AP, Project Architect, Antunovich Associates Architects and Planners

❯ Passion. The education of an architect requires such time and energy that without passion the pursuit of such an understanding is pointless. Communication skills, verbal, written, and graphic, are essential to architectural success. Great ideas never become reality if no one else can understand them and build them.

Allison Wilson, Bachelor of Science Graduate, University of Maryland

43

What are the most important skills an architect needs to be successful?(Continued)

❯ Communication is the most important of all skills. Without the ability to communicate orally, in writing, and through graphics, one probably cannot be a successful architect. Through communications one interacts with clients, the community, and the people with whom one learns and works. Though an architect may have outstanding strengths in one area of communication, few are successful without being professionally competent in all three.

Clark E. Llewellyn, AIA, Dean, University of Hawaii

❯ Architects must have the ability to be creative (which includes the creative use of precedents). They must be able to think at different scales (simultaneously). They must have the ability to inspire confidence (which is conveyed largely by listening). They must have the ability to communicate ideas (either orally or in writing, as well as through drawing). Finally, they must have the ability to be able to tell good stories.

Casius Pealer, J.D., Assistant General Counsel (Real Estate), District of Columbia Housing Authority; Cofounder, ARCHVoices

❯ An architect must be resourceful. The myriad of regulations, building codes, materials, products and rules of thumb are impossible to commit to memory. An architect must know where to go to find answers to best solve the design problem. Moreover, because the architect is responsible for coordinating an entire team of professionals, he/she must have very good organization skills and people skills. Finally, the ability to imagine objects in three dimensions is paramount.

Kathy Denise Dixon, AIA, NOMA, Associate Principal, Arel Architects, Inc.

❯ All architects must be able to communicate well in a variety of media. Other important skills include speaking, writing, critical thinking, and problem solving. Also, an understanding of business finance is important, as the measure of a successful project is more than aesthetics and function. My personal goal on every project is to learn at least one item that will enable me to increase my creativity or productivity.

Kathryn T. Prigmore, FAIA, Project Manager, HDR Architecture

❯ Architects require collaboration, visionary ideas, persistence, optimism, and the scale of pragmatism and idealism, tipping more toward idealism.

Patricia Saldana Natke, AIA, Principal and President, Urban Works Ltd.

❯ As cliché as it sounds, communication is the most important skill an architect uses. The language we use when we talk among ourselves is unintelligible to most clients. Even our visual expressions are often misinterpreted or misunderstood. The sophisticated computer programs we employ are no substitute for confident and articulate face-to-face communication.

W. Stephen Saunders, AIA, Principal, Eckenhoff Saunders Architects, Inc.

❯ An architect's most important skills are interpretive in nature so that the problems and needs of the client can be solved and provided for in a way that addresses the previous question. A broad understanding of how spatial relationships and proportions influence and enhance the lives of people who use certain buildings is also important. The leadership skills necessary to implement those designs through advocating and describing their advantages are also important.

Ambassador Richard N. Swett (r), FAIA, President, Swett Associates, Inc.

Teaches about People and Places

KATHRYN H. ANTHONY, PH.D.

Professor

School of Architecture

Department of Landscape Architecture

Gender and Women's Studies Program

University of Illinois at Urbana-Champaign

Champaign, Illinois

Why and how did you become an architecture professor?

❯ I have had a lifelong fascination with architecture, especially the social and psychological relationships among people, places, and spaces. My father is a retired professor of city planning who also studied architecture, and while in France he worked for LeCorbusier. I have early memories of visits to my father's office in Avery Hall at Columbia University, intrigued by all the architectural drawings and models displayed throughout the corridors. I was also fortunate to travel with my family throughout Europe. Several visits were to contemporary urban design projects and new towns, topics of my father's university lectures.

Why and how did you decide on which school to attend for your architecture degree? What degree(s) do you possess?

❯ I was an undergraduate student in psychology at the University of California, Berkeley. During my final year, I discovered the new field of environmental psychology and enrolled in a course on this subject. After purchasing all three required textbooks, I could not put them down. I read them

all during the first week of the term. This had never happened before, and I realized that I had found my niche. After I received my bachelor of arts in psychology, I remained at Berkeley to complete my Ph.D. in architecture with a specialty in social and behavioral factors in design.

You have written two books that help inform both the education and practice of architecture—Design Juries on Trial: The Renaissance of the Design Studio *and* Designing for Diversity: Gender, Race, *and* Ethnicity in the Architectural Profession. *How can architecture students learn from your research on design juries?*

❯ My research on design juries has much to offer architecture students about both the jury process and, more generally, the design studio. The traditional academic design jury is an outmoded model that is all too often inefficient and ineffective. After reading my book, students will become more empowered to take charge of their academic careers.

By reading about the experiences of over 900 students, faculty, and leading practitioners, students will have greater confidence to prepare and present their design projects both in school and in professional practice. They will learn how to work more efficiently in design studio, and how to use research to better understand the design program at hand. *Design Juries on Trial* presents students and faculty with several alternate models to evaluate design work that involve greater student participation and higher levels of learning.

How did you first become interested in diversity?

❯ My ethnic heritage is 100 percent Greek. When I was ages three, six, and nine, my family spent

Next stop: Paradise. A Hospice for Spiritual Healing—Master's Thesis by Christina A. Mooney at the University of Illinois at Urbana-Champaign. Faculty: Kathryn H. Anthony, Ph.D.

the summers in Greece visiting relatives in Athens and on the island of Skyros. I was struck by the unusual ways that Greeks used time and space. For example, mid-day siestas allowed young children to play outside late at night in busy *plateias* (plazas) while their parents dined with friends and neighbors at the local taverna. Small-scale private spaces encouraged greater use of the public realm.

As a graduate student I spent three years in the International House at the University of California, Berkeley, where over 600 students, half American, half from all over the world, ate three meals a day together and lived under one roof. Short of living abroad, it is hard to imagine a more immersive environment to learn about cultural and ethnic diversity. Even today, some of my best friends are those I met at I House.

Why is the topic of "diversity" important for architects?

❯ Diversity is one of the most important issues for today's architects. The built environment reflects our culture, and vice versa. If our buildings, spaces, and places continue to be designed by a relatively homogenous group of people, what message does that send about our culture? The lack of diversity in the architectural profession impedes progress not only in that field but also in American society at large.

Discrimination in the architectural profession can lead to discrimination in how we all use the built environment, and it has done so for years. Architects must pay greater attention to the needs of women, persons of color, gays and lesbians, and persons with physical disabilities, all of whom—until recently—have historically been treated as second-class citizens in the built environment. So-called "minorities" have already become the majority in many American cities and that trend will only increase.

What do you like about research, teaching, and writing?

❯ By far the most appealing aspect of research, teaching, and writing is creativity. Research and writing offer the opportunity to examine issues that have been previously unexplored. One has a chance to carve out new ground, and this is exciting. For example, while *Design Juries on Trial* is not the final word on this topic, it was one of the first examples of empirical research on design juries, and for this it remains significant. This is also true for my second book, *Designing for Diversity*, one of the first books to address how women and persons of color fare in the architectural profession compared to their white male counterparts, and it too is based on empirical research.

As a female scholar in architectural education, my writings have had a special slant, and I believe that I have made a mark in the field. My aim in both books has been to create a more humane environment in both architectural education and practice.

Teaching is another creative endeavor. One of my favorite aspects of teaching is to see a student flourish outside the university. An idea that started as a casual discussion during office hours germinates into a significant body of work presented at a national venue. It is an amazing metamorphosis, and it is gratifying to watch students discuss their work with leading scholars from around the world. Similarly, I appreciate hearing from alumni long after they

graduate and learning about their accomplishments, both professional and personal. It underscores how fortunate we are as educators to cross paths with them during their most formative years.

How has architecture and design impacted your everyday life?

❯ My historic 1924 Dutch Colonial house, where I have lived for almost 25 years, always had plenty of character, charm, and curb appeal. Yet it also had two major drawbacks: a tiny apartment-sized galley kitchen and only one bathroom. Together with URBANWorks Ltd., a Chicago architectural firm that promotes diversity, we designed an unusual "21st century octagon," a kitchen/bath addition that received an award from our local Preservation and Conservation Association. Top priority throughout the design process was to integrate with and enhance the architectural integrity of the original structure. With sun streaming in from all directions

▼ 1924 Dutch Colonial Residence, Urbana, Illinois. Architect: URBANWorks, Ltd./Codesigner and Client: Kathryn H. Anthony, Ph.D. PHOTOGRAPHER: LARRY KANFER, LARRY KANFER PHOTOGRAPHY. ©LARRY KANFER PHOTOGRAPHY, WWW.KANFER.COM.

1924 Dutch Colonial Residence, Urbana, Illinois. Architect: URBANWorks, Ltd./Codesigner and Client: Kathryn H. Anthony, Ph.D. PHOTOGRAPHER: LARRY KANFER, LARRY KANFER PHOTOGRAPHY. ©LARRY KANFER PHOTOGRAPHY, WWW.KANFER.COM.

and gorgeous views of nature, the new space totally transformed my home. Some of my favorite design surprises: a full moon shining from the clerestory windows, reflecting prisms along the walls when the sun shines on my silestone countertops, and, on a wintry day, feeling like I'm in the middle of a snow globe. At its best, architecture can work magic.

Who or what experience has been a major influence on your career?

❯ No doubt that my father's career as a professor of city planning and a principal in a city planning consulting office was a major influence. Without it, I may have chosen a career in healthcare, as a counselor or therapist, or in journalism—but probably not in architecture. My mother taught me the value of listening and understanding.

My mentors in graduate school also had a strong influence. Robert Sommer, a psychologist at the University of California at Davis, taught me the importance of writing scholarly research for a wide variety of audiences along with the value of writing in a style that the average layperson could understand.

Clare Cooper Marcus, a retired professor of architecture and landscape architecture at the University of California at Berkeley, taught me the need to examine environment-behavior research topics that could have far-reaching psychological impacts. Galen Cranz, a professor of architecture at Berkeley, provided thoughtful critiques of my student work and helped me become a much better writer than before.

After I joined the faculty of the University of Illinois, my colleagues James Anderson and Sue Weidemann provided excellent role models as scholars who engaged in high-caliber environment-behavior research and who interacted well with their students and colleagues.

My late husband, Barry Riccio, a historian, was an excellent wordsmith and a top-notch writer who often critiqued my manuscripts. He helped me come up with the title for *Design Juries on Trial* and other publications. Several have alliteration in their titles—a favorite trademark of his. My personal experiences with Barry's seven-year long battle with a rare form of cancer also had an impact on my career.

Architecture: Connectivity + Community

PATRICIA SALDAÑA NATKE, AIA

Principal and President

Urban Works Ltd.

Chicago, Illinois

Why and how did you become an architect?

❯ I grew up on the south side of Chicago, in an area referred to as Back of the Yards—the famed "Stockyards" of Chicago. I am a first generation Mexican American; both of my parents are from Zacatecas, Mexico. One day, my parents needed to go to downtown Chicago to address passport renewal issues. We took a long bus ride (or what appeared to be a lengthy ride for an eight-year-old). When we arrived in the center of the Chicago Loop area, I was mesmerized by the skyscrapers, the expanse of the green space in Grant Park, and the reflectiveness of the windows and metal on the building skins. I recall being breathless as I entered the Federal Building (Mies)—the sheer size of lobby and the simplicity of the materials. I wanted to know why there were not any majestic places and green spaces where I lived? I did not know what an architect did—but I knew that I wanted to change my neighborhood for the better. Therefore, I became an "architect" at a very early age.

Why and how did you decide on which school to attend for your architecture degree? What degree(s) do you possess?

❯ I wanted to attend a school somewhat close to home. Since I lived in Chicago, I applied to Illinois Institute of Technology (IIT) and University of Illinois at Urbana Champaign (UIUC). I was accepted at both and chose UIUC after attending a minority recruitment event at which my mother and I were invited to spend the weekend on the campus. I earned a bachelor of science in architectural studies from UIUC.

What has been your greatest challenge as an architect/principal?

❯ Time! The flow of creative ideas and desire to search for innovative solutions comes easily, but the execution of the idea requires adequate time. My equally greatest challenge is the educating of clients.

Westhaven Development, Mixed Income Housing, Chicago. Architect: Urban Works, Ltd. PHOTOGRAPHER: ANTHONY MAY PHOTOGRAPHY.

Benito Juarez High School Performing Art Center, Chicago. Architect: Urban Works, Ltd.

This is a challenge that I find exhilarating. Inspiring clients to take a risk, to think outside of the box, to visualize (although technology has finally made a leap), and put full trust in us as designers.

How did you name your firm, Urban Works, Ltd.? Why "urban" and not "architecture?"

❯ Urban refers to the entire realm of the urban city—all major metropolitan cities, local and global. "Urban Works" signifies that we have a unique capacity to convey the shifting conditions of a modern urban city.

Why has the architectural profession been unable to attract more minorities to its ranks, in particular Hispanic?

❯ I believe it may be due to socioeconomic conditions as well as some cultural issues. In addition, there are very few role models in schools, universities, and the work force. I have always led my career path with a mindset that I would overcome all obstacles—and yes the obstacles are greater—but I never expected prescriptive solutions.

You are a past national diversity chair of the American Institute of Architects (AIA) and your firm profile states "celebrate diversity." Why is diversity important in the architectural profession?

❯ The profession has an obligation to the public. That public is diverse. The AIA has finally implemented the funded 2020 Vision for Architecture, developing a cohesive system for collecting demographic data on the profession, and a methodology for analyzing and publishing the information.

You have been involved with a number of community service including professional associations, neighborhoods groups, and area schools. Why is it important for you to be involved with this community service?

❯ There is such under representation in local communities that I merely want to assist in representing the voice of others whom may not be able to voice their opinion. Plus, diverse architects bring valuable perspective to the design and definition of livable communities. Buildings become a part of history—they should be reflective of their current time, place, and inhabitants. Currently, a very large segment of society has little to no influence on our architectural history. It is a crisis!

What are your primary responsibilities and duties?

❭ I am the principal in charge of design. I provide the design direction on key projects in the office. In addition, I handle the marketing and business development for my office.

What is the most/least satisfying part of your job?

❭ Truly the most satisfying is the completion of a space or building. To think back to its genesis, embedded with human thought and labor, and made into a physical object. The least satisfying is contract negotiations. Each time we must negotiate a contract fee, it reminds me that society views our work with a finite value.

Who or what experience has been a major influence on your career?

❭ The greatest honor is to have had inspirational architects/individuals that influenced my career.

■ Carol Ross Barney, FAIA, of Ross Barney Architects—while I was employed at her firm in the 1990s. I am grateful for her vision and persistence.

■ Dan Wheeler, FAIA, of Wheeler Kearns—I taught with him at University of Illinois at Chicago (UIC), and I value his brilliance and optimistic quest for excellence.

■ Rafael Hernandez—He was the executive director of Hispanic American Construction Industry Association (HACIA) and winner of the 2003 AIA Whitney Young Award. I appreciate his endless support and confidence in the potential success of my firm.

■ Stanley Tigerman and Eva Maddox, Archeworks (2002–present)—I taught with them at Archeworks, and I value their tireless commitment to socially responsible design.

■ Bradley Lynch, Brininstool + Lynch (2004–present)—I taught with him at Archeworks, where he taught me of the poetics of elegant minimalism.

Instituto del Progresso Latino Community Center Design, Chicago. Architect: Urban Works, Ltd.
PHOTOGRAPHER: PHILIP SCHMIDT.

Leadership by Design

AMBASSADOR RICHARD N. SWETT (R), FAIA

President

Swett Associates, Inc.

Concord, New Hampshire

Why and how did you become an architect?

❱ There are four clear reasons why I became an architect.

My father was a civil engineer who started, owned, and operated a construction company in the northeast since I was two years old. I grew up in the construction environment and ultimately worked for him as a laborer in the trenches and with him as a partner developing alternative energy biomass power plants and sustainable communities around them to utilize the thermal waste in an efficient centralized heating system in the mid-1980s, long before global warming and sustainable design were publicly discussed.

As a sixth grader, I remember doing a project that fascinated me. It entailed creating an Aztec city on a 4' by 8' piece of plywood that included pyramids and temples, roads and canals, residential districts, and government centers. I learned a great deal about the relationship between transportation, habitation, and the infrastructure required to make living in an ancient city possible and comfortable.

As a junior in high school, I was the student representative on my town's new high school building committee, which oversaw the creation of its own high school. Up to that point, students, like me, attended a regional high school in the neighboring larger community. Serving in this capacity provid-

ed me access and participation rights to the process of designing this new school. Although I did not say much, I watched and took note of the role the architects played in shaping and directing the needs and desires of the town. I was also intrigued by the way everyone had to work out differences and work together to achieve this goal.

While at Yale I had a course that studied the relationship of the architect with the community as he or she worked to gain consensus regarding a project that was being designed. I spent the semester shadowing an architect in Boston who worked for the Boston Redevelopment Authority as he designed a mixed-use senior housing building with retail space on the ground floor in the North End, or Italian neighborhood of Boston. I attended numerous community meetings, discussed with the architect and the community their concerns for the new concept of combining uses in one building, and watched as the architect slowly and successfully brought about consensus where opposition first existed.

These seminal experiences are the foundation upon which my entry into the profession was built. Interestingly, although I also enjoyed drawing and design, my interests lay more with the relationships between architect and client and client and community, antecedents to my entry into the public realm.

Why and how did you decide on which school to attend for your architecture degree? What degree(s) do you possess?

❱ I ended up at Yale University as an undergraduate for several reasons, although I was accepted at all the Ivy League schools to which I applied. My original intention was to study engineering; my father was the greatest influence in my life, and

President Bill Clinton, Ambassador Richard N. Swett, David Putnam of Markem Industries, Keene, New Hampshire

architecture had only recently been introduced as an option. My father was a Yale graduate from the School of Engineering, and being an independent Yankee, I did not want to follow in his footsteps on his coattails, so I was determined to demonstrate my entrance into the collegiate ranks on my own. When all my applications were accepted at Harvard, Penn, Brown, and Yale, I could matriculate to New Haven without feeling it was only because of the legacy relationship.

At Yale, I was also intent on playing football and using that as a springboard into professional sports. I figured that any injury I might endure, if a career stopper, would not diminish my professional poten-

tial, as I would still graduate with an Ivy League degree. Well, two things changed my plans of being an engineer who played football into being an architect who aspired to compete in the Olympics. I was able to attend the Montreal Olympics where I saw Bruce Jenner win the gold medal in the decathlon, and I found my courses in architecture more to my liking than my engineering courses at Yale. So I dropped out of the football program, took up the decathlon on the track team, and switched my major to architecture. I graduated from Yale College with a B.A. in architecture and as the holder of the university decathlon record (which I still hold). In the professional world I applied and was accepted to seven graduate architecture programs as well as several business schools, but I never attended any of them as I was fully occupied with professional pursuits having obtained my professional license in the State of California through the apprentice program in place at the time.

What has been your greatest challenge as an architect?

❭ My greatest challenges exist at opposite ends of my career. In the beginning, when I first went out on my own, I had a design build firm in California. One of my first projects was a residential project that was with a client that refused to pay a substantial portion of the project cost. It ended up being the business school education I had decided not to attend as a graduate student, both in what I learned from it and what it cost me, financially.

The other is my recent position as a managing principal in one of the country's largest architecture and engineering firms. I came into an office in Washington, DC, that was without leadership and without a backlog of work. For the last year I had been rebuilding these two very important components necessary for success back into the office's operations. This work is now challenged by the greatest recession, possibly depression, since the depression of 1929. Still, the firm made tremendous strides and I am confident the office will emerge at the other end of the economic down cycle more vibrant, productive, and profitable than it was.

What led to your involvement in leadership roles in your professional and public life?

❯ My stint as a developer of alternative energy biomass power plants was the part of my professional life that politicized me the most. I had to act and understand how to work with community planning organizations, environmental groups, etc., as a developer. As I became more familiar with the political process and how to engage in it, I realized how narrow and polarized most participants' viewpoints were. My natural inclinations as an architect and consensus builder made me move naturally into leadership positions where I served to build bridges between groups that otherwise were at an impasse.

How did your background in architecture prepare you as a U.S. Representative and Ambassador to Denmark?

❯ When I ran for the U.S. House of Representatives, one of my slogans I liked to use was, "I am running to serve in the People's House, and every house deserves a good architect." Throughout my first campaign I drew the analogy of managing the government's budget, which was in the worst deficit condition ever in the country's history to how Americans manage their own homes. I would say we would not build additions to our houses as much as we would like to if we did not have the money to do so, so why should we continue to expand the government's budget? At the time we were entering the savings and loan crisis, a milder form of today's troubles, and the analogy had resonance with the public.

In Denmark, I built my service on four cornerstones of activity, drawing upon my experience gained in Congress. Knowing that our foreign service tended to be reactionary instead of proactive to events, I set out four ways that we could engage with our host country that would establish long-term relationships worthy of preservation. That way, when difficulties came, everyone would be motivated to work for their solution because there were greater relationships to be preserved at stake. The four cornerstones we identified were Regional Security, Economics and Trade, Human Rights Issues, and Design Diplomacy. The last category was an obvious tip of our hat to the Dane's wonderful sense of design and the high value they placed in it. My architectural background gave me the ability to identify with this important aspect of their national character and to engage with them in ways that enabled them to positively influence America's somewhat lower commitment to design quality and its positive impact on the quality of life in the community.

Why did you write Leadership by Design: Creating an Architecture of Trust?

❯ I was frustrated, and still am frustrated, by the divisive and polarized quality of our elected officials' service. As the only architect to serve in Congress in the twentieth century, I am also painfully aware of the lack of leadership the profession is providing to fix this problem. In fact, our lack of interest in developing our leadership skills impacts our own practices and profession in immediate ways that make it difficult to manage day-to-day operations, let alone influence national public policy.

The book was written for three reasons: (1) as an outlet for the frustrations that had built up inside me as I went through the various stages of my career and saw the problems that could be solved by

Ambassador Richard N. Swett, Secretary of Defense William S. Cohen.

leaders with the inclusive problem-solving skills similar to those used by architects in the design process, (2) as an instructive manual to motivate members of the design professions to step up and become leaders in their professions and communities, and (3) as an instructive manual to motivate members of the broader community to think about how public leaders can actually be inclusive problem solvers who engage the community at large in the process of finding solutions to the difficult problems they face.

Why is it important for architects to be leaders in their community? How do they become involved?

❯ This is the million-dollar question. During the 2008 presidential campaign, we witnessed two candidates calling out for change and unity. Both come to this position from different places. One has little experience working across the aisle, so to speak, while the other has been doing so for many years, although at times with a lack of diplomacy that has offended his own party. They both have no real experience of working in a systematic way to solve

problems that looks across the political horizon for solutions from both sides of the political spectrum. This is where the design process and architects could be very useful, for they are professionals who are energized by the opportunity to broaden their horizon of creative solutions, not reduced to fearfully restricting themselves to a narrow band of options defined by a single ideology. By being advocates for the use of the design process as a way to improve the quality of life for all members of their communities, design professionals have the ability to apply this approach to all aspects of that community, not just to enhancing the built environment and preserving the natural environment.

In Denmark, the Folketing, or Parliament, has a "design review" of all legislation to determine if it is in the best interest of the broadest swath of the population to be affected by it. This is a quality control check that truly believes that good design is a quality-of-life issue.

Becoming involved in the political process is both easy and difficult. It is easier to befriend public servants to help them understand the inclusive problem-solving process used by the design professions and incorporate these ideas into their platforms. It is more difficult in that it takes abundant time and energy to be persuasive in getting these points heard and adopted. More difficult still is the proposition of running for office. That can be very expensive and time-consuming, and it opens one to personal attacks that, if taken personally, can be quite painful. But is there much of an alternative as we see the quality of our public leaders continue to decline and diminish in their ability to solve these divisive and complex problems that face our world?

What is the most/least satisfying part of your career as an architect?

❯ The most satisfying part of my architecture career is being able to reshape the world around me into a better place by engaging the community at large to the best extent possible in that process. The least satisfying is working with people in my profession who possess the potential to have the most positive impact but are just not able to realize their potential or sense the responsibility to do so.

Who or what experience has been a major influence on your career?

❯ I continue to believe that public service can be and is a noble service that requires the vision and problem-solving expertise possessed by architects, engineers, and people of the creative professions. My years of service in the public realm have taught me this and convinced me that we should strive to increase our influence and broaden our impact in order to improve our communities and the world around us.

The Architecture of Leadership

CAROLYN G. JONES, AIA

Director, Callison

Seattle, Washington

Why and how did you become an architect?

❯ After taking an Introduction of Architecture class at a summer camp program in junior high, architectural design became one of my favorite hobbies. I would spend summers at my drafting table designing floor plans and building foam core models of houses. Despite my interest in architecture, I never thought of it as a career I wanted to pursue. I started college as an international studies major without even considering architecture as an option. During the second semester of my freshman year, I decided to try Introduction to Architecture. Three weeks later I was an architecture major. There was no one reason I can name that convinced me to switch, I think that I was just instantly captivated by the buildings we were studying and could not imagine anything more rewarding than creating the built environment for a living.

Why and how did you decide on which school to attend for your architecture degree? What degree(s) do you possess?

❯ I have a five-year bachelor of architecture degree from the University of Notre Dame. Since I

STOREFRONT

Coldwater Creek International Plaza Retail Store, Tampa, Florida. Architect: Callison. RENDERING: BRIAN FISHER, PRESENTATION ARTS.

did not go to college to study architecture, it was pure luck that I even ended up at a school with an architecture program. I chose Notre Dame for its well-rounded liberal arts undergraduate program, its size, the campus atmosphere, and the student life it provided. It was more important to me to be at a school that felt like a great fit for me overall, with the strength of the specific program I was interested in being a secondary consideration.

As it turned out, I believe the specific program there did provide me with a very strong background and foundation for the study and practice of architecture. However, I truly believe that the most important part of my education, which has helped make me the architect as well as person that I am today, was based more my *entire* Notre Dame experience and less on the specifics of the architecture program.

What is retail design and how might it be different from architecture design?

❯ What makes retail design unique is the focus beyond just the traditional shell building to the interior architectural design as well as the visual merchandising. The design of the entire built environment, down to the smallest detail of a merchandise fixture, is part of what makes a retail space function.

I have never felt that interiors and architecture are two separate, distinct fields, and in retail design, the two are inseparable. From the architectural standpoint, retail design needs to be a seamless connection between interior and exterior spaces and forms.

The key is that in retail, the architecture serves as a backdrop to display the merchandise. You have to understand how product is displayed, how it best sells, how the customer interacts in or "shops" the space, the impact of lighting, and the importance of setting a certain atmosphere through a combination of built environment, furniture, fixtures, and finishes.

What are your primary responsibilities and duties?

❯ As a project manager, my primary responsibilities are full oversight over the design and construction of a project from start to finish. Starting with monitoring the initial design and setting up the project team, schedule, and budget, I help lead the entire process all the way through construction. In the earlier project phases, I am primarily responsible for managing the internal project team and consultants to produce the documents, communication with the client's project manager, reviewing design decisions, working with the developer or landlord on coordination issues, and dealing with schedule, budget, and permitting. During construction, in addition to these activities, I work closely with the general contractor to keep the project moving forward in all aspects of contract administration, including biweekly site visits to monitor progress.

As a director at my firm, my responsibilities are much broader than working on individual projects. I help to manage a large client account that involves many skills beyond those necessary to execute projects. We work with the client directly to help manage workflow, project quality, schedules, and budgets. Internally I work with staffing to keep the project teams balanced with the right individuals. I also spend an extensive amount of time on personnel issues, helping others set and work towards their goals, dealing with problem situations, helping to maintain morale of the staff, etc. Directors also work with other groups and leadership throughout the firm on initiatives, task forces, and other business functions that affect broader aspects of how the office runs.

What has been your greatest challenge as an architect?

❯ My greatest challenge as an architect has been learning the necessary skills for my position that were not taught in school, mainly teamwork, management, and leadership. School focuses heavily on the achievement of the individual, but in the working world, success relies on working with others. It took me quite a few years to realize that my own hard work or talent meant very little, and in the end would not lead to much success, if I did not cooperate with and respect the input and contributions of others.

In some ways, I am less confident now than I was when I was first starting out in architecture. The longer you practice, the more you know, but you also become increasingly more aware of what you do not know. Sometimes that can be very overwhelming, but in the end you have to remember that you have an amazing support system in the resources and colleagues you build up over the years. Those people become part of your professional "team" who can help you achieve more than you ever could on your own.

What challenges do you find in being both an architect and a mother?

❯ In most ways, I face the same challenges as a working parent in any profession. Balancing work and family is never easy, and with architecture there is the occasional added pressure to work extra hours or late nights on project deadlines. Learning to work more efficiently in the time you do have is critical and often feels counterintuitive to what we have learned since the studio model in school. (Of course, the past experience of pulling all-nighters probably helped prepare me for life

Nordstrom, Fashion Island Mall, Newport Beach, California. Architect: Callison. RENDERING: AMY DIMARCO, AIA.

with a newborn!) I think most working parents would agree that it is frustrating to feel like you are ever really able to give 100 percent either at work or at home. It can be difficult to realign expectations of yourself and your career after working so hard to succeed at what you do.

What I do find very challenging specifically as an architect is the lack of role models of other working moms at the leadership level. Perhaps this is not unique to our profession, but it has been difficult to find many women in more advanced roles who also face the challenges of parenting young children. Many of the women in leadership have chosen not to have children and the others often have children quite a bit older, so I have found myself to be an exception in this regard. What I have come to realize is that I need to embrace the fact that I actually *am* that role model. It is an honor to be an example for others as a young firm leader and mom, learning the ropes of balancing a career and a family every day. I hope, by being a role model in this regard, I can help encourage the next generation of young architects, men and women, to find their own work/life/family balance. As a bigger vision, I also hope to help find a way to keep more talented women architects in the profession in the long run by encouraging them to find creative solutions to balancing their own families and careers.

What is the most/least satisfying part of your job?

❱ What we often refer to as people issues are the both the most and least satisfying parts of my job. On the least satisfying side is dealing with office politics, staffing problems, or personnel issues. This might include how I get along with and fit in with other leaders in the company who I do not always agree with or who have different agendas, as well as helping staff who do not get along with each other learn to cooperate. More downsides include delivering tough messages to staff that are having serious performance issues and, in the worst case, having to lay off or even fire coworkers. Many days, the architecture challenges we face on projects seem quite manageable compared to keeping so many talented and unique individuals working together in a positive, constructive way.

On the flip side, people issues are also the most rewarding part of my job. One of my favorite activities is working with staff to help them create and work towards their professional goals. Whether through our performance review process or more informal day-to-day coaching and mentoring, it is very rewarding to help facilitate the growth and learning of those around me. Although seeing a building you worked on get completed is still the pinnacle of satisfaction for me as an architect, it is followed closely by seeing people around me grow and succeed in their careers. It can often be challenging to find the time to spend with others in this development capacity, especially when you have so many pressing needs on your own projects, but the time spent connecting one-on-one with those you work with has intangible rewards. It is an honor to be in a leadership position where I can be a role model and mentor for other young architects.

Who or what experience has been a major influence on your career?

❯ By far the greatest influences on my career have been the mentors I have had. Two individuals in particular were extremely supportive of my career growth and were champions for me at a young age. As a result, I have enjoyed rapid growth in my career and a chance to expand my skill set and knowledge base very quickly. These opportunities have helped fuel my success within my firm as well opened up opportunities for me to learn new skills on various project types.

Although finding a mentor is not always a clear or defined process, there are things a young architect can do to help facilitate finding one. I have found that the more interest, initiative, drive, and enthusiasm you show in your career, the more likely you are to attract the attention of a mentor who can support you along the way. Look for others that you respect or have an interest in, and do not be afraid to reach out to them and find out more about their career path.

Nordstrom, Topanga Mall, Canoga Park, California. Architect: Callison. PHOTOGRAPHER: CAROLYN G. JONES, AIA.

To Lead, To Serve

CATHERINE A. MCNEEL FLORREICH, ASSOCIATE AIA

Architectural Intern

Eley Guild Hardy Architects PA

Jackson, Mississippi

Why and how did you become an architect?

❯ My father is an architect who has his own practice. I grew up around the business and was exposed to art and other cultural events, travel, and museums. The professional organizations around our state are relatively small and family-oriented so I also got to know other architects and their families through conventions, beaux-arts balls, and the like.

I knew that I wanted a design degree but considered becoming a fashion designer, a graphic designer, or an industrial/product designer. When I was researching colleges and career options, I realized that I was really looking for an education that allowed flexibility and various means of studying a problem. I decided to attend architecture school but was not sure if I wanted to enter traditional practice. However, I felt confident that I could use my broad-based education in a number of professional settings.

Why and how did you decide on which school to attend for your architecture degree? What degree(s) do you possess?

❯ Once I decided to pursue an architecture degree, I researched several universities in the southeastern United States. I looked at architecture programs that were accredited by the National Architecture Accrediting Board (NAAB) and considered both the five-year degree programs and 4+2 degree programs. I decided to attend Mississippi State

University, which offers a five-year bachelor of architecture degree. Mississippi State is tied closely to the profession, encourages collaboration between multiple design disciplines, and continuously develops new technology resources. Community service is also encouraged within the School, and this effort has been magnified to respond to ongoing Hurricane Katrina recovery efforts in our state.

What has been your greatest challenge as an intern thus far?

❯ One of my greatest challenges as an intern thus far has been finding my own voice in the profession. I have struggled to find a successful balance of responsibility, accountability, authority, and mentorship within the context of project teams. Sometimes it is hard to overcome the barriers in getting your opinion out of your mouth and into the project.

What are your primary responsibilities and duties?

❯ My role and responsibilities include but are not limited to conceptual design, construction docu-

Stephen Covey Conference and Retreat Center, Gulfport, Mississippi. Architect: Eley Guild Hardy Architects PA.
PHOTOGRAPHER: RICHARD SEXTON.

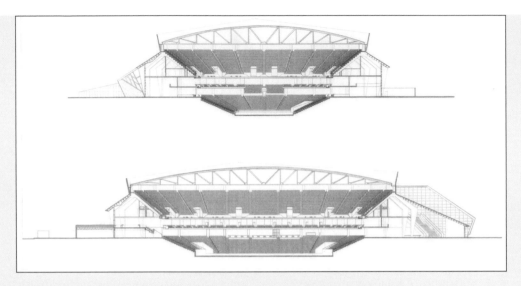

The Entergy Center City of Jackson by Catherine A. McNeel at Mississippi State University.

ment production and management, and consultant coordination and management. Our firm is switching to building information model (BIM) technology, and I am assisting other users with this implementation. The firm is completing many commissions dealing with Hurricane Katrina Recovery efforts on the Mississippi Gulf Coast.

Throughout your career, you have been involved with both the AIAS and the AIA. How have these experiences contributed to your career?

❯ The AIAS and the AIA have played a huge role in my professional development. I became involved with my local AIAS chapter, serving as secretary, chapter president, and Freedom by Design chair.

I attended the AIAS FORUM during school and really enjoyed the national efforts and voice provided by the AIAS. I decided to run for national vice president and was elected at the 2005 FORUM in Cincinnati. I lived in Washington, DC, as the 2006–2007 AIAS national vice president. The vice president serves on many committees and has the opportunity to visit each collateral organization

office and learn more about the governance of the overall profession. The knowledge gained and relationships formed have created many more opportunities to serve the profession.

After my wonderful year in Washington, DC, I moved to Jackson, Mississippi, and was elected to serve as the 2008–2009 AIA Gulf States regional associates director (RAD). I was also elected to serve as the National Associates Committee's (NAC) 2008 advocacy director.

My firm has been extremely supportive of my involvement in professional organizations. I believe that firm-wide support is critical to one's ability to effectively serve in leadership positions.

Being involved in the AIA is extremely rewarding. I am working with fellow AIA associate members and interns to lead the future of our profession and engage in dialogue about initiatives that affect emerging professionals. I feel more a part of the profession through my involvement at the national level, and I feel that I have a greater understanding of the way the profession works and the challenges it faces.

I encourage more people to become involved, at either the local or the national level. There are opportunities for you, no matter what your interest or background. I have always found that I receive much more than I provide. Our profession is continuously changing and it is important to be a part of that change, instead of watching from the sidelines.

What are your 5-year and 10-year goals relative to architecture?

❯ My immediate goal is to complete IDP and become a LEED Accredited Professional; also, I wish to become a licensed architect. I plan to complete the ARE by early 2010. I hope to find new ways to learn and broaden my professional experience and capabilities. Looking ahead 10 years, I would like to own a practice or be a managing partner in an existing firm. And I would like to serve as the president of AIA Mississippi and as the AIA Gulf States regional director.

What is the most/least satisfying part of your career as an architect?

❯ The most satisfying part is . . . making an impact on the community and bringing the vision of a collaborative team to life. Under the best circumstances, architects are hired for their vision and abilities to lead a team towards a shared goal. Being trusted with such lofty expectations is incredibly humbling and rewarding.

The least satisfying part is . . . dealing with the more mundane aspects of the project delivery method: conflicting regulatory authorities, redlines, poor communication and documentation of decisions, and lack of responsibility.

Who or what experience has been a major influence on your career?

❯ My parents have been the most influential presence in my life and my career. I was always told that I could be whatever I wanted to be and do whatever I wanted to do. I would say that I am a good combination of both of my parents: my father is strong willed and a leader. . . . My mother dedicates a lot of her time to being involved in the community; she is compassionate, giving, and strong. These traits have made me into the person I am today.

My husband, Ryan, has also been an incredible part of my career development. We met in architecture school and found the support system to be undeniably strong. Although we now work for competing firms, we compare our experiences and give advice. It is great to have a husband who truly understands where I am coming from and what I am faced with on a daily basis. He has been my support through all of the challenges and personal growth of internship.

St. Martin High School, Ocean Springs, Mississippi. Architect: Eley Guild Hardy Architects PA. RENDERING: ELEY GUILD HARDY ARCHITECTS PA.

Teaching Architect

MAX UNDERWOOD, AIA

Professor of Architecture

School of Architecture and Landscape Architecture

Herberger Institute for Design and the Arts

Arizona State University

Tempe, Arizona

Why and how did you become an architect?

❯ Because my father was involved in construction as a high-voltage electrician, I grew up within the building industry and became an architect primarily by osmosis. Some of my fondest childhood memories are of accompanying my father to his construction sites at Disneyland, Kaiser Steel, MGM Studios, and the Huntington Library Gardens.

In addition, I spent many hours of my youth working with my hands, building custom furniture and rebuilding my 1955 Oldsmobile, in our well-equipped shop in the family garage. In high school, I excelled in chemistry and physics. Because of my love of conceptual thinking and open-ended discovery, and of art and drafting, I worked summers for several local architects and contractors.

Why and how did you decide on which school to attend for your architecture degree? What degree(s) do you possess?

❯ During my senior year of high school I was recruited in physics at Caltech and University of Southern California (USC). After attending their respective university-wide open houses, I decided to enroll in a dual physics and architecture major at USC.

In the mid-1970s, the architecture program at USC had a wonderful mix of European and Southern

California professionals who had commissions throughout Los Angeles. In addition, the larger university offered exciting classes in film, urban geography, computer science, and, of course, physics, taught by some of the leading physicists of the NASA Jet Propulsion Lab in Pasadena.

The larger architectural and physics cultures of Los Angeles were exhilarating at the time with Aldo Rossi visiting at UCLA, the newly formed energy of SCI-ARC and Richard Feynman lecturing at Caltech. During my junior year of the bachelor of science in architecture program, I worked in the office of Charles and Ray Eames, a truly life-altering and formative experience of my subsequent career as both an architect and educator.

I attended Princeton University and received my master of architecture degree, within a small intimate program, situated close enough to New York, so you could be part of its vital energy and still get your work done.

What are your primary responsibilities and duties as a "teaching architect," an architect and a faculty member?

❯ True education is not only imparting a body of professional knowledge but to question and advance it through a collaborative investigation of the discipline of architecture by both the student and teacher, whether in school or in a professional office.

Education is a forum where the distinctions between teacher and student have been replaced with the notion of collective inquiry and discourse. The condition is not one of students in competition with one another, but where everyone is discovering something that was unfamiliar a moment before, until this new situation arose,

Spaces of Silence,
Kyoto, Japan.
Architect: Soami.
PHOTOGRAPHER:
MARC MONTY.

and where all are willing to help each other clarify their ideas, methods, and work.

Education begins with a response to each student's individuality and talent. The student and teacher must first jointly find out where the individual is relative to their own personal growth, and then establish how to further develop the student's self discipline, motivation, expertise, and individuality. Education, like design, is an act of faith and discipline, where the limits are not clearly defined and the student must discover, define, and act on them. The outstanding students are constantly reaching beyond themselves to develop new ideas, cherishing the difficulties of work that asks hard questions, and forcing themselves to experience the world differently and to change. The pleasure of teaching comes from the firsthand participation in an individual's discovery of the previously unrealized power of their innate abilities in the formation of their own ideas, investigations, and self-criticism.

Next, education should focus upon the development of each individual's processes of inquiry, invention, and making, grounded by an emphasis on making connections between cross-cultural references, other disciplines, and architecture. Therein lies a concern to integrate interdisciplinary knowledge and critical inquiry from the arts, humanities, and sciences alike, but in ways that suit the problems and purposes of the present.

Students should develop a personal attitude and vision in their inquiry of architecture, test it, and realize it through their critically made work. They must be encouraged to doubt, question givens, and generate acute alternatives to what architecture is today. Familiarity with that evolving body of knowledge we call *tradition* and its progression of ideas, helps students obtain a critical breadth of personal vision and understand why certain questions being explored by other disciplines are essential to their evolving body of work. Students must develop representational media and notational devices that capture the spirit of their design inquiry, and allow them to clearly visualize, refine, and communicate its qualities to other people. They must remember that the most challenging professional and intellectual problems of contemporary architecture require integrating the knowledge of several disciplines into broader understanding, insight, and action.

Who or what experiences have been major influences on your career?

❯ Working for the office of Charles and Ray Eames in the mid-1970s was one of the most profound and life-altering experiences of my career. Their office allowed me to experience firsthand exemplary professional practice and what hap-

pens if you "make design your life, and life your design." It was a rich and provocative environment for celebrating the inquiry of the unknown. Everyone in the office became personally engaged in thinking deeply and differently, going beyond the point where others had stopped, satisfied. I saw endless speculation, prototyping, and when a promising revelation was arrived at, celebrating its beauty through film so anyone, even a child, could share in the enjoyment of the discovery. Charles would always ask you one question at a desk critique, "What is interesting?"

Creator of Space

JOHN W. MYEFSKI, AIA

Principal, Myefski Cook Architects, Inc.

Glencoe, Illinois

Why and how did you become an architect?

❯ I wanted to shape the future built environment. I feel that architects have such a profound impact on the way we live that I thought it would be great to create. I also had the chance to work for an architect as a high school senior. This experience really set the stage for my future.

Why and how did you decide on the University of Michigan to attend for your architecture degree? What degree(s) do you possess?

❯ I grew up in the upper peninsula of Michigan, and the idea of going to a school that was in the Midwest was important because of cost; cost was a strong consideration when selecting the University

of Michigan. I was fortunate to have one of the best public schools in my state. I attended the pre-architecture program at Northern Michigan University for my first two years. All of my credits transferred to the University of Michigan. This saved me cash and allowed me to flourish in a small university before graduating from Michigan with my bachelor of science. Because I really enjoyed the architecture program, I stayed to graduate with my master of architecture two years later.

After receiving your master of architecture, you had the opportunity to study abroad in Denmark as the recipient of a Fulbright Fellowship. Please describe this experience and how it shaped your career as an architect.

❯ Because I received both my degrees from the same school, I felt that my education needed a boost or outside shock to complete my studies as a well-rounded student. My solution was to attend a program in Europe; the Fulbright provided me

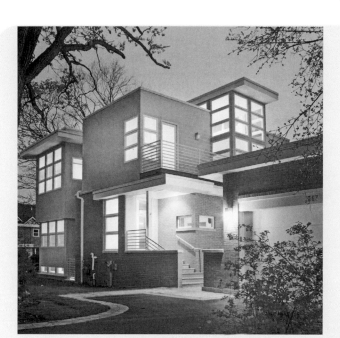

◀ Private Residence, 317 Adams, Glencoe, Illinois. Architect: John W. Myefski, AIA, Myefski Cook Architects, Inc. PHOTOGRAPHER: TONY SOLURI PHOTOGRAPHY.

▼ Principal Mutual Life Insurance Company, Des Moines, Iowa. Architect: John W. Myefski, AIA, Murphy/Jahn.

that opportunity in Copenhagen, Denmark. The Royal Danish Academy was a great chance to study abroad and spend the time traveling throughout Europe. I cannot tell you how this changed my life as an architect and person. The exposure to living in Denmark and what I saw enriched my soul and improved my work. Travel is the most important part of your education!

Wakefield Memorial Building, Wakefield, Michigan. Architect: John W. Myefski, Myefski Cook Architects, Inc. PHOTOGRAPHER: MYEFSKI COOK ARCHITECTS.

What has been your greatest challenge as an architect?

❭ Waiting to peak! Being in my mid-forties, I am just getting started on where I want to go with my work. It takes time to build a practice and even more time if you want your work to be substantial and not a momentary flash in a magazine. When you start your practice you need to succeed in many ways and it is basically like building a home. First you start with a solid foundation and then keep working your way up. At this point I feel that I am starting on the second floor—cannot wait to get to the roof! I think most architects really getting going at age 55–60 so I have plenty of time to improve.

What are your primary responsibilities and duties as the principal of your own firm?

❭ Everything! In a practice of 15 architects with two principals you really do everything. That is the best part. I find the work, do the design, oversee the building of the project, maintain contact with the client, fix just about any problem that exists, and

run the day to day of a business. Most people do not understand that it is the architect's job to solve problems. Life is a series of logjams, and I am constantly trying to keep the water flowing.

Why did you decide to open your own firm?

❭ I had been working for Helmut Jahn and loved my job but needed to look to the future and develop my own work. I started the firm because I found a historic home that I was saving by literally moving it to a new site; it went so well that the owners of the home asked me to take over the new home they wanted. This was my first job, and saving the home made me a hero in my small community—the rest is history.

When designing a project, how do you begin? What is your inspiration?

❭ I pull the pen out and sketch on whatever I can find. The ideas are created from inside but they are influenced by the program, client, site, locale, history, etc. I love to feel and experience the site and its surrounding context. Buildings do sometimes have a metaphor but mainly it comes from someplace within. I think if you could discover the exact point, you would unlock the future.

Who or what experience has been a major influence on your career?

❯ My childhood was key and that is because I spent much of it traveling. The exposure opened my eyes and I have a hard time closing them to this day. My education was a strong second and that is because I had great professors and a wonderful facility to explore at the University of Michigan. It is simple; you need pen and paper; the rest comes from your exposure and professors. My first position at Murphy/Jahn was the best and gave me the chance to work on wonderful projects.

NOTES

1. Rand, Ayn. (1943). *The Fountainhead.* New York: Penguin, p. 16.

2. *The American Heritage Dictionary.* (2000). Boston, MA: Houghton Mifflin.

3. Kostof, Spiro. (1986). *The Architect: Chapters in the History of the Profession.* New York: Oxford University Press, p. v.

4. Cuff, Dana. (1991). *Architecture: The Story of Practice.* Cambridge, MA: MIT Press, p. 153.

5. Raskin, Eugene. (1974). *Architecture and People.* Englewood Cliffs, NJ: Prentice-Hall, p. 101.

6. U.S. Department of Labor. Bureau of Labor Statistics Occupation Outlook Quarterly. (2008). Retrieved May 26, 2008, from http://www.bls.gov.

7. NAAB Report on Accreditation in Architecture Education. (2009). Retrieved May 14, 2009, from http://www.naab.org.

8. National Council of Architectural Registration Boards. "2008 Survey of Registered Architects." (2008). Retrieved December 10, 2008, from http://www.ncarb.org.

9. American Institute of Architects. (2006). The Business of Architecture: The 2006 AIA Firm Survey. Retrieved August 17, 2008, from http://www.aia.org.

10. U.S. Department of Labor. Bureau of Labor Statistics. "Occupational Employment Statistics. (December 2007). Architects, Except Landscape and Naval." Retrieved August 13, 2008, from http://www.bls.gov/oco/ocos038.htm.

11. Design Intelligence. (2009). *2009 Compensation and Benefits Survey.* Norcross, GA: Greenway Communications, LLC.

12. American Institute of Architects. (2008) *2008 AIA Compensation Survey.* Washington, DC: AIA.

13. Anthony, Kathryn. (2001). *Designing for Diversity.* Urbana, IL: University of Illinois Press, p. 22.

2 The Education of an Architect

The architect should be equipped with knowledge of many branches of study and varied kinds of learning, for it is by his judgment that all work done by the other arts is put to test. This knowledge is the child of practice and theory. Practice is the continuous and regular exercise of employment where manual work is done with any necessary material according to the design of a drawing. Theory, on the other hand, is the ability to demonstrate and explain the productions of dexterity on the principles of proportion.

VITRUVIUS POLLIO, *The Ten Books on Architecture* (ed. Morris Hicky Morgan)

TO BECOME AN ARCHITECT, there are three major steps: education, experience, and exam. The most critical may be education. While completing your formal education (obtaining a National Architectural Accrediting Board [NAAB] accredited degree) may take five to seven years in college, your actual architectural education will continue throughout your lifetime. This chapter will help you learn how to prepare for an architectural education, discuss the degree paths, outline the selection process, and describe the experience of an architecture student.

Depending on where you are on this path, the process of becoming a licensed architect may take a total of 10 to 15 years, from entering an architecture program to passing the Architect Registration Examination (ARE). Where does this process begin? Based on interactions with those wishing to become architects, it starts very early. Some say their interest in becoming an architect began in elementary school or even earlier. For others, it was later—after college or later in life.

◀ Alexandria Central Library, Alexandria, Virginia. Architect: Michael Graves + Associates/PGAL. PHOTOGRAPHER: ERIC TAYLOR, ASSOCIATE AIA. PHOTO © ERICTAYLORPHOTO.COM.

Where does their desire to become architects come from? Some say they enjoyed drawing; they enjoyed constructing or building with blocks, Legos, Erector Sets, and similar toys. In addition, a drafting course may have piqued an interest in architecture.

What should you do if your desire to become an architect emerges in high school? From the academic coursework you choose to a part-time position in an architectural firm, you can pursue many activities to further your interest in architecture and begin the process of becoming an architect. If you have completed a degree in another discipline and now wish to become an architect, many of these same activities may be helpful.

Preparation

TOYS

Over the past century, numerous toys with an architectural theme have been developed. Many are variations of blocks; all provide children with a sense of design, discovery, and creation. For example, Legos are one of the more popular children's toys that architecture students say helped them become interested in the field. John Lloyd Wright, the son of the famous architect Frank Lloyd Wright, invented Lincoln Logs in 1916. Introduced just prior in 1914, Tinkertoys and Erector Sets allow children to construct and build their ideas. A more basic toy that almost all children play with is blocks. Sets of wooden blocks can be used to build everything from patterns to elaborate structures, houses, and skyscrapers.

A less well-known toy, used by Frank Lloyd Wright as a child, is Froebel Blocks, a series of wooden stacking blocks developed in the 1830s by Friedrich Froebel, a German educator and the originator of the kindergarten, for children to learn the elements of geometric form, mathematics, and creative design. Wright described their influence on his work: "The smooth shapely maple blocks with which to build, the sense of which never afterwards leaves the fingers: so form became feeling," and "A significant idea behind the blocks is the importance for developing minds of examining things around them in a freely structured manner."

Another set of wooden building blocks to consider is Kapla. Made of pine from renewable French forests, Kapla are small rectangular planks all measuring $1" \times 4^{1}/_{2}" \times {1}/_{4}"$. Children of all ages can create just about anything without any glue, screws, or other fasteners.

BOOKS

Many books tell stories featuring architecture or buildings. Some targeted at younger children have good illustrations of architecture, while others have plots that engage the reader with houses, castles, trees, and imaginative environments.

ACTIVITIES

Cultural institutions sponsor events or activities meant to expose children to the world of architecture. For example, the National Building Museum in Washington, DC, holds a Festival of the Building Arts each fall. During the festival, visitors of all ages can build a brick wall, participate in a nail-driving contest, try stone carving and woodworking, learn the techniques involved in surveying, build a city out of boxes, or create a sculpture out of nuts and bolts. The Frank Lloyd Wright Home and Studio near Chicago offers an opportunity for young teens to serve as tour guides. Contact area museums or other cultural institutions for exhibits, lectures, or classes related to architecture and the built environment.

PROGRAMS

Organizations such as Center for the Understanding of the Built Environment (CUBE), Built Environment Education Program (BEEP), Chicago Architecture Foundation, Learning by Design in Massachusetts, and Architecture in Education host programs for both individuals and teachers.

SELECTED BOOKS ON ARCHITECTURE FOR CHILDREN

13 Buildings Children Should Know (Hardcover) by Annette Roeder (ISBN: 3791341715)

Architects Make Zigzags: Looking at Architecture A to Z by Diane Maddox (ISBN: 047114357X)

Building Big (Paperback) by David Macaulay (ISBN: 0618465278)

Discover America's Famous Architects by Patricia Browne Glenn (ISBN: 0471143545)

Draw 50 Buildings and Other Structures by Lee J. Ames (ISBN: 0385417772)

Frank Lloyd Wright for Kids: His Life and Ideas by Kathleen Thorne-Thomsen (ISBN: 155652207X)

Great Building Stories of the Past (Hardcover) by Peter Kent (ISBN: 0195218469)

Houses and Homes by Ann Morris (ISBN: 0688135781)

Housebuilding for Children, 2nd Edition by Les Walker (ISBN: 1585679062)

How a House Is Built by Gail Gibbons (ISBN: 0823412326)

Iggy Peck, Architect by Andrea Beaty & illustrated by David Roberts (ISBN: 081091106X)

Math in the Real World of Architecture by Shirley Cook (ISBN: 0865303428)

Round Buildings, Square Buildings, and Buildings That Wiggle Like a Fish by Phillip M. Isaacson (ISBN: 0394893824)

The Picture History of Great Buildings (Hardcover) by Gillian Clements (ISBN: 1845074882)

Willits House, Highland Park, Illinois. Architect: Frank Lloyd Wright. PHOTOGRAPHER: R. LINDLEY VANN.

who desire to help younger children learn about architecture. CUBE brings together educators with community partners to effect change that will lead to a quality built and natural environment. BEEP, a program for young students sponsored by the American Institute of Architects (AIA) California Council, encourages in elementary students an awareness of the built and natural environments, architecture, urban planning, and seismic safety, as well as how citizens can influence growth and planning in California.

An element of the Boston Society of Architects, Learning by Design gives young people the opportunity and the skills they need to communicate their ideas about the built and natural environments, about community, and about themselves. This organization has developed children's design workshops with themes that include designing dream houses, designing the community, neighborhood walking tours, places to learn, history through structures, block play, and block design.

Many of these programs and others are listed in A+DEN—Architecture + Design Education Network (www.adenweb.org), an online resource of programs designed to help students learn about the design process and built environment.

ACADEMIC COURSEWORK

Because becoming an architect requires a college education (in most states), your high school academic curriculum should focus on college preparatory courses, including four years of English and mathematics. Pursue as many honors and advanced placement (AP) courses as possible; by taking and passing advanced placement exams, you may receive college credit and bypass required entry-level courses. (*Note:* The number of credit hours you can receive varies by college.) In addition, AP credit allows you to carry a lighter academic load or pursue additional coursework, such as electives or minors.

While the mathematics requirement may vary among architecture programs, most either require or encourage you to take calculus. You should pursue or take the highest-level math course your high school offers.

Although some high schools do not require or offer physics, you should take an entire year of high school physics rather than biology or chemistry if possible. A good year-long physics course is excellent preparation for college physics and structures courses. If you have already completed college, note that many graduate programs require or strongly encourage your taking calculus and physics as prerequisite courses; these typically can be done at area community colleges, but check the requirements of the graduate program. A handful may also require completing a history of architecture course. Again, check with each program as to its requirements.

In addition, take art, drawing, and design classes rather than architectural drafting or computer-aided design (CAD). Your interest in architecture may have surfaced from a drafting course, but art courses will be more helpful in your preparation to become an architect. Art, drawing, and design courses develop visual aptitude and literacy, while expanding your ability to communicate graphically. Take a freehand drawing course or a three-dimensional course such as sculpture or woodworking. In addition, art courses provide you with material for your portfolio, a requirement for some architecture programs; this is especially true if you apply to graduate programs, as all will require a portfolio for admission.

Do your best with every academic course you take! While grades are not the only criterion by which college admissions offices judge applications, they certainly are one of the more important ones.

Besides academics, what can you do to begin your preparation for a career in architecture? Consider the following:
(a) exploration of the built environment,
(b) visits to architecture firms and schools,
(c) participating in a summer program sponsored by an architecture program, and
(d) participating in an after-school program.
All these provide you a head start on the path to becoming an architect.

Piazza d'Italia, New Orleans, Louisiana. Architect: Charles Moore.
PHOTOGRAPHER: ISABELLE GOURNAY.

EXPLORATION

An important skill to acquire in becoming an architect is the ability to see. By learning to observe buildings, spaces, and their relationships, you become sensitive to issues that concern architects. Explore your surroundings by looking closely at the built environment every day.

> What detail can you describe from memory about a building you know well—a school or nearby store, for example? Now, visit the building and note all the details you did not remember or notice before. Draw sketches of the overall building or details.
>
> MARGARET DELEEUW, University of Maryland

Tour and observe your neighborhood or city, and take visual notes about the architecture you encounter. Seek out guided tours of significant buildings in your city, and learn about their architectural features.

Purchase a sketchbook and begin to teach yourself to draw. Sketch from real life to develop your drawing skills and sharpen your awareness of the existing environment. Sketching from life trains you to observe, analyze, and evaluate while recording your surroundings. Do not worry about the quality of the sketches; focus instead on developing your skill of seeing.

> When I was a summer intern, I sat outside and sketched during my lunch break. One day I sketched a landscape, as the office overlooked a waterfall. Another day I drew my shoe or my handbag. Yet another day I found some object in the office to draw, like a lamp. Some days I sketched my hand or my foot. This simple exercise was greatly beneficial, as it taught me that the key to producing an excellent drawing is to train your eyes to see.
>
> MARGARET DELEEUW, University of Maryland

One way to develop your drawing skills is to dedicate a specific amount of time—one or two hours—per day to sketching. Be committed to drawing each day. Practice, practice, and practice!

Begin reading books, magazines, and newspapers articles on architecture and the profession of architecture. Check your local public library for ideas.

VISITS

Tour the design studios of a nearby school of architecture to become acquainted with the experiences of an architecture student. Speak with current architecture students about what they do. If possible, attend a few classes to learn about the courses you may take. As most schools sponsor evening lectures highlighting architects and their work, consider attending one. Typically, these are free and open to the public.

Visit with a local architect to gain a broader understanding of the nature of an architect's work and the value of the profession. To locate an architect, contact the local chapter of The American Institute of Architects (AIA, www.aia.org) listed in the phone book. Ask your parents, teachers, or friends of your family if they know any practicing architects. Try not to be intimidated as you call to meet with an architect. Remember, these connections may be valuable when you apply to architecture programs or for possible summer employment opportunities.

Visit construction sites to learn how buildings are constructed. Talk with carpenters, builders, and others in the building industry to learn their perspectives on architecture. In addition, travel throughout your community, throughout your region of the country, or to other countries to experience architecture from various perspectives. As you visit, sketch!

SUMMERS

Many colleges and universities offer summer programs (archcareers.org/summerprograms.html) designed for high school students, college students, or adults who desire to learn about the field of architecture. Lasting from one to several weeks, these programs are an excellent opportunity to determine if architecture is the right career choice. Most include design, drawing, and model-building assignments; field trips to firms or nearby buildings; and other related activities. These can all assist you in determining if architecture is for you. Summer programs are also a good way to learn about the architecture program of a particular institution.

Each summer, the Graduate School of Design at Harvard University offers Career Discovery, a six-week program during which students of all ages are introduced to design through a core program of morning lectures, panel discussions, and field trips. Over 50 schools nationwide offer such summer programs. Entitles such as museums and community park districts may also offer such programs.

While growing up, I wanted to be an architect, but I really did not know much about the profession or architecture school. To learn more, I attended the Discovering Architecture Program at the University of Maryland the summer before my senior year of high school. Completing the program solidified my interest in architecture. During the three-week program, we took field trips to Baltimore and Washington, DC; listened to lectures about the basics of architecture; and designed and modeled our own memorial. I loved how the program was hands-on and encouraged interaction with faculty and graduate students. Most important, it was located in the architecture building on campus so I could experience architecture school and college life.

DANA PERZYNSKI, University of Maryland

If possible obtain a summer internship with a construction company or architectural firm; you may be limited in the tasks you do, but the experience will be far more rewarding than typical summer positions. If you are unable to secure a summer internship, find an architect to shadow for a day or a week. Many high schools offer programs designed to connect students with career professionals.

If such opportunities are not possible, consider volunteering at or providing community service with a design-related organization such as a museum. Depending on your location, volunteer with Habitat for Humanity; always look for opportunities to become involved with the built environment.

AFTER-SCHOOL PROGRAMS

An after-school program that exposes you to the profession is the ACE (Architecture, Construction, and Engineering, www.acementor.org) Mentor Program of America. ACE is for high school students interested in learning about career opportunities in architecture, construction, and engineering. Throughout the school year, professionals mentor students, who work on a design project and learn about the career fields of architecture, construction and engineering.

Other after-school programs include the Boy Scouts of America Explorer Post and Odyssey of the Mind. One program, Saturday Sequence, offered by Carnegie Mellon University in partnership with Carnegie Museum of Art, is offered during eight consecutive Saturdays in the fall and winter and includes hands-on projects and three-dimensional representation. Additionally, there are competitions that you may enter; the Newhouse Program and Architecture Competition, sponsored by the Chicago Architecture Foundation and the Chicago Public Schools, offers opportunities year-round for students interested in architecture and design. Contact various organizations within your community, including local AIA chapters or architectural foundations to determine if they have programs designed to connect you with the built environment.

Seaside, Florida.
PHOTOGRAPHER:
ISABELLE GOURNAY.

> What advice would you provide to someone who wants to be an architect?

> Have passion and patience. Is that enough advice?

Robert M. Beckley, FAIA, Professor and Dean Emeritus, University of Michigan

> Build, build, build at whatever scale you can because it informs how assemblies come together which will give one a better understanding when designing.

Mary Kay Lanzillotta, FAIA, Partner, Hartman-Cox Architects

> Draw, read, or write about architecture every day. Create! Take all the art, math, and science classes you can. Do not waste a moment!

Diane Blair Black, AIA, Vice-President, RTKL Associates, Inc.

> Keep your eyes open and look at the full spectrum in which architects operate. Seek where you can best use your unique education and individual talents and grow.

Randall J. Tharp, RA, Senior Vice-President, A. Epstein and Sons International, Inc.

> The architecture profession and the role of the architect are changing. Architecture is becoming less and less a purely design oriented function and is reverting back to the role it once played which was that of the master builder, or someone who gives direction to the shape, form and organization of society or the subsets of society that occupy and operate within the built environment. My advice would be to approach the profession from the perspective of fulfilling this type of role and not from the traditional role of only designing buildings after internal programs and activities, site selection, economic and political negotiations have all been concluded.

Ambassador Richard N. Swett (r), FAIA, President, Swett Associates, Inc.; Managing Principal, Leo A. Daly

> Take a design course, intern with a firm, read architectural magazines, visit buildings, and, once you are confident with your decision to pursue architecture, identify schools that provide what you want from your education. Choose a school with a curriculum that is strong in your interests—design, sustainability, theory, technology, urban planning, historic preservation, etc.

Margaret DeLeeuw, Marketing Director, Celli-Flynn Brennan Architects & Planners

> Have a passion for observing the environment around you. Learn to translate what you see into lines on paper.

H. Alan Brangman, AIA, University Architect, Georgetown University

> Keep an open mind. Pursue the aspect(s) of architecture that you are most passionate about with reckless abandon. Surround yourself with intelligent and creative people. Enjoy the journey and learn from all of your experiences. Architecture can be grueling work, but if you apply an open mind, passion, inspiration, and wisdom to the process, it can be even more rewarding.

Margaret R. Tarampi, Associate AIA, Doctor of Philosophy Candidate, University of Utah

> I would suggest a period of self-reflection. It is a challenging and competitive career that one cannot enter half-heartedly. If the desire and determination are there, then I would encourage the person to pursue it.

Kathy Denise Dixon, AIA, NOMA, Associate Principal, Arel Architects, Inc.

What advice would you provide to someone who wants to be an architect? (Continued)

❯ I would stress the importance of two points: that architecture is very much an intellectual pursuit, and that architects must be interested in craft, making, etc.

Douglas Garofalo, FAIA, Professor, University of Illinois at Chicago, President, Garofalo Architects, Inc.

❯ I recommend that everyone, no matter what his or her aspirations, seek one or more individuals for help with career development. I have had two primary mentors—one for nearly 30 years and one for almost 25 years—and many friends and associates along the way who contributed to my success. I would not have achieved as much as I have without their support. I also developed a 25-year plan early in my career. This too has been invaluable.

Kathryn T. Prigmore, FAIA, Senior Project Manager, HDR Architecture, Inc.

Fishing Boats, Styrso, Sweden. PHOTOGRAPHER: MICHAEL R. MARIANO, AIA.

❯ Shadow an architect before deciding to attend an architecture school; several shadowing experiences are ideal. Take all classes available in freehand drawing, painting, photography, sculpture, furniture making, and related arts and crafts. Invest in a sketchbook. Explore a new part of your city or take a trip to a different city. Participate in the summer high school programs offered by many architecture programs.

Elizabeth Kalin, Architectural Intern, Studio Gang Architects

❯ Talk to individuals in the profession, both those pursing a traditional career in a design firm and those following an alternative career path. Realize that architecture can take you on paths as varied as publishing, graphic design, and documenting historical buildings. The problem-solving skills inherent in an architecture degree are valuable in many occupations that have nothing or little to do with architecture.

Tamara Redburn, AIA, LEED AP, Project Architect, Fleming Associates Architects, P.C.

❯ Develop a passion for architecture and design in order to truly enjoy the field. As you will invest much time in becoming an architect, you must enjoy and learn from this time-consuming, dedicated work. Although becoming an architect is not easy, you will learn from the process.

Brad Zuger, Architectural Designer, Shanghai MADA S.P.A.M.

❯ Try architecture, but do not rule out other careers without adequately exploring them. Keep an open mind about your future—but once you have decided on this field, do not let anything stop you.

David R. Groff, Master of Architecture Candidate, Virginia Tech–Washington Alexandria Architecture Center

❯ First, you must always remember that there is more to life than a career. The education of an ar-

Celebration, Celebration, Florida. Architects: Cooper, Robertson with Robert A. M. Stern Architects. PHOTOGRAPHER: GUIDO FRANCESCATO.

chitect must begin with a framework for developing personal consciousness—that is, an avenue for instilling the value and manifestation of being fully awake and aware as a thinking, feeling, and contributing member of our evolving world.

Be encouraged to doubt, question givens, and generate keen alternatives to what architecture is today. In the real world, enlightened clients seek the conscious architect, rather than the trained architect, to identify and propose solutions to the unprecedented conditions of our rapidly changing world.

Second, immerse yourself in the emerging conditions of the world around you. Ask yourself what is changing, and why. What forces and conditions are causing these changes? The broader your understanding of the human experience, the better design you will produce.

Max Underwood, AIA, Professor, Arizona State University

❯ Motivation is paramount. Studying and practicing architecture takes an enormous amount of time and energy. The academic studio environment is a microcosm of the profession. Not all students instantly take to the studio setting, but when used creatively, it has a great deal to offer.

Kathryn H. Anthony, Ph.D., Professor, University of Illinois at Urbana-Champaign

❯ Be open; do not limit yourself to the traditional definitions and boundaries of the practice of architecture. Learn to observe and to be a good listener. Understand the design process and become a master of your own process. An architecture degree is rich and diverse training for many design-related careers. The process of solving problems creatively translates broadly and does not limit your career possibilities. Because opportunities present themselves unexpectedly and often, be open to them. Know and believe in your unique talents and how these opportunities can be best used.

Barbara Crisp, Principal, bcrisp llc

❯ Intern, intern, intern. Do whatever it takes to gain a summer position in an architecture firm and discover what professional practice is really like. Find out as much as you can about the profession and the career paths you can pursue, but be open to all sorts of experiences. Stay flexible and open to new challenges. Realize that, even after college, your education in architecture has hardly begun; your career path can be a rewarding adventure.

Carolyn G. Jones, AIA, Director, Callison

What advice would you provide to someone who wants to be an architect? (Continued)

❯ Set your sights high! Go find amazing architects and work with them. Go knock on Alvaro Siza's door or travel to London and work for Hadid.

William J. Carpenter, Ph.D., FAIA, Associate Professor, Southern Polytechnic State University; President, Lightroom

❯ Architecture is a fabulous profession with social relevance. The field is so multifaceted that anyone with an inner drive for building in the physical environment will succeed.

Patricia Saldana Natke, AIA, Principal and President, Urban Works Ltd.

❯ Architecture is passionate. Being an architect is not just a career decision—it is a lifestyle. Architecture can be rewarding if you have realistic expectations about what to expect from it. Truly understand what an architect does, and commit your life to that.

Know why you want to be an architect—to end homelessness, to become rich and famous, to serve others, to get published. This goes back to the passion. Talk to practicing architects to see if the profession can really meet your career objectives.

Grace H. Kim, AIA, Principal, Schemata Workshop, Inc.

❯ Gain a liberal arts training; do not focus exclusively on skills that apparently are required to be an architect (e.g., drafting). Written communication is a large part of being an architect and should not be overshadowed by drawing or computer skills.

Lynsey Jane Gemmell, Project Manager/Associate, Holabird & Root

❯ Discover more about what architects do beyond the naïve things you hear. Take as many drawing, painting, and sculpture courses as you can. Learn software applications that expand your ability to tell a compelling story about what you are trying to do. Even though the ability to write well is not usually emphasized, it, along with the ability to

speak well, is of great importance. A clear narrative, whether written or oral, has the most impact.

Thomas Fowler, IV, AIA, Professor and Director, Collaborative Integrative-Interdisciplinary Digital-Design Studio (CIDS), California Polytechnic State University–San Luis Obispo

❯ You must love buildings. You need many skills to become an architect, including drawing, math, and other creative problem-solving capabilities. However, a passion for the art of building is essential to being an architect.

Edward J. Shannon, AIA, Director of Design, Benvenuti & Stein Design, LLC

❯ Work hard and be patient—the process of becoming an architect is one of the most demanding AND rewarding experiences you will have in your life. Also do not be afraid to pursue an alternate career in architecture. Having an architecture degree and being a licensed architect prepares you for a number of related and non-traditional careers in architecture.

Jessica Leonard, Associate AIA, LEED AP, Campus Planner/ Intern Architect, Ayers Saint Gross Architects and Planners

❯ Keep in mind that the architecture profession encompasses many careers and many firms, each with its own distinctions.

Eric Taylor, ASSOCIATE AIA, Photographer, Taylor Design & Photography, Inc.

❯ GO FOR IT! Architecture is an amazing profession providing many opportunities and rewards. Architecture education is purposely broad in scope and prepares graduates to make a difference in the world, in any numbers of ways. Architects are called to have vision, provide leadership and input, create uplifting places, and be the stewards of resources. It is a challenging profession that requires lifelong learning and a continuous building of one's skill sets and abilities. I would tell someone

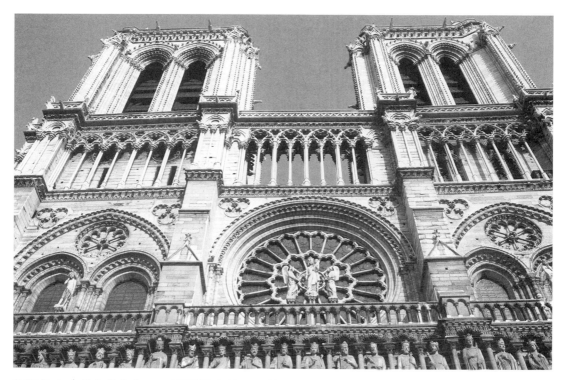

Notre Dame de Paris, Paris, France. PHOTOGRAPHER: R. LINDLEY VANN.

interested in becoming an architect to figure out what interests them about the profession and pursue it to the fullest.

Catherine McNeel Florreich, Associate AIA, Architectural Intern, Eley Guild Hardy Architects PA

❭ Try it. The reality is different from the popular idea of the profession. Architecture is a diverse discipline with a wide range of opportunities for specialization.

Lois Thibault, RA, Coordinator of Research, U.S. Architectural and Transportation Barriers Compliance Board (Access Board)

❭ Intern in an architecture office to gain a better idea of what the profession is really all about. An architectural intern may find that perception and reality are very different in terms of what actually occurs in an architect's office on a daily basis.

Robert D. Roubik, AIA, LEED AP, Project Architect, Antunovich Associates Architects and Planners

❭ Be passionate! You must feel in your heart that you want architecture to be a part of your life. Learn to be creative and to challenge linear thinking. Expand your world through travel, reading, drawing, conversation, music, and every other way possible. Learn to enjoy and be rewarded by the challenges of discovery and risk.

Clark E. Llewellyn, AIA, Dean, University of Hawaii

❭ As the profession of architecture is vast, do not be afraid to take an unusual path. Often we are taught we have just a single path to take in order to be a successful architect, but this is not so. Succeeding at architecture requires you to make your own path. Individuality is rewarded in this profession.

Lisa A. Swan, Residential Designer, Design Forward

What advice would you provide to someone who wants to be an architect? (Continued)

❯ Take courses in art, math, and science. Once you learn to draw and how buildings are put together you can stand proud of your hard work and dedication and explain to the next generation how it is all worth it.

Jennifer Jaramillo, Architectural Intern, Dekker/Perich/Sabatini, LLC

❯ Take time. Take a great deal of time to understand what undergraduate education and institution is the best fit for you. Select an education that gives you a broad understanding of the world so your work in architecture can engage as much context as possible.

Admit no money barrier. Go to both the best-fit and finest school you can possibly attend without regard for the expense—you can pay it back.

Seek out faculty. Get to know your teachers well and try to have work experiences that confirm the nature of practice. Verify what works and what does not with respect to your developmental needs; if you discover you really like to be in the woods, or in nature, another profession may be a better fit for you.

Travel. Observing and talking to people may be the greatest teacher.

It is okay to fail. Follow the maxim of IBM's Thomas Watson Jr.: "Want to succeed faster? Accelerate your rate of failure!"

Joseph Bilello, Ph.D., AIA, Professor and Former Dean, Ball State University

❯ There is no better *discipline* for those that like to be creatively involved in the lives of others, but the *profession* needs a lot of work. Share your insights, engage within communities, seek help/expertise when you need it and, most of all, do no harm.

Wayne A. Mortensen, Associate AIA, NASW, Project Manager/Urban Designer, H3 Studio; Lecturer, Washington University

❯ Earn a professional degree if you want, but do not let anyone tell you what to do with it or how to use it. Get out in the real world—by which I do not mean corporate practice. The real world requires you to get your hands dirty. The real world expects you to take initiative in doing mundane jobs. And the real world exists within, but also beyond, the borders of the United States and other Western nations. The corporate world will still be here and will value the real-world experiences you bring back.

Casius Pealer, J.D., Assistant General Counsel (Real Estate), District of Columbia Housing Authority; Cofounder, ARCHVoices

❯ Travel as much as possible. Experience as much as you can and find buildings that inspire you. Be artistic. Drawing, painting, sculpting, and photographing all develop your eye. It will allow you to analyze things you never even saw before. Be passionate. Architecture is very demanding but it is worth the sacrifice if you love what you do.

Marisa Gomez, Bachelor of Science Candidate, University of Maryland

❯ First, choose the right school for you. Speak to architects about what they do, visit their offices, and ask where they went to school and why. Most important, explore the physical world around you. Do you want to change it? Then, think about what part of architecture interests you—design, planning, engineering, business, development, preservation, residential, commercial, or something else. You need not choose right away but, with direction, the course of your training and work experience can be adjusted periodically to be sure you stay on track.

Christopher J. Gribbs, Associate AIA, Senior Director, American Institute of Architects

❯ We are a profession of generalists; you have to know a little about a lot of different things. You cannot be egotistical and think you know how to design without the involvement and successful collaboration with a variety of experts. You need to make sure that you ask the right questions. Schools need to be involving more and different disciplines. The traditional way of thinking about design is dead.

Robert D. Fox, AIA, IIDA, Principal, FOX Architects

❯ Studying architecture and practicing architecture are different. When you study architecture, you focus solely on the expression of your vision. As a professional, however, you cannot escape service and the imperative to accommodate other people's visions. If you wish to become an architect, be tolerant and flexible. Seek people who are doing what they want to do and spend time with them.

W. Stephen Saunders, AIA, Principal, Eckenhoff Saunders Architects

❯ Do not let them talk you out of it—most importantly, a strong skill set in math does not matter.

John W. Myefski, AIA, Principal, Myefski Cook Architects, Inc.

❯ Become a student of life and be familiar with the realms of design, communication, marketing, philosophy, history, computers, psychology, and engineering, to name a few. You should be knowledgeable not just about the design and construction industry but about nearly everything you experience with your senses.

Finally, you do not have to become an architect if you do not want to. If you are in the process of becoming an architect and want to take another path, *do it!* Use the diversity of your architectural education to your advantage and find a career path that really fits.

F. Michael Ayles, AIA, Principal, Business Development, Antinozzi Associates

❯ Live. Experience the built environment. Go see buildings and have experiences in them. Understand why you like certain spaces and not others. Think about the spaces that you live, work, play, and worship in and the characteristics that they have that make your activities more or less enjoyable. Pursue a wide variety of experiences so that when you design a building you can imagine a variety of situations for which its spaces will be used.

Allison Wilson, Bachelor of Science Graduate, University of Maryland

❯ Architects come in many forms. Some are public architects working for communities and city governments; others design skyscrapers, schools, hospitals, churches, houses, and everything in between. Reach out to architects and ask questions. Develop a feel for the challenging and rewarding world that lies before you.

As you follow your dreams, reach out to an architect in your community. Even if you do not know one, pick up the phone book and look some up, give them a call, and simply ask to tour the office. Ask lots of questions—what they like and dislike, what school they went to, what type of projects they work on. Stay in touch with them as you go through your education.

Last, be a heads-up professional. While the profession emphasizes mentorship, know that you must be responsible for your own development by being aware of what you are working on and how it fits in with the overall process, and by asking questions. When you seek increased responsibilities in the office and exercise your judgment when needed, you will find your opportunities to grow are limitless.

Shannon Kraus, AIA, MBA, Vice-President, HKS Architects

Succeeding in the Built Environment

H. ALAN BRANGMAN, AIA

University Architect

Georgetown University

Washington, DC

Why and how did you become an architect?

❭ I became an architect because I have always had a fascination with building things.

Why and how did you decide on which school to attend for your architecture degree? What degree(s) do you possess?

❭ I initially went to school at the University of New Hampshire to study civil engineering. At the beginning of my sophomore year, I met an art professor who had been a former instructor at Cornell University. He suggested that I transfer to Cornell. My degree is the bachelor of architecture.

What has been your greatest challenge as an architect?

❭ My greatest challenge as an architect has and continues to be convincing other professionals that architects are capable of doing much more than just architecture.

How is working as a university architect different from the more traditional role of an architect?

❭ My job responsibilities are more in line with those of a principal in a real estate development firm. I am responsible not only for the hiring and oversight of design and planning consultants, providing program, planning, and design oversight for all university facilities but also for all real-estate-related matters.

McDonough School of Business, Georgetown University, Washington, DC. Architect: Goody, Clancy.

How and why did you pursue what might be considered a nontraditional career path as opposed to a more traditional one?

❭ Initially, I did so because I had an interest in something more than just designing buildings. I spent nine years with the Oliver T. Carr Company, a real estate development company in Washington, DC. That opportunity opened my eyes to the breadth of the built environment and provided me with a much more global perspective on place making.

McDonough School of Business, Georgetown University, Washington, DC, Architect: Goody, Clancy.

During your career, you worked in the Design Arts Program for the National Endowment for the Arts, an Independent agency of the federal government. Can you describe your role in this agency?

❯ I was the deputy director of the Design Arts Program. The program was primarily responsible for grant making and supporting initiatives to spread the word about the benefits of good design. The initiatives that I enjoyed the most were:

■ Mayors Institute on City Design, a series of national forums dedicated to improving the understanding of the design of American cities through the bringing together of mayors and urban design professionals.

■ Your Town—Designing Its Future, national workshops geared to teach the importance of design to those who can influence and make decisions about the way rural communities will look and work in the future.

■ Design For Housing Initiative, a national workshop dedicated to bringing together representatives from the housing delivery system to spur a better understanding of "Good Design" and its application to affordable housing.

■ Presidential Design Awards, an honor award program done in conjunction with the White House given every four years by the president to projects that came about as a result of federal involvement.

The first three initiatives were partnered with universities that had schools of design such as University of Virginia, MIT, University of Minnesota, Tulane, UC Berkeley, Georgia Tech, and University of Maryland. These initiatives were typically run as a three-day seminar and not only involved decision makers like mayors, in the case of the Mayors Institute, but also involved nationally renowned design professionals, planners, landscape architects, real estate developers, economists, sociologists, and educators.

▲ Multi-Sports Facility, Georgetown University, Washington, DC, Architect: Hughes Group Architects.

◀ SW Quadrangle, Georgetown University, Washington, DC, Architect: Robert A. M. Stern/ EYP. PHOTOGRAPHER: H. ALAN BRANGMAN, AIA.

Why did you pursue the additional credentials of a Real Estate Development Primer Certificate at Harvard Graduate School of Design and Wharton School of Business?

❯ When I started my career in real estate development, I had been counseled to consider obtaining an M.B.A. At the time I did not want to commit the time required to return to graduate school. Besides, the president of the firm did not have a business degree and seemed to be doing quite fine. I decided to pursue the path of learning through experience. Besides I had been schooled as an architect and architects are taught to solve problems. I was able to manage any of the issues or problems that were part of my job responsibilities quite well. After having gotten a few years under my belt, I took the primer courses as a way of confirming what I had learned. It worked.

What is the most/least satisfying part of your job?

❭ The least satisfying aspect of my current job is the pace at which things are accomplished in an academic environment—very slow. Entrepreneurship is not something that is typically associated with academia.

Who or what experience has been a major influence on your career?

❭ Bob Smith, AIA, associate principal, RTKL, was very influential in encouraging me in 1979 to look to real estate development as a possible career to pursue.

Oliver T. Carr, Jr., The Oliver T. Carr Company, was a mentor in my early years; through my employment at Carr. He provided me with the opportunity to preside over 5,000,000 gross square feet of commercial development in downtown Washington, DC.

Neuro-Architecture: How Design Designs Us

MARGARET R. TARAMPI, ASSOCIATE AIA

Doctor of Philosophy Candidate

University of Utah

Salt Lake City, Utah

Why and how did you become an architect?

❭ Like many people who pursue architecture, a proficiency in mathematics, science, and art pointed me towards this discipline. I enrolled in a summer program in architecture to find out if it was really what I should pursue in college. The creative and technical aspects of architecture enthralled me. My view of the world and my thinking was transformed. Yet at the end of that summer I was still not satisfied. I had been raised in a culture of directly touching the lives of others. My mother is a doctor and three of my grandparents were teachers. At the time, I could not see how architecture could directly enrich the lives of others as the pursuits of my mother and grandparents did so clearly.

I sought advice from my summer studio professor, Laura A. Lee, FAIA. Little did I know that what she would say to me would affect me for the rest of my life. She simply stated, "People spend 95 percent of their days in the built environment. You cannot help but believe that architecture affects them." At that moment I understood the great power of architecture; it can improve the quality of life for all people. My work now focuses on understanding how architecture affects human experience (behavior and cognition) using neuroscience as the foundation for discovery.

Why and how did you decide on which school to attend for your architecture degree? What degree(s) do you possess?

❭ I earned a bachelor of architecture from Carnegie Mellon University with minors in psychology and architectural history. I primarily looked at universities with five-year bachelor of architecture programs in the northeast United States so that I could be close to home. I chose Carnegie Mellon University (CMU)

Bus Stop + Reflect designed by Margaret R. Tarampi and Eric Egenolf. RENDERING: ERIC EGENOLF.

because of its strength in the arts and sciences and because of its emphasis on interdisciplinary collaboration. It was a smaller university where I would be taught by top-rate professors (as opposed to graduate students) and given a lot of personal attention. On the other hand, CMU also had all of the resources and opportunities available at a larger institution.

Later I pursued a post-professional master of architecture from the Washington Alexandria Architecture Center (WAAC) of Virginia Tech. WAAC was more theoretical and provided a good counterpoint to the architectural philosophy of CMU. It followed a Bauhaus style of teaching, which was very appealing and challenged my existing notions of architecture.

Currently I am pursuing a Ph.D. in cognitive psychology at the University of Utah. At the moment, I am completing a master of science in psychology as part of my doctoral program. I specifically chose the University of Utah so that I could work with my advisor Sarah Creem-Regehr, Ph.D., on space perception and spatial cognition research.

What was your greatest challenge as an architecture student?

❯ My greatest challenge as an architecture student was effectively managing my time. I was (and continue to be) interested in many aspects of the process and the product of architecture. However I knew that had to choose a select group of topics on which to focus and dedicate my time and energy. This continues to be a challenge as I pursue architecture issues.

After your professional bachelor of architecture degree, you pursued a master of architecture (post-professional) and are now pursuing a doctoral degree. Why did you decide to pursue additional education?

❯ The bachelor of architecture provided a fantastic foundation and understanding of the whole process of architecture, but because it is so comprehensive and intensive it does not leave a great deal of room to explore any one topic in depth. The question of how architecture affects human experience was always in the forefront of my mind. While I was able to pursue a minor in psychology during my undergraduate studies, I felt I was just beginning to address that question. The master of architecture gave me a new perspective on the discipline of architecture from a different school of thought. I was able to explore the question further from an architectural standpoint. As I became more immersed in the question and in collaborative work with scientists through the Academy of Neuroscience for Architecture (ANFA), it became clear that in order to investigate the question fully I would need to pursue a doctoral degree in the sciences. By also earning my credentials in the sciences, I can pursue scientific research funding and utilize resources available in both fields. Hopefully this also means that my research work will be respected in both the architecture and the science fields.

What Is neuro-architecture?

❭ Jonas Salk argued that creativity was the merging of intuition and reason. Within this framework we can think of the design process as being made up of two distinct parts—design development (the intuition part) and construction (the reason part). While a wonderful base of knowledge is developing on the construction end of the design process (materials, assembly, building performance, etc.), we do not have a great deal of research to apply to design development (programming, schematic design, etc.).

Historically, architects have relied on intuitive observations to inform their designs. These observations also need to be understood scientifically to comprehensively understand the implications of our work. While we cannot prove that good design is important, science is our best means of understanding the relationship of architecture's effect on human experience. Neuroscience is one part of the puzzle; it is the study of the nervous system

addressing how we think, move, perceive, learn, and remember. This fundamental level of inquiry provides the foundation for addressing the broader question about the relationship between architecture and cognition. This is neuro-architecture. However, it will take a multidisciplinary approach to truly understand this relationship. By investigating the question on multiple levels, we can uncover applicable research results.

How did you become involved with the discipline?

❭ When I graduated from CMU I was considering graduate school in psychology, sociology, or anthropology. It was knowledge from these sciences that I believed could shed light on the effect of architecture on human experience. As I was searching for graduate programs, I came across the work of John P. Eberhard, FAIA. At the time, John was heading a research initiative at the American Institute of Architects (AIA) exploring this very question with a basic science approach. When seeking advice from John about graduate school, I was surprised when he offered me a job at the AIA working as a research consultant. I spent several years working with John on the neuroscience and architecture initiative at the AIA and later at the ANFA. It was through this relationship that I was given the opportunity to do neuroscience laboratory rotations at the Salk Institute for Biological Studies and at the University of California San Diego. This immersive experience in science led to my current pursuits in graduate school.

Can you elaborate on the connection between neuroscience and architecture?

❭ We intuitively believe cognitive functions are affected by their architectural setting. Neuroscientists have recently shown that the adult brain is plastic, or changeable, and can be affected, for instance, by modifications in behavior and the environment.

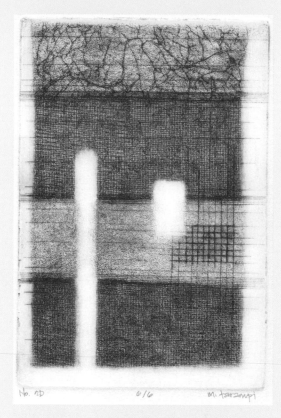

No 2D, Edition: 3/5. Medium: Intaglio Print. ARTIST:
MARGARET R. TARAMPI, ASSOCIATE AIA.

Generally, research has found that enriching both
behavioral and environmental factors leads to cognitive improvements and anatomical changes in animal
models. It is research by neuroscientists such as Fred
H. Gage, Ph.D., at the Salk Institute that has given
us a positive indication that our environment has an
effect on cognitive function. Dr. Gage has shown that
neurogenesis, or the birth of new neurons, persists
throughout adult life in a few key structures of the
brain. One of these structures is the hippocampus,
which is important in the formation of memories.
An important aspect to this finding is that in prior
studies Dr. Gage found that mice that were placed in

an enriched environment, or an environment with
more stimulation, had up to 15 percent more neuron
birth compared to mice that lived in standard cages.

It should be noted this finding has not been corre-
lated to humans nor does an enriched environment
for a mouse compare to what might be considered
an enriched environment for humans. The connection in humans might be very subtle, and we have
to figure out how we can tease out that connection.
Examples in which poor architectural design have
negative consequences on human society as well
as the life of individuals, such as the low-income
housing projects of the mid-twentieth century,
suggest that similar environmental and behavioral
factors might have similar effects in humans. This
shows how important neuroscientific research in
this field might prove in the future for improving the quality of living. A clearer understanding
of how people respond behaviorally to particular
environmental surroundings, such as architectural
design, and what neural mechanisms underlie
these effects, could then be used as a foundation
for architectural decisions. Architects could rely
less on intuition and thereby reduce the variability
in the design process. This does not imply that
the creative aspects of architectural design will be
compromised. But rather this intersection has the
potential to engage and amplify the imagination
in the design process just as new computer technologies allowed architects such as Frank Gehry to
experiment with new structural systems and form.
This is all unexplored territory with limitless potential for advancing the field of architecture.

What is the most/least satisfying part of pursuing an alternative career in architecture?

❯ The most satisfying part of pursuing an alternative career in architecture is addressing a question

in our profession that potentially has overarching effects to the way that architecture is practiced with the intent of improving everyone's quality of life.

The least satisfying part of pursuing an alternative career in architecture is not being able to engage in the design process on a daily basis. I miss design and construction a great deal. I try to fill that void by pursuing art, submitting to architecture design competitions, and by volunteering with Habitat for Humanity.

Who or what experience has been a major influence on your career?

❯ I have been blessed to have several significant and influential mentors in my career. Laura A. Lee, FAIA, supported my development as an architect while

I was at Carnegie Mellon. She was responsible for encouraging me to pursue architecture and teaching, and to take on a leadership role through AIAS. John P. Eberhard, FAIA, informed and structured my ideas about how architecture affects human experience. He saw potential in me that I had not yet realized and provided me with fantastic opportunities for growth. The wisdom of his life experience has been invaluable and has forever altered the direction of my career. Esther M. Sternberg, MD has provided sage advice and encouragement in my scientific pursuits. She has given me crucial insights into the field of science and was a direct influence on my decision to pursue a doctoral degree.

These individuals along with many others have served as role models and catalysts in my development as an architect and human being. I hope that others have people in their lives that believe in them and support them to the extent that these mentors have shaped my life. Individuals such as these are of key importance to anyone's career development.

▼ Songs of Freedom designed by Margaret R. Tarampi, Associate AIA; Eric Egenolf; Lawrence Fabbroni; Jef Leon; Christopher Reynolds. Submission for Pentagon Memorial Competition. MODEL: MARGARET R. TARAMPI, ASSOCIATE AIA; ERIC EGENOLF; AND LAWRENCE FABBRONI.

Recent Graduate, Young Global Professional

BRAD ZUGER

Architectural Designer

Shanghai MADA S.P.A.M

Shanghai, China

Why and how did you become an architect?

❯ Having grown up in a small Midwest town, I have always been fascinated with the city. As a child, I never lived in an urban setting, yet always questioned what the city was like to live in. Since then, I have studied in Dublin, Los Angeles, and various cities in China and also traveled extensively through Europe, Asia, and North America. Because of this global exposure, I now begin to question how architecture can better perform for the current demands of our society and how the future of urbanism will need to change to meet these new demands. The opportunity to investigate such possibilities is why I am now in the design field.

Why and how did you decide on which school to attend for your architecture degree? What degree(s) do you possess?

❯ I graduated with a bachelor of science in design at the University of Nebraska-Lincoln in May 2006. This program was diverse in teaching with a small design community offset in a large university. In May 2008, I received a master of architecture and urbanism from the University of Southern California, which had a globally minded graduate program focused on urban issues and technology. Los Angeles presents a complex and experimental setting in which to study architecture, as well as an exciting design community.

What has been your greatest challenge as an architecture student?

❯ Being an architecture student continues to challenge me, which I truly enjoy. My greatest challenge has been the long nights at architecture hall, common to most students. Each project possesses a new

Chair with Jacket—Charcoal Drawing by Brad Zuger at University of Nebraska.

Cruise Ship Terminal by Brad Zuger at University of Southern California.

challenge, and solving all of the issues involved in a design project takes much time.

Why did you choose to pursue the four + two Master of Architecture degree?

❯ When looking at schools, my decision did not depend on whether the school was a five-year or six-year program because I figured that both were professional degrees. However, I did think at the time that I would get more out of a program with a master of architecture because I would be spending more time on my education.

What interests have you developed as a graduate student?

❯ My interests in graduate study have stemmed from international travel and studios that focused on generative design. These interests culminated in my graduate thesis, which investigated the relationship between design and making and how technology interfaces with making. The project investigated the role of technology in a relatively low-tech environment in China, stating that simple building methods and advanced technologically driven design are not incompatible. The result used a generative system where rules negotiated between a physical and digital system. Other systems of ecology, material performance, and global culture were used as input for the design solution. These interests have now transcended this project, as I am now working in China on topics related to these issues.

What has been the most satisfying part of your education?

❯ I enjoy building with my hands and making things. The best and most interesting way to test and experiment with design systems is to actually build them. One of the things that drew me to become an architect is my desire to actually make what I am thinking and to challenge how things are made. As a young designer, I am continually ex-

Valley City Green Infrastructure by Brad Zuger at University of Southern California. Exhibited at the 2007 Shenzhen-Hong Kong Bi-City Biennale of Urbanism and Architecture.

ploring new ideas and investigating new problems, which is the most satisfying part of my career.

What do you hope to be doing 5 to 10 years after graduation with regard to your career?

❭ I definitely want to be involved with my community, the university, and the AIA. Also, I want to gain a wide variety of experience with different firms in different areas with different specialties. Eventually, I want to be working in my own design firm.

Who or what experience has been a major influence on your education/career?

❭ During graduate school at USC, I participated in a program called the Delta Investigation and

Inquiry Program (DIIP). DIIP aims to strategically identify and investigate localities with the new global matrix that present rich cultural conditions and volatile ecological situations in need of urban and architectural solutions. In the summer of 2007, I worked in a team of about 30 students from three universities who traveled to the tropical island of Hainan, China. There we worked on an ecologically sensitive master plan for a retirement community of 30,000 inhabitants. The program focused on wellness and eco-tourism in a tropical environment. This experience in China was a turning point in my education, exposing me to a multitude of possibilities and ideas, hence changing my viewpoint about the role of architecture in society.

Adventures in Architecture

ALLISON WILSON

Bachelor of Science in Architecture Graduate

University of Maryland

College Park, Maryland

Why did you decide to become an architect?

❯ At the university, I learned that I enjoy the problem solving that goes with my coursework and the camaraderie I share with my fellow students. I like that there are so many different aspects to architecture and that I never stop being a student. Even after class, I still learn about architecture by being in and around the built environment. The variety of experiences that I have had as a student, as well as an intern, keep me confident that architecture will never stop offering me new opportunities. The bottom line is that architecture is something I really enjoy doing, and hopefully since it is enjoyable, it will never really feel like work.

Why did you decide to choose the school that you did—the University of Maryland?

❯ I chose Maryland because I was offered admission to the honors and Gemstone programs and a scholarship. As a New Jersey native, the location was relatively ideal because it let me get away from home but be within driving distance. The proximity to Washington, DC, was also a selling point for me because of the many wonderful opportunities the city offers. Because of the architecture program is a solid 4+2-year degree format, I have had the opportunity to pursue architecture and also explore other interests. Ultimately after I accepted though, it was the people that made me stay at Maryland without even thinking about transferring.

Why did you choose to pursue the four-year pre-professional bachelor of science in architecture degree?

❯ By nature, I am a generalist, and while I love to learn about architecture, there are many other disciplines that interest me. Because of the format, I have had the opportunity to explore other academic programs. Aside from my bachelor of science in architecture, I graduated with a minor in English because I had open credits in my sophomore year that allowed me to take more electives. I also became involved with several student groups outside of architecture early on because I was not immediately overwhelmed with studio courses. I think knowing people and having experiences outside of architecture has ultimately helped my design work because it has given me a broader range of experience to draw upon for inspiration.

Solar Living Pavilion, Model 1 by Allison Wilson at University of Maryland.

Machu Picchu, Peru.
PHOTOGRAPHER:
JENNIFER KOZICKI.

What has been your greatest challenge as an architecture student?

❯ My greatest challenge is determining when to walk away from studio. There are always deadlines, but if design solutions do not come, I must walk away. Architecture students get the equivalent of writer's block when good ideas just fail to materialize. It can be frustrating with deadlines looming, but sometimes I need to walk away and do something else and then come back to my design work later with a clear head.

You have had the opportunity to study abroad twice (Peru and Italy) during your undergraduate studies. How were these experiences valuable to your education?

❯ Studying in Peru and Italy opened the door, literally, to a much larger world for me. These experiences allowed me to explore the values of other cultures through architecture and provided me the opportunity to learn a great deal in a short amount of time. In Peru, I learned about Incan and precolonial architecture and how occupation by an invading force alters the architectural style. In Italy, I learned from both ancient and modern architecture. Ancient Roman architecture has such a clear ideal design aesthetic, where the big idea behind the architecture is well articulated and comprehensible. The modern buildings in Italy have great respect for energy conservation as costs are so high.

Study abroad has been a valuable addition to my education because it has provided incredible experiences that have now prepared me to design buildings for a whole new set of parameters. Everyone should study abroad at some point, regardless of discipline, but especially in architecture. There is so much to gain from understanding why another culture creates buildings the way they do.

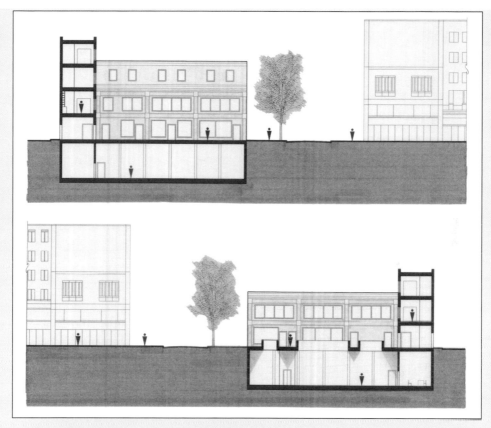

Art Gallery by Allison Wilson at University of Maryland.

What is the most/least satisfying part of being an architecture student?

❭ The most satisfying part is the community within my school. Although the University of Maryland has 35,000 students, the architecture program has about 250 students. For me, the university seems small because I know my classmates by name. I like knowing everyone and having everyone know me; however, I have access to the resources of a large university.

The feeling of success after a project is also incredibly satisfying. After a project and design reviews are done, my class celebrates.

Sometimes I have an unsatisfying day, one where my design just is not coming together or I have gone backwards so I can go forward again. Sometimes it gets frustrating in the middle of the design, but eventually it always passes and the design gets somewhere. On the unsatisfying days it is usually best for me to just walk away from my work for a few hours and do something else that gets my brain engaged and then try to come back to it later.

What do you hope to be doing 5 to 10 years after graduation with regard to your career?

❭ I desire to be designing sustainably green buildings as well as educating people about them. I would like to be able to come back as a visiting faculty member at a university. I may be working for someone else, but I tend to be independent; I may be self-employed, although probably not in the next 5 to 10 years.

Who or what experience has been a major influence on your career?

❯ I have become interested in sustainability because of a short trip to visit family in West Virginia. Due to weather conditions, the most direct route took us over Mount Storm. Among other things, Mount Storm is home to a coal-burning power plant that connects to the Washington DC power grid as well as a set of approximately 38 windmills. With its glowing red security lights and smokestacks, the image of power plant belching smoke into the dark snowy sky burned into my memory. The image has stayed memorable, and I keep a photograph of both the power plant and the windmills on my studio desk to remind me why it is so important to design ecologically but also to remind me that there is hope for the future in those windmills.

Paths to an Accredited Degree

Before selecting a particular architecture program, you need to understand the different paths to obtaining a National Architectural Accredited Board (NAAB) (www.naab.org) accredited degree. Because there is more than one path, this can be confusing. Each path is designed to offer a particular level of expertise and enable you to make a variety of career and educational choices. To become an architect, you will need to set an educational goal to obtain a professional degree accredited by the NAAB.

NAAB accredits three different professional degrees: the five-year bachelor of architecture (B.Arch.); the master of architecture (M.Arch.), which can accomplished by first pursuing a four-year pre-professional undergraduate architecture degree or the four-year undergraduate degree (B.A./ B.S.) in a field other than architecture; and the doctor of architecture (D.Arch.), available solely at the University of Hawaii.

While your eventual goal will be to obtain an NAAB-accredited professional degree, you may wish to consider starting the path at a community college or an institution offering only a four-year degree in architecture. Further still, you can pursue an undergraduate degree in any discipline related or not to architecture.

BACHELOR OF ARCHITECTURE (B.ARCH.)

The bachelor of architecture is an undergraduate five-year degree for students coming directly from high school. It is the oldest professional degree offered at the university level in the United States. Some schools, including Drexel University and the Boston Architectural College (BAC), offer the B.Arch., but completing the degree may take more than five years because of work programs required by these schools.

At most schools, enrolled students begin intensive architectural studies in the first semester and continue for the duration of the program. If you are highly confident in your choice of architecture as your academic major, pursuing a B.Arch. may be the ideal choice. If, however, you think you may not ultimately choose architecture, the five-year program is not forgiving, meaning that changing majors is difficult. Of the institutions offering an accredited degree in architecture, approximately 50 offer the B.Arch.

Recently, a handful of institutions began offering a five- or five-and-a-half-year master of architecture. How are these degrees different from the traditional bachelor of architecture? Contact each institution and ask.

PRE-PROFESSIONAL BACHELOR OF SCIENCE (B.S.) AND MASTER OF ARCHITECTURE (M.ARCH.)

Sometimes known as a four + two, this path to the accredited degree involves first obtaining a pre-professional architecture bachelor of science (B.S.) degree followed by the professional master of architecture (M.Arch.). Pre-professional degrees are four-year degrees that prepare candidates for pursuing a professional degree. These degrees may have different actual titles—bachelor of science (B.S.) in architecture, bachelor of science in architectural studies (B.S.A.S.), bachelor of arts (B.A.) in architecture, bachelor of environmental design (B.E.D.), bachelor of fine arts (B.F.A.) or bachelor of architectural studies (B.A.S.). The amount of architectural work in the program may vary from school to school and determines the length of time required to complete further professional architectural studies, the M.Arch. Most pre-professional degrees are within universities that also offer the professional M.Arch. degree; however, others are offered within four-year liberal arts institutions. Note that your undergraduate degree may dictate the eventual length of your graduate program. Some graduate programs may be three years in length even though you have a pre-professional degree, although you may receive advanced standing or course waivers. Contact each graduate program for more details.

Another viable option for this particular route is to begin your studies at a community college. Often, the first two years of a B.S. degree are predominantly general education courses that can be taken at a community college. It is important, however, to be in touch with the institution at which you plan to continue studies about what courses to take and when to apply. Depending on the institution, it may be worth transferring early rather than receiving an associate's degree from the community college.

Note that if you graduate with the pre-professional degree, you will not be eligible to become licensed in most states. Therefore, if you desire to be a licensed architect, you should continue your studies and pursue the professional M.Arch. degree program. There are a few states in which you can pursue licensure with a pre-professional undergraduate degree, but you would not be able to obtain the National Council of Architectural Registration Boards (NCARB) Certificate (see Chapter 3) necessary for reciprocal licensure.

The professional M.Arch. is a graduate-level degree that typically lasts two years and offers a comprehensive professional education. This combination of the B.S. degree with the M.Arch. offers flexibility, as you can choose to take any number of years off to gain experience between the two degrees. Plus, you may choose to attend a different institution for your graduate studies. Of the institutions offering an accredited degree in architecture, approximately 75 offer the pre-professional architecture degree and accredited M.Arch.

A handful of schools offer an M.Arch. lasting less than two years that follows a pre-professional undergraduate degree. However, these degree programs may be limited to candidates from the same institution. For example, the Catholic University of America (CUA) offers a master of architecture with advanced standing (one and a half years) for select individuals who graduate with the B.S. in architecture from CUA, but those with a B.S. in architecture from other institutions must take two years to complete the master of architecture. At other institutions, the M.Arch. may be less than two years in length because of a switch in the nomenclature of their accredited degree from B.Arch. to M.Arch., but it may require either intersessions or summer sessions.

Finally, a few institutions offering the M.Arch. for individuals with the pre-professional architecture degree will require three years of study; these include most of elite institutions, but candidates may be eligible for some advanced standing.

UNDERGRADUATE DEGREES (B.A./B.S.) IN FIELDS OTHER THAN ARCHITECTURE AND MASTER OF ARCHITECTURE (M.ARCH.)

A professional master of architecture program is available for candidates with an undergraduate degree in a field other than architecture. It offers a comprehensive professional education. Depending on the institution, this accredited M.Arch. will require between three and four years of study to complete. Some institutions require that calculus, physics, and freehand drawing be taken before admission. Depending on your particular educational background, you may need to fulfill these prerequisites. Of the institutions offering degree programs in architecture, over 60 offer this M.Arch.

Some of these programs have the student begin work in the summer before the first semester, while others require full-time study during a later summer semester. Be sure to explore the curricular differences among the programs you are considering.

DOCTOR OF ARCHITECTURE (D.ARCH.)

As a professional degree, the doctor of architecture (D.Arch.) is currently available only at the University of Hawaii. The program is seven years in length and is unique in that it allows the graduate to fulfill the educational requirements for taking the licensing exam, whereas the post-professional doctoral degrees do not. As the D.Arch. is an accredited degree, you are encouraged to contact the University of Hawaii if you are interested in this path.

POST-PROFESSIONAL DEGREES

Besides offering professional degree programs, slightly more than half of the institutions offer post-professional degree programs intended for study as an advanced degree after the professional accredited degree. Although these degrees have different titles (master of science in architecture, master of science in building design, master of urban design), they all allow candidates to focus on a particular field of study—for example, urban design, architectural theory, computer-aided design, housing, sustainability, or tall buildings. The typical candidate pursues this degree after working within the profession for a few years. In addition, a handful of institutions offer a doctor of philosophy (Ph.D.) for those with the master of architecture.

If you have the professional bachelor of architecture, you may wish to consider pursuing the post-professional master degree if you have an interest in teaching within an architecture program. Most architecture programs require a master degree, either the professional or post-professional, as the minimum terminal degree for faculty. However, you may be able to teach as an adjunct faculty with the bachelor of architecture.

Decision-Making Process

Regardless of the degree you may pursue, how do you select an architecture program? After learning about the many degree programs, choosing among them may seem a daunting task; over 125 institutions in the United States and Canada offer professional architecture degree programs. However, if you analyze the criteria that are most important, you can quickly narrow your search and manage this process.

Consider that your education in architecture is only one-third of the path to architectural licensure. There are three Es to complete before becoming an architect: (1) education—an NAAB-accredited degree (Canadian Architectural Certification Board [CACB-CCCA] in Canada), (2) experience—fulfilling the requirements of the Intern Development Program (IDP), and (3) exam—satisfactorily passing the Architect Registration Examination (ARE). All told, it may take 8 to 12 years to complete the three Es.

When choosing the institution where you will pursue your architecture degree, strongly consider the following:

Ensure that the degree program is accredited. Degree programs are accredited by the NAAB (or the CACB-CCCA in Canada), not the institution itself. (For a current list of institutions offering accredited programs, see Appendix B.)

Be sure to understand the possible paths to obtaining your professional degree: (1) bachelor of architecture; (2) master of architecture, following a pre-professional architecture degree or a degree from another discipline and (3) doctor of architecture. Each path has advantages and limitations. Consider which is best suited for you, which will help narrow your choices.

Identify the typical coursework offered in most, if not all, architecture programs: design studio, structures, systems, graphics/drawing, architectural history, general education, computer, site, professional practice, programming, and architecture electives.

You know the degree programs, the list of architectural programs, and the typical courses offered, but what is most important to you? Think about the criteria listed below in the following categories: You, Institution, and Architecture Program. Take time to think about answers to the questions posed and write them down.

By going through this process, you will be better matched with your eventual college choice and more confident in your decision. As you develop criteria on which to base your decision, certain degree programs and universities will surface as logical choices.

YOU

Consider the following attributes prior to selecting a school and an architecture program:

National Museum of Canada, Ottawa, Canada. Architect: Moshe Safdie.
PHOTOGRAPHER: RALPH BENNETT.

Level of confidence: How confident are you in your choice to become an architect? Do you want options as you progress through college, or do you want to dive right into architecture?

For example, if you are not completely confident in becoming an architect, you may consider a program that offers the pre-professional four-year bachelor of science; this way you can begin to explore architectural studies but not in full force, as in a professional B.Arch. program.

Personality type: What type of person are you? Will you feel more comfortable at a large school or a small school? This is a difficult criterion to nail down but also a critical one. Ask yourself, "Will I be comfortable here?"

Closeness to home: How close do you wish to be to home with respect to miles or time? Proximity to home is typically a top reason for selecting a school. If it is important to you, draw a circle on a map around your hometown indicating your desired distance from home.

What schools are inside the circle you have drawn? However, challenge that notion and select the school that is best for you regardless of its location. You should consider each of the over 100 accredited architecture programs. Narrow the choices later based on other criteria.

Budget: Do you and your parents have a specific budget for college? Obviously, with college costs increasing at a rate greater than inflation, cost is an important criterion. Recognize that your college education is an investment in your future and not something that disappears. Remember, once you have your education, no one can take it away.

INSTITUTION

Attributes to consider when selecting an institution include:

Type of school: While most individuals refer to all post–high school institutions as *colleges,* there are different types from which to choose. Most probably consider the university, typically a cluster of colleges under a single administration. However, just as possible is a four-year college, which is usually smaller and places less emphasis on research. Other choices include an institute of technology or polytechnic institute; these focus primarily on engineering and the sciences. Another choice is a two-year college or community college—a viable option, but one that will require transferring to a four-year program to complete your undergraduate degree.

Locale: Where is the institution located? Is it in an urban or a rural setting, or somewhere in between? To what extent is a program's location important to you? Programs located in cities such as New York, Chicago, or Philadelphia consider this urban location an asset, as it gives proximity to architecture to be studied and to architects and other professionals.

Institution size: How many students attend the institution? What is the faculty-to-student ratio for courses, both in the major and in other fields? How much do class and institution size matter to you? For example, a small number of architecture students may be an advantage of a small school, but a larger institution may have more robust resources to offer.

Public versus private: Is the school private or public? Public institutions tend to be less expensive than private institutions because of the support they receive from the state, but they may have higher student enrollments. For international and other out-of-state students, tuition differences between public and private schools may be insignificant.

Cost: What is the overall cost of tuition, room and board, and other expenses? Be careful about using cost as the primary criterion for your initial selection (see Financial aid, below). Cost is and always will be an important consideration, but do not eliminate an institution because of the advertised tuition rate alone. Be sure to gain complete cost information that includes tuition, room and board, books and supplies, travel, and personal expenses.

Financial aid: What amount of financial aid will you receive in the form of grants, scholarships, and loans? Financial aid should be an important consideration, especially at the beginning of the search process. Realize that at a given institution, a large percentage of students receive financial aid. Many schools have full-tuition scholarships that save you as much as $100,000. You will never be eligible for such scholarships if you do not apply to or consider these schools. Also, do not only consider financial aid upon entry to the program; ask what financial aid is available for upper-class students. Many programs award scholarships on a merit basis.

ARCHITECTURE PROGRAM

Because you will spend the largest portion of your college career within the architecture program, consider the following factors as you make your decision:

Degree: What professional architecture degree programs are offered? Does the school have joint degrees with other disciplines? The type of degree program varies from institution to institution. Many academic units have joint degrees with engineering, business, urban planning, and so on. These opportunities may be attractive to you but not available at all schools.

Academic structure: Where is the architecture degree program housed within the institution? Is it within its own college, school, or department? Is it with other departments in a school of engineering, art, design, or other discipline? The location of the architecture program can have an impact on its culture.

During my graduate studies at Arizona State University, the School of Architecture was housed in the College of Environmental Design. Beside architecture, the college offered degree programs in interior design, industrial design, and landscape architecture. We had the chance to study in close proximity to students who would eventually be our professional peers in the workforce. In addition, courses in these other programs were easily available to us as electives.

LEE W. WALDREP, Ph.D.

Philosophy/approach: What is the philosophy of the academic unit and of particular faculty? Some schools are technically oriented, while others are design oriented. Does the school lean in one direction more than the other? What is the mission statement of the architecture program? The approach of the programs you consider should be in concert with your own ideas of architecture. Learn about these differences in approach and decide which fits you.

Reputation/tradition: How long has the school been in existence? What is the reputation of the school among architecture professionals? Reputation is difficult to measure. Decide how important reputation is to you. Ask architects in the profession if they have heard of the school. If possible, contact alumni or current students to obtain their perspective.

Accreditation: What is the program's current term of accreditation? Even though it may be the full six years, what was the outcome of the last accreditation visit? When was the last visit? If the program is fully accredited, accreditation may not be a strong criterion for you, but the program's *Architecture Program Report (APR)* and last *Visiting Team Report (VTR)* may be helpful.

Enrollment: How many students are in the architecture program or in each academic class? Just as institution size can affect your decision, so can the enrollment of the program itself. Consider the overall enrollment of the program and the number of students in each graduating class as well as the student-faculty ratio for architecture courses, especially the studio courses. The number of students in a program could be a reason to strongly consider or not consider a particular school.

Academic resources: What kind of studio space is available to students? What other spaces or resources exist for students—resource center (library), shop, computer labs, digital fabrication lab? Because you will be provided a personal workspace in a studio, the quality of the facilities must be considered carefully—more so than for many other majors. The culture of the studio and access to it can directly affect your choice. What are the hours of the studio? Other facilities such as the shop, architecture library, and computer labs are also worth investigating.

Special programs: What opportunities beyond the classroom does the school offer its students? Lecture series? Study-abroad programs? Dual-degree programs? Minors? Individually designed programs? Experienced-based programs (co-ops, internships, preceptorships)? What special enrichment programs appeal to you? Do you wish to study abroad during college? If so, attending a program with a required study abroad program might be essential. How about a lecture series? Although not a formal part of the academic coursework, an engaging lecture series can be a plus.

Faculty: Who are the faculty? How many are pure academicians versus practicing architects? Are they new to the profession or seasoned faculty? What is the diversity of the faculty? Faculty bring academic courses to life. Read the faculty biographies in the catalog or online and ask to attend a class or meet a faculty member when you visit the school. Do the faculty seem like they would inspire you, motivate you, help you learn? Pay attention to how many faculty members are practitioners first and educators second. What difference does that make in the quality of teaching?

Student body: Who are the students? Where are they from? What are the demographics of the student body (gender, age, ethnicity, etc.)? In searching for a graduate program, consider the educational backgrounds of your future classmates. What proportion are international students, and from what countries do they come? Attending a program with international students can enhance your architectural education. You will spend a great deal of time with your fellow students, and you should be comfortable with them. Consider that many institutions have more than one architecture degree program, which means you may interact with students in degree programs other than your own.

Duomo, Florence, Italy. PHOTOGRAPHER: R. LINDLEY VANN.

Career programs: What programs are in place to assist you in gaining direct experience in the field? Cooperative education? Internships? Exposure to practicing architects? What programs are in place to assist you in gaining direct experience in the field during summers or after graduation? How does the program connect with the professional community and its alumni? Some schools, including the University of Cincinnati; Drexel University; University of Detroit, Mercy; and Boston Architectural College, have cooperative education programs that require students to work in the profession while in school. For more details on these school/work programs, refer to the next chapter.

Postgraduate plans: What happens to the school's graduates? Where are they employed? How long did it take them to find a job? For those who graduate with the pre-professional bachelor of science in architecture, do the graduates continue with the master of architecture degree? If so, what institutions do they attend? Do they continue at the same institution at which they obtained their undergraduate degree? Ask the career center for the annual report on graduates, or obtain the names of recent alumni from the alumni office and contact them.

Resources

The following are resources to assist you in your decision-making process.

PROMOTIONAL MATERIALS, VIDEOS, CATALOGS, AND WEBSITES

The first resource you are likely to receive from any school is the promotional materials that accompany the application for admission. Be sure to contact the architecture program as well as the central university admissions office. In some cases, the program provides additional information or materials. All of these materials are helpful in learning more about the university and its architecture program; however, recognize that they are designed to persuade you to select the institution. Review the materials alongside materials not produced by the program or visit the campus to see for yourself.

GUIDE TO ARCHITECTURE SCHOOLS /ARCHSchools.org

Compiled approximately every five years by the Association of Collegiate Schools of Architecture (ACSA), the *Guide to Architecture Schools* ([8th ed.] Washington, DC: Association of Collegiate Schools of Architecture [ACSA]) is a valuable resource. Its primary content is a compilation of two-page descriptions of the over 100 universities offering professional degree programs in architecture.

In 2008, ACSA launched a companion, online Web-based version (archschools.org) to the *Guide to Architecture Schools*, providing the same information as the book but with the added ability to search the institutions and programs by a number of different criteria, including location (school, state, region), degree, population (female, minority, international, and out of state), curriculum (related disciplines and specialization), and financial factors (scholarships, tuition, residence, and degree level). While both resources provide valuable information, recognize that the programs themselves write and report the information.

CAREER DAYS IN ARCHITECTURE

While many high schools host annual college fairs, these events do not focus specifically on the discipline of architecture. However, there are two annual events that do.

Typically held each October, the New England Career Day in Architecture is a great opportunity to learn more about a career in architecture by interacting with professionals; attending workshops on selecting a school, career options, and financing your education; and meeting with admissions representatives from over 35 programs. For more information, contact the Boston Society of Architects (BSA) (architects.org).

Held during Forum over the winter holiday break, AIAS hosts the College and Career Expo (archcareers.org) connecting students with architecture programs.

CAMPUS VISITS/OPEN HOUSES

One of the most helpful resources is the campus visit. Campus visits are an absolute must, especially for your top choices. When arranging one, consider spending the night with a current student to get an inside feeling about the institution. If possible, request that you stay with an architecture student. In addition, visit with a faculty member or administrator within the architecture program, ask for a tour of the program's facilities, and monitor a class.

In the fall, most schools host open houses as an opportunity for prospective students to meet with faculty and students and to learn more about curricular opportunities. While these are excellent opportunities, recognize that they present the campus at its best. In addition to these planned events, visit unannounced to see the campus, including the design studios, in its normal setting. Many graduate programs in architecture host an open house in the fall for prospective candidates and a parallel one in the spring for admitted candidates. Take advantage of these opportunities to learn more about a program and make an impression.

ADMISSIONS COUNSELOR/ADMINISTRATOR

As you narrow your choices, one of the best resources is an admissions counselor or an administrator (director, advisor, or faculty member) from the architecture program. Remember, the task of these individuals is to assist you in learning more about their university and the architecture program. Develop a personal relationship with them to obtain the information you need to make an informed decision. Do not hesitate to keep in touch with them throughout the admissions process.

STUDENTS, FACULTY, ALUMNI, AND ARCHITECTS

An often neglected but important resource is conversations with individuals associated with the architecture program—students, faculty, and alumni. During campus visits, ask for an opportunity to speak with students and faculty. Request the names of a few alumni in your area, both recent and older graduates, to ask their impressions. Finally, seek out architects and ask them their opinions about the schools you are considering for admission. If you are unable to visit a program, request the email addresses of students or recent alumni to ask questions.

NATIONAL ARCHITECTURAL ACCREDITING BOARD (NAAB)

As noted in the appendix, the NAAB is the sole agency that accredits architecture programs in the United States. Their website (naab.org) provides a simple search for accredited architecture programs by degree program, state, or region. Each listing provides contact information for the program as well as details on the program's accreditation.

ARCHITECTURE PROGRAM REPORT (APR)/VISITING TEAM REPORT (VTR)

As part of the accreditation process administered by the National Architectural Accrediting Board (NAAB), a team representing the profession, educators, regulators, and architecture students visits each program in architecture every six years, assuming that it has received a full term of accreditation. As part of the accreditation process, each institution prepares a related document called the *Architecture Program Report* (APR). The APR can be an excellent resource as you make your decision. It provides details of the program and describes the institutional context and resources; the document is public information and available from the academic unit on request. It may be too long for the institution to send to you, but it should be available in the institution's library or may be listed online.

Another useful document, the *Visiting Team Report* (VTR), also should be available to you upon request. The VTR conveys the visiting team's assessment of the program's educational quality as measured by the students' performance and the overall learning environment. It includes documentation of the program's noteworthy qualities, its deficiencies, and concerns about the program's future performance.

While all this information may be overwhelming, these documents may be helpful to consider because they provide both an overview of the program from the academic unit itself and a review of the program by an outside group.

RANKING OF ARCHITECTURE PROGRAMS

While rankings are a popular method of assistance in selecting an architecture program, be cautious. Do you know what criteria the book or magazine article uses when ranking programs? Are the criteria used important to you? You should use your own set of highly subjective criteria when determining which program is best for you. Consider that none of the associations involved with architectural education attempt or advocate the rating of architecture programs, beyond their term of accreditation. Qualities that make a school good for one student may not work that way for another. You should consider a variety of factors in making your choice among schools.

Although few would argue that certain programs, particularly those at the Ivy League schools, are excellent, the fact is that if a degree program is accredited by the NAAB it is valid for you to consider.

One resource, DesignIntelligence (di.net), attempts to assess the best architecture schools each year by asking practitioners to comment on how recent graduates from different schools fare in the marketplace. This report provides valuable information but also urges critical evaluation of the research results.

Application Process

After you narrow your choices and receive application materials, the next step is to complete the applications by the stated deadlines. Be cognizant of these deadlines, as many universities have set earlier and earlier deadlines within the academic calendar; some deadlines are as early as December 1.

Also, remember that the purpose of the admissions process is to select highly talented, diverse individuals who will succeed in that program. Institutions use the application materials—application, test scores, transcripts, portfolio, and recommendations—to measure performance to date and project future performance. Schools also want to know about you as a person; contact the school directly for more insight on what you can do to maximize your application for admission.

APPLICATION

At first, you might think that applications are designed to be complex and difficult, but if you simply read the instructions and review what is being asked, completing the application is easy. In most cases, the application is a series of questions related to you and your background. Do not make it hard! If you do not understand an aspect of the application, contact the admissions office for clarification. More and more universities are using online applications. Do not be intimidated by this trend; instead, just print out such applications and complete them by hand to ensure accuracy when you submit them online.

ESSAY QUESTIONS/PERSONAL STATEMENT

As part of the application, you may be asked to write a personal statement. Undergraduate applicants may have a choice of topics. For example, applicants to Carnegie Mellon University may write on one of these topics:

Evaluate a significant experience or achievement that has special meaning to you.

Discuss some issue of personal, local, or national concern and its importance and relevance to you.

Indicate a person who has had significant influence on you, and describe the influence.

For graduate students, the personal statement is an integral part of the application file. Rather than a topic, most graduate programs request a personal statement describing your background, interest in architecture, and how the institution will assist in fulfilling your goal of becoming an architect. Most will have a word limit, so be sure to check.

TEST SCORES

SAT/ACT: Most institutions will require you to take the standardized SAT or ACT. Which test you take depends on the region of the country you live in. Some students perform better on one than on the other; for this reason, consider taking both. Many institutions use these test scores as an indicator of your probable success in college, so you will want to do your absolute best. Some people, however, are not good test takers. If your results are not at the level required for a particular institution, discuss them with the admissions office.

GRE: If you are applying as a graduate candidate, you may be required to submit Graduate Record Examination (GRE) scores with your graduate program application. Institutions vary in how much weight they give to these scores. Study hard and take the practice test. You may consider tak-

Royal Library, Danish Ministry of Culture, Copenhagen, Denmark. Architect: Schmidt, Hammer & Lassen. PHOTOGRAPHER: GRACE H. KIM, AIA.

ing the GRE while you are still an undergraduate in anticipation of pursuing graduate studies. Most schools accept scores even if they are a few years old.

TRANSCRIPTS

All institutions to which you apply will require that transcripts be submitted. The admissions reviewers will, of course, look at your overall grade point average; however, just as important are trends in your academic record. If there is something in your academic background that is less than flattering, do not hesitate to include a letter explaining the situation.

PORTFOLIO

Unlike most other majors, undergraduate architecture programs may require a portfolio; this is especially true for bachelor of architecture degree programs. All graduate architecture programs will require a portfolio. Requiring a portfolio does not mean you have to be a talented architect prior to admission. Rather, the portfolio demonstrates your level of creativity and commitment to architecture.

What is a portfolio? For admission purposes, it is a compilation of creative work you have done on your own or as part of a class. It may include freehand drawings, poetry, photographs, or photographs of three-dimensional models or work. A portfolio is a means used by the admissions office to determine technical skills, creative ability, motivation, and originality. To gain a better understanding of what to include, question the admissions office. Despite the temptation, it is typically recommended not to include any drafting or computer-assisted design (CAD) work; again, check with the individual school for exact requirements.

RECOMMENDATIONS

All admissions offices require evaluations from counselors or teachers (high school students) and faculty or employers (graduate students) to aid them in making their decision.

Counselor or teacher: The application package typically includes an evaluation form for counselors or teachers to complete. For many high schools, this is the last step, and the counselor will forward your application, high school transcripts, and the evaluation form to the college or university.

Faculty or employer: Applicants to graduate programs must supply letters of recommendation as part of the application. While most programs allow current or former employers to submit a letter on your behalf, you are far better off obtaining letters from your undergraduate professors. This may be difficult if you have been out of school for a few years, but it is worth the time to track them down. In all cases, the individuals should know you fairly well, particularly your academic abilities.

Most schools enclose a checklist with the application materials asking for an evaluation on specific personal qualities such as:

Clarity of Goals for Graduate Study

Potential for Graduate Study

Intellectual Ability

Analytical Ability

Ability to Work Independently

Ability to Work with Others

Oral Expression in English

Written Expression in English

Teaching Potential

Research Potential

Most programs also accept letters written on the letterhead of the recommender.

Now you know all there is to know about selecting an architecture program. From the degree programs to the resources available, you have the information you need to make an informed choice. But just as important is determining how you will pay for your studies.

SCHOLARSHIPS/FELLOWSHIPS/COMPETITIONS

Once you have made an informed choice on where to pursue your architecture degree, an additional criteria to consider is your financial resources to pay for tuition, fees, and other related expenses; more than ever, cost is one of the leading factors in determining where to attend school. But to the extent possible, do not let money limit your choices. Work hard to secure funding to make your number one choice a reality.

Aside from need-based financial aid, there is an abundance of scholarships/grants available from companies, organizations/associations, and universities. To start, search the internet. Next, contact your institution of choice to fully understand what is available; be in touch with both the university and academic unit. Also, discuss what scholarships are available to incoming students and inquire about possible scholarships available in future semesters.

One source for scholarships is the American Institute of Architects (AIA); each academic year, scholarships (renewable for two years) are given to minority/disadvantaged high school seniors or college freshmen who plan to study architecture in an NAAB accredited architecture program, in amounts ranging from $500–$2,500. The AIA, through their local components, provides scholarships to architecture students in a professional degree program accredited by NAAB. Other scholarships/fellowship programs available include the Richard Morris Hunt Fellowship and the RTKL Traveling Fellowships administered by the AIA, and the Rotch Traveling Scholarship administered by the Boston Society of Architects.

If you are applying to architecture programs from high school, please recognize that most aid available will probably come from the university; however, this is not always the case. For example, the College of Architecture at Illinois Institute of Technology (IIT) offers a single five-year full-tuition scholarship named the Crown Scholarship for candidates entering their bachelor of architecture. Most architecture programs provide scholarships to upper-level undergraduate students or those participating in study abroad programs. Bottom line, ask questions of your academic unit.

When applying as a graduate student, you must first understand the process of applying for merit-based scholarships, grants, fellowships, and assistantships from your programs of choice. Typically, there are more funds available to graduate students. One source worth pursuing is graduate assistantships because they provide opportunities to teach or develop research skills in addition to providing additional financial benefits beyond the stipend; for some public institutions, assistantships provide tuition remission and provide tuition at the in-state rate for out-of-state students.

Another source of possible funds is design competitions; each academic year the Association of Collegiate Schools of Architecture (ACSA) and the American Institute of Architecture Students (AIAS) and other organizations host design competitions open to architecture that provide prize money and public recognition.

In addition to scholarships/fellowships targeted at students, there are others available when you graduate and begin your architectural career. Again, search the Web but possibilities include the following: SOM Foundation Traveling Fellowship, Steedman Fellowship in Architecture, Moshe Safdie & Associates Research Fellowship, AIA/NAC Jason Pettigrew ARE Scholarship, Frederick P. Rose Architectural Fellowship, and the prestigious Rome Prize.

Baptism by Fire

ROBERT D. ROUBIK, AIA, LEED AP

Project Architect

Antunovich Associates Architects and Planners

Chicago, Illinois

Why and how did you become an architect?

❯ Growing up, I had an affinity for art and I was very detail-oriented. I liked to draw and was an avid model builder. My friends and I used to build model rockets, and I took great care in the crafts-manship of each model and would spend hours meticulously refining their construction. I was equally concerned about how the collection was presented in my room, as each model rocket was hung from the ceiling in a location based on the proportions of the overall collection.

When I went to college, I started out in the College of Engineering and transferred into the Architecture School a year later—not necessarily because I wanted to be an architect, but because I knew that I did not want to be an engineer. At that time, I was still uncertain about what career I want-ed to pursue. However, when I took my first archi-tectural studio course, one of the first principles that the instructor taught us was the importance of presentation, proportion, and attention to detail in architecture. It was almost like a light bulb went on, and it seemed like a natural fit for me. It was soon apparent that architecture was the direction that my career should be headed.

Catholic Theological Union, Chicago. Architect: Antunovich Associates Architects and Planners. PHOTOGRAPHER: SEBASTIAN RUT.

Why and how did you decide on which schools to attend for your architecture degrees? What degree(s) do you possess?

❯ My home state university, the University of Colorado at Boulder (CU), is a very well-respected public university that has one of the most beauti-ful campuses in the country. For these reasons, in addition to receiving in-state tuition, I had always

planned to attend CU. It was here where I received a bachelor of environmental design with an emphasis in architecture. After I finished my pre-professional degree at CU, I decided that I wanted to pursue my professional degree at a school that had very different strengths. I also wanted to study in an urban center, since I was aware that most architectural graduates ended up practicing in close proximity to where they attended school—and cities offered more opportunities for architects.

Although I had visited Chicago only a few times in my life, I knew that it had a great architectural history and tradition. In addition, my father was originally from Chicago and moving there would give me the opportunity to reconnect with some family that I did not know very well. I applied and was fortunate enough to receive a scholarship that allowed me to attend the Illinois Institute of Technology (IIT). While I did not know a great deal about the school prior to attending, I was aware of the legacy of Mies van der Rohe and had studied Crown Hall in my architectural history courses at CU. At IIT, I received my master of architecture degree.

How has your career developed since graduation with your professional degree?

❯ My thesis advisor referred me to a local well-respected firm in Chicago. She knew a few people who worked there and felt that it would be a good place for me to start my career. It was known as a corporate firm that targeted high-profile projects. This firm gave me opportunities to get well-rounded experience ranging from graphic presentations to working drawings. However, during my four years there, only one (small) project that I worked on actually got built. It was demoralizing to continually work on projects and have them fail to be completed.

Then, an opportunity arose when a friend of mine from another local firm contacted me about a position at his firm, Antunovich Associates Architects (AA). I knew that AA had a reputation for good work, had a high success rate for getting projects built, and was generally less corporate. I set up an interview and was fortunate enough to be offered a position. I have been at AA ever since (over five years). At AA, my role as a project architect has developed with a focus on the managerial and technical design aspects of the profession.

What has been your greatest challenge as an architect?

❯ During a stretch of about 18 months from 2001–2002, I experienced my first economic downturn as an architect. The office where I was working, which six months earlier had been bustling with activity and more work than we could handle, suddenly did not have enough work to sustain the current staff. In that time period, I witnessed five rounds of layoffs and a 40 percent reduction in staff. It was very disheartening to watch qualified and capable colleagues lose their jobs. This made for an uneasy working environment—since it was never clear when another round of layoffs would occur and who would be targeted.

Why did you pursue becoming a LEED AP Professional?

❯ As architects, I felt that it is our responsibility to do our part to help the environment by designing energy-efficient buildings. In addition, with the advancement of energy codes, sustainable design is going to evolve from an ethical decision to a legal obligation.

What are your primary responsibilities and duties?

❯ Currently, I am functioning as project architect for West Broad Village, a mixed-use development in suburban Richmond, Virginia. I lead a team of 10 in the design, development, documentation, and construction administration for the buildings of this 115-acre development. As the construction for this project is phased, my primary responsibility involves keeping the team focused, organized, and moving forward. I orchestrate the daily tasks of everyone on the team while being the primary point of contact with the owner and contractor. I also review all drawings for code compliance and coordinate our work with our engineering consultants.

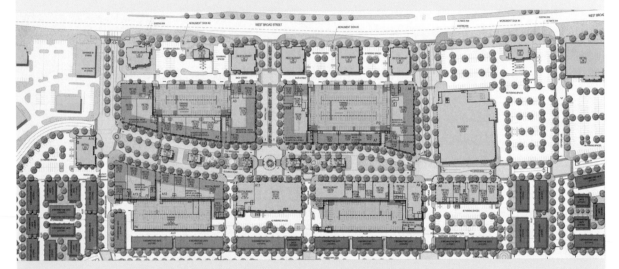

West Broad Village, Henrico County, Virginia. Architect: Antunovich Associates Architects and Planners.

West Broad Village, Henrico County, Virginia. Architect: Antunovich Associates Architects and Planners.

What is the most/least satisfying part of career as an architect?

❭ The most satisfying part of being an architect is seeing our work get built. The process of designing a building can be an arduous, painstaking, stressful one—and what makes it all worthwhile is to see the tangible fruits of our labor.

The least satisfying part of being an architect is the compensation. Although it is improving, the pay is not always commensurate with the time, responsibility, and stress that are an integral part of an architect's daily work life.

Who or what experience has been a major influence on your career?

❭ The most influential experience of my career so far has been my first project functioning in the role of project architect (PA). I had been working as a staff architect on a team of four on the schematic design of an institutional project called the Catholic Theological Union (CTU). A staff architect typically works on the design and documentation of individual components of a building, but ultimately the PA leads the team and is responsible for all drawing issues and construction administration.

About midway through the permit process, the PA for the project left the firm to pursue other opportunities and my boss asked me to the lead. Suddenly, I was thrust into an unfamiliar role, with responsibilities that were new to me. It was "baptism by fire." Somehow I got through it and completed the project—which turned out to be very successful in terms of client satisfaction, budget, and schedule. The time period from when I took over as PA to the completion of construction was about two years—and it was the most stressful time in my professional life. However, I have no regrets, as the CTU experience enabled me to gain the experience and confidence necessary for helping me to grow as an architect.

World of Possibilities

ELVA RUBIO

Executive Vice-President, Creative Director

Bruce Mau Design

Associate Professor, School of Architecture

University of Illinois at Chicago

Principal, Rubio Studios

Chicago, Illinois

Why and how did you become an architect?

❯ I have always been interested in the visual arts, design, and environmental experience. I also spent my entire childhood surrounded by social agendas and unconventional life experience. My matriarchal side has a legacy of art practice and my father was dedicated to healthcare for the underprivileged as a psychiatrist in a state mental hospital. It took me some time to become an architect; I think mostly due to generational issues for women and the profession.

Why and how did you decide on which school to attend for your architecture degree? What degree(s) do you possess?

❯ I hold a master of architecture from Washington University in St. Louis, Missouri. Quite honestly, I chose Washington University based upon practical reasons. I had been working at HOK for eight years in St. Louis and had longed for a professional architectural degree. Attending Washington University offered the opportunity to remain in my familiar surroundings, allow my three-year old daughter to stay with her school and friends and continue to work part time at HOK. It was the best career choice I have made in my life. Washington University was a very dynamic school filled with

Center On Halsted, Chicago. Architect: Gensler. PHOTOGRAPHER: CHRIS BARRET, HEDRICK BLESSING.

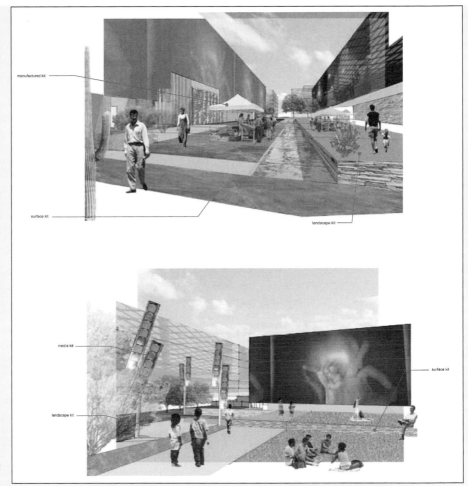

Martha & Mary
(M&M), Phoenix,
Arizona. Architect:
Gensler.

current and contemporary viewpoints and people with experience from around the world.

What has been your greatest challenge as an architect?

❯ The most difficult issue I have faced in my career has been the position of women in the field of architecture. This has been at the forefront of debate for years in the profession and addressing it has not met with a lot of success. If you go to any website of a major architectural firm, you will see that design leadership is a male majority. I have worked in large firms for a major portion of my career, and I have usually been the only woman in a design leadership role. This is equally true for the academy with predominately male faculty. This has been a real, physical and challenging problem that has crippled my generation of women.

Recently, I have had the amazing opportunity to see the generational shifts through teaching, and there is a real difference in attitude and position in the most recent groups of architectural graduates. This will alter the profession and the discipline in the future.

What are your primary responsibilities and duties?

❯ I am currently the design director for Bruce Mau Design, which involves direction and management of projects and studio teams. I am also responsible for business, financial, and marketing initiatives of the studio. I am also a full-time faculty member at the University of Illinois at Chicago School of Architecture. As an associate professor, I mainly teach design studios and electives in the graduate and undergraduate program. I also currently produce at least one small built project a year through Rubio Studios.

During your career, you have received a number of AIA awards for your work. What do you feel/think when you are recognized by your peers?

❯ The work was timely, moving, and inspiring in unconventional contexts. I have had the oppor-

Hyatt River Front, Chicago. Architect: Gensler.

tunity to work with many talented people who have helped the work become exceptional on many levels, including communications. I have also had the great opportunity to work with a phenomenal photographer, Steve Hall of Hedrich Blessing, for the last 20 years. As we all know, it is also a matter of "luck" to have the right clients and opportunities. I have had that great fortune in those precious moments throughout my career.

As both a practitioner and educator, how has one aspect of your career informed the other?

❯ The worlds inspire and inform one another. I could not grow intellectually, spiritually, and visually without the academic and student influence. This is also true of work itself; the profession would become richer if there were a more collaborative relationship between academia and the profession. Graduating students bring so much to a firm, and at the same time academia can offer an incredible wealth of knowledge and thinking that does not get the proper exposure in the built world. I also believe, if the work remains in the theoretical and conceptual realm, there is a limit to true contribution and meaning. The most satisfying moments have been when these two worlds have come together in a true collaboration.

Who or what experience has been a major influence on your career?

❯ The lush and tropical backyard of my grandmother in Miami, Florida.

Retiring Optimist

ROBERT M. BECKLEY, FAIA

Professor and Dean Emeritus

Taubman College of Architecture and Urban Planning

University of Michigan

Ann Arbor, Michigan

Why and how did you become an architect?

❭ My father recommended architecture as a career when I was in junior high school because I liked mathematics and to draw. After that I never considered another option though my career has taken me to the farther reaches of what one might consider a traditional career in the profession of architecture.

Why and how did you decide on which school to attend for your architecture degree? What degree(s) do you possess?

❭ I have a bachelor of architecture from the University of Cincinnati (1959) and master of architecture from the Harvard Graduate School of Design (1961).

I was born in Cleveland, Ohio. My father had a very modest income, and I knew I would have to provide the majority of my support in school. The University of Cincinnati had a cooperative education program in architecture that combined school with work after the second year. This program

▼ Bellevue Downtown Park, Bellevue, Washington. Architect: Beckley Myers, Architects with MacLeod Reckord Landscape Architects. PHOTOGRAPHER: ROBERT M. BECKLEY, FAIA.

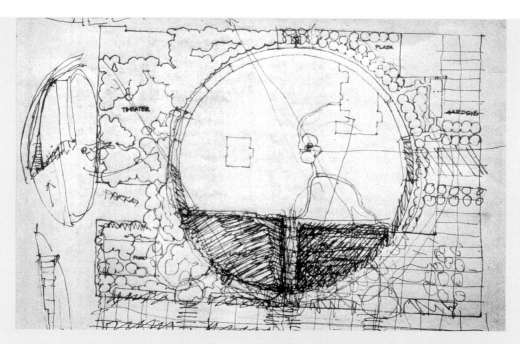

Bellevue Downtown Park – Concept Sketch, Bellevue, Washington. Architect: Beckley Myers, Architects with MacLeod Reckord Landscape Architects. PHOTOGRAPHER: BECKLEY MYERS, ARCHITECTS.

took an additional year to complete the bachelor degree, six rather than five years, but the benefit of having employment income from my chosen profession while I was still learning was attractive as I struggled with how to pay for my education. As it turned out the professional experience I gained through the co-op program while a student was a formative part of my education and directly contributed to my attending graduate school.

One of my first co-op positions was working for a trio of faculty who had recently graduated from Harvard and were teaching at the same time they were establishing their own architectural practice. They became my mentors, and it was their encouragement that led me to consider furthering my education so that I myself might teach as well as practice.

What has been your greatest challenge as an architect?

❯ The greatest challenge for an architect is getting the vision for a project realized. I have tried to produce projects that have a strong conceptual basis. Starting with a strong concept provides a reference point from which decisions can be made. Those decisions relate to programmatic adjustments, budget, construction, time, etc. I try not to lose sight of the vision for a project and try to vest everyone related to a project with that same vision. Without a clear vision you seldom end up with what you started with as an idea.

Our design for the Bellevue Washington Downtown Park was conceived as a circular "great lawn" defined by a canal, walkway, and alley of trees with other park activities located between the circle and surrounding streets. The project has had four construction phases thus far over nearly two decades, but this simple concept has endured through each phase.

Another example is our master plan for the Milwaukee Theater District (now called the Milwaukee Center). The concept was to create a linear galleria that would connect different elements of the project to each other and the surrounding streets and river. The master plan was changed several times in response to differing economic mandates, but each variation respected our original concept of a public galleria connecting different buildings and activities.

I have taken the liberty of using the title "retiring optimist" from the University of Michigan Taubman College newsletter. How are you a retiring optimist?

❯ The term "retiring optimist" came from the journalist who interviewed me for an article on my retirement from the university. I guess she saw in my answers to her questions a tendency to put a positive spin on my answers to difficult questions. I think that comes from my personal conviction that we can, we must, learn from our mistakes.

In other words, mistakes are okay as long as you learn from them. That is why I have enjoyed teaching so much. Teaching has provided me with the opportunity to work with students in asking questions. And, even though we don't always come up with the correct answers, we learn in the process of conducting "our patient search."

One of my favorite stories comes from a biography of Leonardo da Vinci. The book described an event during his lifetime when he and his assistants were in a town being besieged by an army. One of his staff ran to Leonardo and told him soldiers were using his equestrian statue located in the public square for target practice. Leonardo picked up his sketch pad and went outside to sketch the soldiers in the act of destroying one of his works. Leonardo turned what others considered a disaster into a creative opportunity. Leonardo was an optimist.

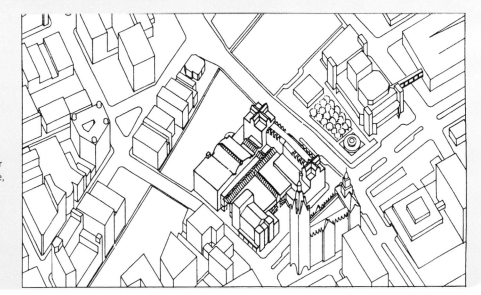

Milwaukee Theater District, Milwaukee, Wisconsin.
Architect: Beckley Myers, Architects.
PHOTOGRAPHER: BECKLEY MYERS, ARCHITECTS.

As a professor of both architecture and urban planning, can you describe the differences between the two?

❯ For me there is not much difference because I have always thought of architecture within its (urban) context and planning as it affects architectural decision making. I think the two are closely related. But, as these two professions developed over the latter part of the twentieth century, they grew further apart. Planning and planning education has become more concerned with policy and sociopolitical issues and less with the built environment. My teaching and professional endeavors have tried to see planning and architecture as part of a larger whole, a whole that considers aesthetic, human and natural, ecological and behavioral issues as one, regardless of scale.

How do you balance your two primary career roles—faculty member and architect?

❯ In a large research university, faculty are expected to make a creative contribution to their chosen field referred to as scholarship or research through writing and presentation of scholarship (the commonly accepted form of dissemination of knowledge in higher education) but also by built work, competition entries, funded and non-funded research and theoretical projects. What is critical is peer review when the work of faculty is evaluated. It is not good enough just to produce work.

In this way teaching and practice are closely related. But, the qualifier here is that the educator/architect is expected to make a creative contribution to the field at a high level and be able to show evidence that his or her work is considered a contribution to

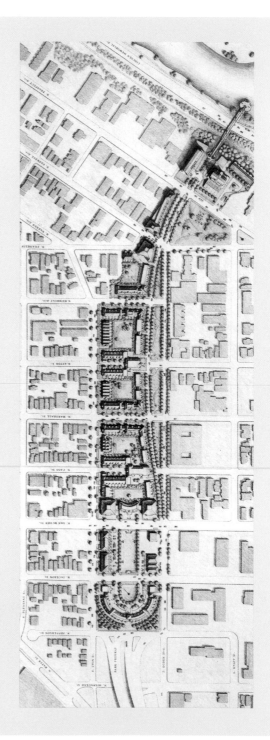

Park East Development Plan, Milwaukee, Wisconsin. Architect: Beckley Myers Flad, Architects. PHOTOGRAPHER: BECKLEY MYERS FLAD, ARCHITECTS.

the profession of architecture. So built, and unbuilt work must be published and reviewed or entered into competitions, presented at conferences, etc. I think those are standards that should apply to anyone teaching.

Who or what experience has been a major influence on your career?

❭ My faculty mentors in undergraduate school were terribly influential in my professional life. They opened my eyes to aesthetic possibilities I had not imagined before. They served as role models, combining teaching with an active and exploratory practice, and they inspired and encouraged me to raise expectations for my own career.

Finally, I would say I have been influenced and inspired by many others—students, who always teach you as much as you teach them, colleagues, and collaborators. It is important to keep in mind that architecture is a team sport, both as it is taught and as it is practiced. One's success has to be measured by the success of the team. You have to know how to block as well as run.

Creative Dual Careers

W. STEPHEN SAUNDERS, AIA

Principal

Eckenhoff Saunders Architects, Inc.

Chicago, Illinois

Why and how did you become an architect?

❭ I started learning to be an architect when I was 11 years old. I'm now 58 and I'm still learning. I have always been fascinated by how things look and by how they are built. Becoming an architect was an opportunity to spend my life exploring both.

Why and how did you decide on which school to attend for your architecture degree? What degree(s) do you possess?

❭ I hold a bachelor of arts degree in architecture from Washington University. Washington University was my first choice among the four schools I applied to when graduating from high school. My school counselor recommended all of my college selections.

What has been your greatest challenge as an architect/principal?

❭ The greatest challenge any architect faces is getting his or her best design effort built. All designs must stand the test of the client's budget, the contractor's expediency, and public scrutiny. Coming up with a good idea is not the hard part, it is having the confidence and belief in the idea to defend and sell it without being emotional, possessive, or combative.

As a principal, my greatest challenge is keeping our firm moving in a direction that motivates and fulfills staff expectations while maintaining our clients' confidence and trust.

Westell Corporation Headquarters, Aurora, Illinois. Architect: Eckenhoff Saunders Architects, Inc. PHOTOGRAPHER: DON DU BROFF.

What are your primary responsibilities and duties?

❯ A founding principal in a 40-person firm, I am involved in all aspects of the business with the exception of production. I spend about 30 percent of my time on business administration (i.e., contracts, proposals, invoicing, insurance) and the remainder on architecture (business development, design, project administration, and client relations).

On the projects that I bring to the firm, my role is to define the goals of the project and provide design oversight and team guidance as we move from conception to implementation.

What is the most/least satisfying part of your job?

❯ Unquestionably, the most satisfying aspect of practicing architecture is seeing a design come to life. The transformation of lines on a sheet of paper to steel, concrete, and glass is an experience very few professions offer. I am fortunate that as I have matured as a professional, the design projects I undertake have become more complex and demanding.

On the other hand, confronting the disparity between the amount of talent, personal will, and technical knowledge that is required to design a building and the public perception of what an architect does is the most frustrating. The public is unaware of how complex and unpredictable the process of producing buildings is. This perception gap permeates the entire building process—it undermines fee negotiations with clients; it denigrates the architect in the public review process; and it weakens our effectiveness on the job site, where we are charged with protecting the owner's interests.

Since graduating from your college, you have worked for five firms prior to establishing Eckenhoff Saunders Architects. Did you know that you eventually wanted to establish your own firm upon graduation or did it just happen?

❯ The idea of branching out on my own evolved over time. In my late twenties (around six to eight years out of school), I felt my career was stagnating. I think this is common in architecture: you know the basics of how to put a building together and are ready to take on your own project, but your firm has pigeonholed you as a producer and not a designer.

The opportunity to open my own firm arose when a friend and former college classmate had reached the same point in his career and we both felt it was time to try. What started as an experiment has

disciplines. In architecture, two-dimensional sketches become three-dimensional buildings, while photography reverses the process by condensing the world into silver halide crystals on a sheet of paper. Making photography is a solo experience that serves as a refuge from the challenges of working with hundreds of people to get a building designed, approved, and constructed.

◀ DuPage Medical Group, Glen Ellyn Clinic, Glen Ellyn, Illinois. Architect: Eckenhoff Saunders Architects, Inc. PHOTOGRAPHER: MARIUSZ MIZERA.

▼ Private Residence, River Forest, Illinois. Architect: Eckenhoff Saunders Architects, Inc. PHOTOGRAPHER: W. STEPHEN SAUNDERS, AIA.

become a successful 40-person firm with a mature portfolio of work in five market sectors. We own our own building in downtown Chicago and have started to transition to the next generation of ownership. I can honestly say that if I had not established my own firm 25 years ago, I probably would not have stayed in architecture as a profession.

Besides being an architect, you list yourself as an architectural and landscape photographer. How do the two disciplines—architecture and photography—complement each other?

❯ Architecture and photography both require visualization of a finished work expressed through technical means. Understanding composition, light, texture, void, and solid is common to both

Who or what experience has been a major influence on your career?

❯ Looking back over the past 36 years, my professional belief system has been shaped by one or two college professors, one or two bosses/mentors, and a couple of clients who trusted me before I trusted myself. There was never a pivotal event or person that ignited a lifelong passion. Instead, commitment to a goal and recognizing opportunity has seemed to pay off in the long run.

Jay Pritzker Pavilion—Millennium Park, Chicago, Illinois. Architect: Frank Gehry. PHOTOGRAPHER: W. STEPHEN SAUNDERS, AIA.

Making a Positive Impact

KATHRYN T. PRIGMORE, FAIA
Senior Project Manager
HDR Architecture, Inc.
Alexandria, Virginia

Why and how did you become an architect?

❯ Architecture allows me to make a living doing everything I like and everything I am good at. These are not necessarily the same thing!

My interest in architecture began when I was in middle school. The City of Alexandria Public Library had an extensive collection of architecture books and journals. After I had read all of them, I ventured out to the Fairfax County library and the library at the AIA headquarters. Living in the Washington, DC, area is such a great thing!

Architecture is a dynamic discipline. In all phases of the education process and as a practitioner and educator, it has allowed me to utilize multiple abilities and skills to expand my knowledge base or that peak my interest in other ways. I have been able to find satisfying career paths through architecture as I have matured or as life situations created challenges and opportunities—often unexpected.

2001 M St., Washington, DC. Architect: Segreti Tepper Architects, PC. PHOTOGRAPHER: KATHRYN T. PRIGMORE, FAIA.

Why and how did you decide on which school to attend for your architecture degree? What degree(s) do you possess?

❯ My high school physics teacher suggested I apply to Rensselaer Polytechnic Institute (RPI), partly because at least a dozen of my classmates were applying to my first choice school and he knew the program was just as good, although not as well known. I visited RPI and immediately became intrigued with studying architecture there. The university was smaller than most of the other programs I had applied to, and it was in the heart of a small, very "walkable" city. I also liked the fact that the school of architecture was relatively self-contained and that the entire faculty had active professional practices. Although located within a technical university, the creative aspects of architecture were clearly fundamental to the pedagogical approach.

Another reason I decided to attend RPI was that I would be able to obtain two degrees within five years—a bachelor of science in building science and the accredited bachelor of architecture degree. After I began to take courses, I found out that it was very easy to receive minors and that my advisor did not prevent me from taking overloads as long as I did well in my courses. I also took courses during the summer at various universities in Washington, DC. I ended up graduating four years after I matriculated with both degrees, with a minor in architectural history and one in anthropology/sociology, and with a few extra credits related to technology and the Industrial Revolution.

What has been your greatest challenge as an architect?

❯ I am sure there have been lost opportunities because I am both African American and female, but the most blatant discrimination I have faced seems to be because I look 10 to 20 years younger (on a good day) than I am. Invariably when I show up for an interview or to first job meeting, it is clear that

Pentagon Renovation, Wedge Two, Arlington, Virginia. Architect: HDR Architecture, Inc. PHOTOGRAPHER: HDR ARCHITECTURE, INC.

the participants do not believe that a person my age could have my credentials.

What are your primary responsibilities and duties as an architect?

❯ For one project, I was the project manager for the tenant fit-out of Wedge 2, Phase 3 for the Pentagon Renovation Project. We ran tenant-programming meetings and produced documents for over 140 tenants, including the secretary of defense, the chairman of the joint chiefs of staff, and the secretary of the navy over the course of a year.

I developed project-specific, integrated process for working with the design-build contractors, the Pentagon client representatives, and tenant representatives and training staff to do the work. Key to the success of the project was the Process Manual, a multi-level tracking schedule, and HDR network folder and paper file system customized to suit the specific needs of the project.

Challenges of the Pentagon project included managing client expectations, which evolved as they could see that we were able to be more responsive to the schedule and client requirements than the previous consultant had been able to be; creating and documenting a process that could be easily followed as the composition of the team expanded or evolved; and maintaining the morale of a team which worked for months under a relentless schedule.

What is the least/most satisfying part of your position?

❯ The most satisfying aspect of architecture is the ability to make a positive impact on others through my work. On a daily basis, it is building teams or helping a designer and an engineer resolve a problem. In the long term it is seeing the glow on a client's face as they enter a completed building for the first time or having a former student tell you they just got licensed.

I sometimes feel internal conflicts because I like what I do so much that I often work too many hours. This is sometimes to the detriment of maintaining good relationships outside of the workplace.

Previously, you taught at Howard University; why did you choose to teach?

❯ I spent 13 years at Howard University teaching and nurturing the students. About half of these years, I also served as associate dean. Teaching is the most rewarding undertaking I have done, with the exception of being a parent. To teach, you have to learn, especially when you teach technology-based topics as I did.

The ideal career situation for me would be to teach and practice. I started and finished my teaching career doing both, and I plan to return to doing both at some point in the future. In the interim, I have found opportunities at HDR and other firms to satisfy some of the yearnings that draw me to teaching. We have created a professional development team to encourage interns to get licensed, and I am one of the "faculty" for the Architecture Section's monthly educational sessions.

The reward of teaching, however, surpasses everything else I have done as an architect. There are no words to adequately express the satisfaction I feel for the gift of being able to inspire others to learn.

What was your role in serving on the Board for Architects, Professional Engineers, Land Surveyors, and Certified Interior Designers and Landscape Architects (APELSCIDLA) in the state of Virginia? What does a state board do?

❯ State board members are responsible for upholding the laws and regulations related to the practice of architecture. This includes approving candidates for examination and acceptance of individuals for licensure. The board also hears and decides disciplinary cases brought against individuals and entities with professional credentials. During my tenure on the board, we reviewed and updated the regulations and assessed the need for continuing education.

1001 Pennsylvania Ave., N.W., Washington, DC. Architect: Segreti Tepper Architects, PC–Architect of Record; Hartman Cox–Design Architect. PHOTOGRAPHER: KATHRYN T. PRIGMORE, FAIA.

Through my appointment to the APELSCIDLA board, I was able to serve on many NCARB committees. I was a writer and grader for the Architect Registration Exam (ARE) and chaired the Committee on Examination—the committee, which is responsible for development of the ARE. I have also served on the Broadly Experienced Architects (BEA) Committee that reviews the qualifications of individuals without a professional degree to determine if they are eligible for an NCARB Certificate. After completing a number of years of service to the NCARB, I was appointed to the AIA National Ethics Council. All of these service activities support my commitment to improving the profession and to opening up opportunities for younger architects in leadership roles.

I found an article that talked about your mentoring students—do you still mentor students? Why do you feel mentoring is important?

❭ I have been mentoring students since I was in college. A few years ago I found out that a young lady I started mentoring when she was in eighth grade eventually did graduate from architecture school. I continue to mentor many of my former students.

Mentoring is important because it makes a better world for all of us. I also know that mentoring can change people's lives. I have two primary mentors, one for over 20 years and the other for almost 30 years, who have helped me plan my destiny. They have supported my decisions along the way whether they would have chosen the same path or not. Therein lies their legacy to me. Mentors do not dictate; they do not impose their will on their protégées. They listen, offer options and support, and open doors when they can. Like you parents, mentors are there no matter what.

You were one of the first African American women licensed to practice architecture—why do you think that was the case?

❭ I first became licensed in 1981. To the best of my knowledge, I was the 16th African American woman licensed to practice architecture in the United States. As of today there are approximately 225 African American women out of about 1,600 African American architects. There are approximately 260 women fellows. I was the fifth African American women elevated to Fellowship in 2003.

As the legend goes, the practice of architecture is a rich, white, male profession. Even as opportunities opened up, we were often relegated to the back rooms of offices. This practice persisted blatantly well into the 1970s in many firms for both women and minorities. Rather than face discrimination, many opened their own firms, some married partners who were the "face" of the office, but unfortunately many were driven away. Today the hearts of many are in the right place and we are taking our places in the front offices of many firms. For some firms, however, the risk is still perceived as too great.

You Are an Architecture Student

Congratulations! You are now an architecture student and embarking on the first and most critical phase of becoming an architect. To place your education in context, you should become familiar with *The Conditions for Accreditation* (naab.org), including the Student Performance Criteria set by the NAAB (see the sidebar "Student Performance—Educational Realms and Student Performance Criteria").

STUDENT PERFORMANCE — EDUCATIONAL REALMS & STUDENT PERFORMANCE CRITERIA

The accredited degree program must demonstrate that each graduate possesses the knowledge and skills defined by the criteria set out below. The knowledge and skills are the minimum for meeting the demands of an internship leading to registration for practice.

The school must provide evidence that its graduates have satisfied each criterion through required coursework. If credits are granted for courses taken at other institutions or online, evidence must be provided that the courses are comparable to those offered in the accredited degree program.

The criteria encompass two levels of accomplishment[1]:

■ *Understanding*—The capacity to classify, compare, summarize, explain and/or interpret information.

■ *Ability*—Proficiency in using specific information to accomplish a task, correctly selecting the appropriate information, and accurately applying it to the solution of a specific problem, while also distinguishing the effects of its implementation.

STUDENT PERFORMANCE CRITERIA:

The SPC are organized into realms to more easily understand the relationships between individual criteria.

Realm A: Critical Thinking and Representation:

Architects must have the ability to build abstract relationships and understand the impact of ideas based on research and analysis of multiple theoretical, social, political, economic, cultural and environmental contexts. This ability includes facility with the wider range of media used to think about architecture including writing, investigative skills, speaking, drawing and model making. Students' learning aspirations include:

■ Being broadly educated

■ Valuing lifelong inquisitiveness

■ Communicating graphically in a range of media

■ Recognize the assessment of evidence

■ Comprehend people, place, and context

■ Recognize the disparate needs of client, community, and society

[1] See also Taxonomy for Learning, Teaching and Assessing: A Revision of Bloom's Taxonomy of Educational Objectives. L.W. Anderson & D.R. Krathwold, Eds. (New York; Longman 2001).

A.1. *Communication Skills:* Ability to read, write, speak and listen effectively.

A. 2. *Design Thinking Skills:* Ability to raise clear and precise questions, use abstract ideas to interpret information, consider diverse points of view, reach well-reasoned conclusions, and test outcomes against relevant criteria and standards.

A. 3. *Visual Communication Skills:* Ability to use appropriate representational media, such as traditional graphic and digital technology skills, to convey essential formal elements at each stage of the programming and design process.

A.4. *Technical Documentation:* Ability to make technically clear drawings, write outline specifications, and prepare models illsutrating and identifying the assembly of materials, systems, and components appropriate for a building design.

A.5. *Investigative Skills:* Ability to gather, assess, record, apply, and comparatively evaluate relevant information within architectural coursework and design processes.

A. 6. *Fundamental Design Skills:* Ability to effectively use basic architectural and environmental principles in design.

A. 7. *Use of Precedents:* Ability to examine and comprehend the fundamental principles present in relevant precedents and to make choices regarding the incorporation of such principles into architecture and urban design projects.

A. 8. *Ordering Systems Skills:* Understanding the fundamentals of both natural and formal ordering systems and the capacity of each to inform two- and three-dimensional design.

A. 9. *Historical Traditions and Global Culture:* Understanding of parallel and divergent canons and traditions of architecture, landscape and urban design including examples of indigenous and vernacular, local, regional, national settings from the Eastern, Western, Northern, and Southern hemispheres in terms of their climatic, ecological, technological, socioeconomic, public health, and cultural factors.

A. 10. *Cultural Diversity:* Understanding of the diverse needs, values, behavioral norms, physical ability, and social and spatial patterns that characterize different cultures and individuals and the implication of this diversity on the societal roles and responsibilities of architects.

A. 11. *Applied Research:* Understanding the role of applied research in determining function, form, and systems and their impact on human conditions and behavior.

Realm B: Integrated Building Practices, Technical Skills and Knowledge:

Architects are called upon to comprehend the technical aspects of design, systems and materials, and be able to apply that comprehension to their services. Additionally they must appreciate their role in the implementation of design decisions, and the impact of such decisions on the environment. Students learning aspirations include:

- Creating building designs with well-integrated systems.
- Comprehending constructability.

- Incorporating life safety systems.
- Integrating accessibility.
- Applying principles of sustainable design.

B. 1. *Pre-Design:* Ability to prepare a comprehensive program for an architectural project, such as preparing an assessment of client and user needs, an inventory of space and equipment requirements, an analysis of site conditions (including existing buildings), a review of the relevant laws and standards and assessment of their implications for the project, and a definition of site selection and design assessment criteria.

B. 2. *Accessibility:* Ability to design sites, facilities, and systems to provide independent and integrated use by individuals with physical (including mobility), sensory, and cognitive disabilities.

B. 3. *Sustainability:* Ability to design projects that optimize, conserve, or reuse natural and built resources, provide healthful environments for occupants/users, and reduce the environmental impacts of building construction and operations on future generations through means such as carbon-neutral design, bioclimatic design, and energy efficiency.

B. 4. *Site Design:* Ability to respond to site characteristics such as soil, topography, vegetation, and watershed in the development of a project design.

B. 5. *Life Safety:* Ability to apply the basic principles of life-safety systems with an emphasis on egress.

D. 6. *Comprehensive Design:* Ability to produce a comprehensive architectural project that demonstrates each student's capacity to make design decisions across scales while integrating the following SPC: A.2. Design Thinking Skills; A.4. Technical Documentation; A.5. Investigative Skills; A.8. Ordering Systems Skills; A.9. Historical Traditions and Global Culture; B.2. Accessibility; B.3. Sustainability; B.4. Site Design; B.5. Life Safety; B.7 Financial Considerations; B.9. Structural Systems

B. 7. *Financial Considerations:* Understanding of the fundamentals of building costs, such as acquisition costs, project financing and funding, financial feasibility, operational costs, and construction estimating with an emphasis on life-cycle cost accounting.

B. 8. *Environmental Systems:* Understanding the principles of environmental systems' design such as embodied energy, active and passive heating and cooling, indoor air quality, solar orientation, daylighting and artificial illumination, and acoustics; including the use of appropriate performance assessment tools.

B. 9. *Structural Systems:* Understanding of the basic principles of structural behavior in withstanding gravity and lateral forces and the evolution, range, and appropriate application of contemporary structural systems.

B. 10. *Building Envelope Systems:* Understanding of the basic principles involved in the appropriate application of building envelope systems and associated assemblies relative to fundamental performance, aesthetics, moisture transfer, durability, and energy and material resources.

B. 11. *Building Service Systems:* Understanding of the basic principles and appropriate application and performance of building service systems such as plumbing, electrical, vertical transportation, security, and fire protection systems.

B. 12. *Building Materials and Assemblies:* Understanding of the basic principles utilized in the appropriate selection of construction materials, products, components, and assemblies, based on their inherent characteristics and performance, including their environmental impact and reuse.

Realm C: Leadership and Practice

Architects need to manage, advocate, and act legally, ethically and critically for the good of the client, society and the public. This includes collaboration, business, and leadership skills. Student learning aspirations include:

- Knowing societal and professional responsibilities.
- Comprehending the business of building.
- Collaborating and negotiating with clients and consultants in the design process.
- Discerning the diverse roles of architects and those in related disciplines.
- Integrating community service into the practice of architecture.

C. 1. *Collaboration:* Ability to work in collaboration with others and in multi-disciplinary teams to successfully complete design projects.

C. 2. *Human Behavior:* Understanding of the relationship between human behavior, the natural environment and the design of the built environment.

C. 3. *Client Role in Architecture:* Understanding of the responsibility of the architect to elicit, understand, and reconcile the needs of the client, owner, user groups, and the public and community domains.

C. 4. *Project Management:* Understanding of the methods for competing for commissions, selecting consultants and assembling teams, and recommending project delivery methods.

C. 5. *Practice Management:* Understanding of the basic principles of architectural practice management such as financial management and business planning, time management, risk management, mediation and arbitration, and recognizing trends that affect practice.

C. 6. *Leadership:* Understanding of the techniques and skills architects use to work collaboratively in the building design and construction process and on environmental, social, and aesthetic issues in their communities.

C. 7. *Legal Responsibilities:* Understanding of the architect's responsibility to the public and the client as determined by registration law, building codes and regulations, professional service contracts, zoning and subdivision ordinances, environmental regulation, and historic preservation and accessibility laws.

C. 8. *Ethics and Professional Judgment:* Understanding of the ethical issues involved in the formation of professional judgment regarding social, political and cultural issues in architectural design and practice.

C.9. *Community and Social Responsibility:* Understanding of the architect's responsibility to work in the public interest, to respect historic resources, and to improve the quality of life for local and global neighbors.

National Architectural Accrediting Board, Inc. Washington, D.C.[1]

Remember that most states require you to obtain a professional degree accredited by NAAB to become a licensed architect. What is *architectural accreditation*? NAAB provides the answer:

Architectural accreditation is the primary means by which programs assure quality to students and the public. Accredited status is a signal to students and the public that an institution or program meets at least minimal standards for its faculty, curriculum, student services and libraries. The accrediting process is intended to verify that each accredited program substantially meets those standards that, as a whole, comprise an appropriate education for an architect. Since most state registration boards in the United States require any applicant for licensure to have graduated from an NAAB-accredited program, obtaining such a degree is an essential aspect of preparing for the professional practice of architecture.[2]

Through the accreditation process, NAAB dictates to the architecture programs what must be taught, but it does not dictate *how* they are to be taught. This is why not all architecture programs have the same curriculum. The differences among them may be confusing, but they also allow you to find the program that will suit you best.

COURSES

Regardless of which program you select to pursue your architecture degree, the types of courses offered by each program are similar. A typical sequence includes the following: general education, design, history and theory, technology, professional practice, and electives.

Each architecture program will require courses in *general education*—English, humanities, mathematics and science, and social sciences. While you may not enjoy these required courses,

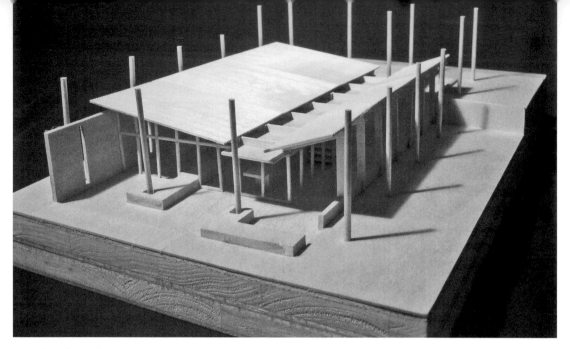

Map Library by Brad Zuger at University of Nebraska, Lincoln.

realize that they will connect to your architectural studies. To the extent your curriculum provides, choose courses that are of interest to you.

As you will quickly learn, *design* is the heart of each architecture curriculum. Once you are in the studio sequence of a degree program, you will be taking design studio each semester, usually for four to six credits. Design studio may meet between 8 and 12 hours contact hours with the designated faculty and countless hours outside of class. Projects may begin in the abstract and deal with basic skill development, but they will quickly progress in scale and complexity. Faculty members provide the program or space requirements of a given building project. From there, students individually develop solutions to the problem and present the results to faculty and classmates. This final presentation, called a *review,* is the culmination of hours of hard work. Comments are provided to the student on the finished project. Just as important as the product is the process. You will learn not only from the studio faculty but also from your fellow students.

Design courses are central to an architectural education, but what is *studio*? More than simply a place to work, studio is where design happens. A central aspect of an architectural education, the studio is the place to work and more. The studio becomes an extension of the curriculum as you combine what you learn from your architecture courses and apply that knowledge to your design work.

As part of your studio course, you will learn architecture in varying methods as described in the following material. At the beginning of a studio project, you, along with your classmates, may do research on the project and site, and perform a precedent analysis. You may take a field trip to the proposed site. The professor may lecture on aspects of the project as you begin the design process. You will work on design during class time and participate in desk critiques, or individual time with the professor to discuss your design and ideas. Depending on the length of the project, there may be pin-ups or interim critiques with your entire studio and professor or subsets of your studio classmates. Eventually, at the end, you participate in the charrette, an intensive burst of energy to complete the project before the stated deadline. Finally, there is the final review or critique, which involves outside faculty or visitors from off-campus.

A vital aspect of the design studio and an architectural education is learning through criticism. Brian Kelly, associate professor in the architecture program at the University of Maryland, offers the following:

> The development of a rigorous design process governed by critical thinking is a central component of architectural education and an essential tool for successful professional practice. Design studios utilize critical review, debate, and consultation with faculty and professional guests to engage a wide range of issues central to the making of architecture. This engagement between students and their critics takes place in a public arena where students can learn from discussions of their own work and that of their peers. For some, the public nature of critique is challenging. Beginning students have been known to mistake comments about their design work as praise of their individual character. "Professor Smith likes me and therefore is always enthusiastic about my work." Likewise, others have confused critical comments focused on the work with evaluation of personal attributes. "Professor Jones has it in for me and always trashes my work." Both of these positions are naïve appraisals of the role of criticism. Criticism is not personal. The role of criticism is to improve students' design processes and thereby lead the way to a higher quality of architecture. Criticism is not simply a matter of "I like it" or "I dislike it." Criticism involves illuminating the principles on which design work is based and evaluating the rational application of those principles. Simply put, criticism is about the work and the process by which the work was conceptualized. It is not about the individual. The goal of criticism is to enable the student to become a competent critic. Both self-criticism and critique of others is an essential tool for architects in practice.
>
> BRIAN KELLY, University of Maryland

All architecture programs require courses in *history and theory* to address values, concepts, and methods. Most curriculums offer courses that provide an understanding of both Western and non-Western traditions across the ages, from ancient Greek architecture to the modern day. In addition, more focused history courses may be required or offered as electives.

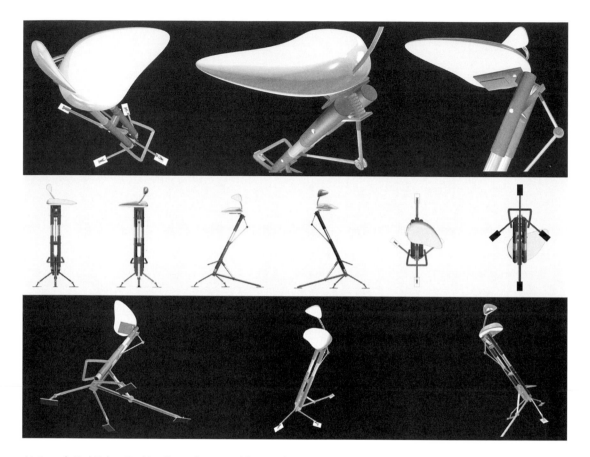

Motorcycle Fork Tubes Stool by Chris Talbott at California Polytechnic State University–San Luis Obispo. Faculty: Thomas Fowler, IV, AIA.

Technology covers structures and environmental systems. Each program teaches these courses differently, but structures will involve basic statics and strength of materials—wood, steel, timber, and masonry. Courses in environmental systems cover HVAC (heating, ventilation, and air conditioning), plumbing, lighting, and acoustics. As well, most programs have courses in construction materials and methods. All of these courses, required by most programs, are taught with the idea that you will connect what you learn in them to your work in the design studio.

As required by accreditation, all programs offer coursework in *professional practice*. This addresses the legal aspects of architecture, contracts, ethics, leadership roles, and business issues.

As well, all programs provide a wide array of *electives* (see the sidebar "Architecture Electives: A Sample"). These may include courses in computer applications, advanced technology, history and theory, urban design, and so on. Some programs permit or require students to take elective courses outside the major in areas such as art, business, or engineering.

ARCHITECTURE ELECTIVES: A SAMPLE

Architect as Developer

Methods in Architectural Design

Computation

History of the City

Daylighting Design

Advanced Freehand Perspective Drawing

The Ideologies of Architecture Theory: The Situations of Theory and the Syntax of History Beyond Postmodern Urbanism

The Cultural Landscape: The Grand Canyon

Finding Purpose: Survival in Design

International Boulevard: The Analysis of Everything Else

Architecture and Corporate Culture

Qualitative and Experimental Structures

Introduction to Crime Prevention through Environmental Design

Understanding Clients and Users: Methods for Programming and Evaluation

Traditions of Architectural Practice

Psychology of Environmental Design

Critical Positions in Architectural Design

The Bone Studio 2: Experimental Concrete Architecture

Interactive Spaces

Legal Aspects of Design Practice

Methods of Presentation, Representation, and Re-Presentation

Seminar in Architectural Philosophy

Issues in Sustainability

TOOLS

Aside from courses, an element of an architectural education is the tools. Unlike those in other majors who have textbooks, architecture students have tools. In fact, while architecture students will need to purchase some textbooks, they will need to purchase these tools. Included are the tools of the profession: parallel straightedge, vinyl board cover, scale, triangles, leadholders with various leads, sharpener, erasers, erasing shield, compass, x-acto knife with blades, circles template, brush, lamp, push pins, and drafting tape or dots. For now, these tools may not be familiar, but they soon will be. Many programs, through their AIAS chapter, sell toolkits with the items just mentioned plus more. It is well worth the money to purchase such a kit to save time and hassles.

Also, consider obtaining a laptop computer and music-playing device with headphones. In recent years, more and more programs are requiring laptops as part of attendance. Regardless, all students are now entering colleges with a laptop or desktop computer. Talk with upperclass students and the program to learn about which platform (Macintosh or PC) is the best and what software is absolutely necessary. You will want headphones for your MP3 or CD player to listen to your favorite music but also to eliminate the distracting noise in the studio.

Academic Enrichment

Beyond the required coursework outlined in the preceding section for a particular degree in architecture, you can enrich your academic experience in many other ways, if you choose.

INDEPENDENT STUDY

Most institutions have a mechanism that allows you to develop an independent study under the direction of a faculty member. (This is rarely undertaken before the upper years of a curriculum.)

The independent study allows you to focus on a chosen topic not typically offered at your school.

Throughout my architectural education, I realized I also had a strong interest in marketing and business in the context of architecture. Because Maryland did not offer a course that addressed this interest, I developed an independent study to understand marketing as a discipline and how it relates to architecture. The course consisted of researching marketing and marketing in architecture by visiting and interviewing two architecture firms of different sizes. Pursuing the independent study was one of my most rewarding experiences in college. It allowed me to work closely with a faculty member, focus on my interests relating to architecture, and start to understand potential career opportunities for my future.

JESSICA LEONARD, University of Maryland

MINORS/CERTIFICATES

If you have an interest in an academic subject other than architecture, consider completing a minor. An academic minor typically requires no fewer than 15 credits (five courses) of coursework, shows structure and coherence, and contains some upper-level courses. Also, students who declare and complete an approved academic minor may receive a notation on their transcript. At the graduate level, certificate programs exist. Parallel in concept to academic minors, certificate programs allow you to gain specific knowledge in an area outside of, but still related to, your degree program.

DOUBLE MAJOR/DEGREES/DUAL DEGREES

For some, a double major/degree/dual degree may be an option. Depending on the institution, you may be able to pursue a double major or degree at the undergraduate level or a dual degree at the graduate level. Because of the time demands of an architectural curriculum, this choice may be difficult at the undergraduate level. A second major or degree would typically require you to complete the academic requirements of two degree programs. If you are interested, consult the undergraduate catalogue. At the graduate level, many institutions have established dual-degree options with the master of architecture. For example, the School of Architecture at the University of Illinois at Urbana-Champaign offers a dual master of architecture/master of business administration, allowing you to graduate with both degrees in less time than if you were to pursue each on its own.

OFF-CAMPUS PROGRAMS (SEMESTER ABROAD)

Many architecture programs offer the opportunity to study abroad. Some architecture programs, including the University of Notre Dame and Syracuse University, actually require study abroad. Other programs offer foreign study as an option. Such programs may occur during the summer or be for an entire semester. Some students may also choose to study at another institution abroad for a full academic year. Regardless, you are strongly encouraged to study abroad during your academic tenure. In fact, faculty will say that you should make it mandatory for yourself. Money is typically an obstacle for some students, but most programs offer scholarships. Remember, once you graduate and enter the workforce, you may not have the same opportunity to travel.

LECTURE SERIES/GALLERIES/REVIEWS

Many architecture programs sponsor a lecture series during the semester. The architecture program will host series of lectures given by practitioners, faculty from other programs, or other professionals, designed to increase the discourse within the school. On occasion, invited lecturers include well-known "star" architects. You should make every effort to attend these lectures to expand your architectural experience. As well, many programs sponsor more informal brown-bag lectures at lunchtime that feature faculty and, sometimes, students. In addition, attend lectures sponsored by nearby schools and chapters of the American Institute of Architects or other institutions. For example, students in architecture programs in the Washington, DC, region frequently attend lectures at the National Building Museum or other cultural institutions because of the close proximity.

Aside from the lecture series, some architecture programs may sponsor exhibits in a gallery within their facility; these exhibitions may be a part of a traveling exhibition from an outside sponsor or be a

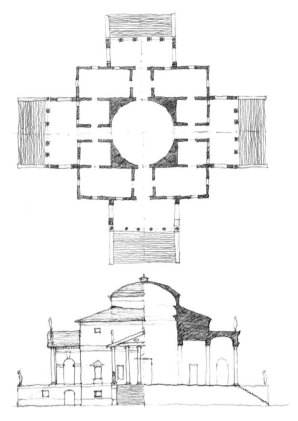

show of student or faculty work. These exhibits are an excellent way to observe and learn from others, either professionals or fellow students.

Finally, attend reviews at the end of the semester to see students' presentations of their work and hear feedback from the faculty or visiting guests. The semester-ending reviews are very instructional in many different ways—you can see firsthand the final presentation drawings and models done by the students, hear their oral presentations, and learn from the critiques from the visiting reviewers.

◀ Villa Rotunda, Study Abroad Program Sketch by Margaret DeLeeuw at University of Maryland. Faculty: Brian Kelly.

▼ Villa Rotunda, Vicenza, Italy. Architect: Palladio. PHOTOGRAPHER: R. LINDLEY VANN.

COMMUNITY SERVICE

A recent opportunity provided by many architecture programs is community service programs. Many institutions participate in Habitat for Humanity International, an organization that works to build or renovate homes for the inadequately sheltered in the United States and in 20 countries around the world, while others assist area schoolchildren through tutoring programs. These programs provide you with an opportunity to give back to the community while developing skills.

A relatively new community service program is Freedom by Design™ sponsored by the American Institute of Architecture Students (AIAS). Freedom by Design[3] utilizes the talents of architecture students to radically impact the lives of disabled individuals in their community through modest design and construction solutions. For the academic year 2008–2009 over 40 AIAS chapters throughout the country worked on projects to enhance the lives of individuals.

Many architecture programs, along with their students, assisted in various ways in the city of New Orleans, Louisiana, and the surrounding region after Hurricane Katrina in 2005. Other organizations that provide opportunities for you to develop your community service as an architect or after graduation include AmeriCorps, Peace Corps, Design Corps, The Mad Housers, Inc., Architecture for Humanity, and Public Architecture. For example, Public Architecture challenges architects to pledge 1 percent of their time to pro bono service to nonprofits organizations in need of design services. The 1 percent program challenges architecture and design firms nationwide to pledge a minimum of 1 percent of their time to pro bono service. The 1 percent program connects firms willing to give of their time with nonprofit organizations in need of design assistance.

Architecture in the Schools, a program led by local chapters of the AIA, matches volunteer architects with public school teachers to enrich the learning experience of children. To test your own architectural knowledge, volunteer to bring architectural concepts to life in any subject area in grades K–12. The bottom line: become involved with community service during both your education and your professional career.

MENTORING

Throughout the history of the architecture profession, mentoring has played a role. Architects mentor and guide their apprentices on the path to becoming an architect. Some schools have both formal and informal mentoring programs to connect you with mentors. One such program is the Mentoring Program of the Architecture Program at the University of Minnesota, the self-proclaimed largest in the nation, which matches students with area architects. Whether or not your school sponsors a program, consider seeking out a mentor from whom you can gain insight and wisdom. Your mentor could be a student further along in the program than you, a faculty member, or a local architect. Also, consider serving as a mentor to a student earlier in the program than you. In this way, you are involved with laddering mentoring—receiving mentoring from someone further along than you and providing mentoring to someone earlier in their career than you.

Through its website, the American Institute of Architects[4] has information on the topic of mentoring, from defining the term to helping you locate a mentor. Mentoring does not end when you finish your formal education; in fact, it should continue throughout your career.

STUDENT ORGANIZATIONS

Become involved with your architectural education by joining one of the student organizations within your university. First, membership in any student organization is a way to develop friendships and leadership abilities, and to have fun. Second, seek involvement with one of the architectural student organizations, the largest of which is the American Institute of Architecture Students (AIAS).

The AIAS (aias.org) operates at both the national and local levels. Located in Washington, DC, the national office sponsors student design competitions, an annual meeting (Forum) and Quad Conference during the academic years, and leadership training for chapter presidents. It publishes a magazine, *Crit,* and serves as one of the collateral organizations representing architecture students to the profession. Most programs in architecture have a local chapter of the AIAS that provides varied opportunities, including social and networking ones, and connections to the profession.

The National Organization of Minority Architects (NOMA) is a national professional association of minority architects that has chapters at over 20 architecture schools. Like AIAS, student chapters of the NOMA organize to connect architecture students with each other as well as architects in the profession. In addition, the NOMA has as its mission "the building of a strong national organization, strong chapters, and strong members for the purpose of minimizing the effect of racism in our profession."

Other student organizations include Arquitectos (for Latino students); Students for Congress for New Urbanism (CNU); Alpha Rho Chi, the fraternity for architecture; and Tau Sigma Delta, the national collegiate honor society. In addition, you may also find others unique to your institution. Also, investigate the value of involvement with student government or committees of your academic unit.

Conclusion

Now that you know how to prepare for an architectural education, select an architecture program based on your criteria, and live the life of an architecture student, consider the following steps of maximizing your education as described by Brian Kelly, associate professor at the University of Maryland:

1. Take charge of your time; you are responsible for your educational experience.
2. Work in the studio.
3. Get to know your peers and faculty.
4. Study abroad; step outside the box.
5. Take time for yourself; your health is paramount.

Uniting Education and Architecture

AMY YURKO, AIA

Founder/Director, BrainSpaces

Chicago, Ilinois

Why and how did you become an architect?

❯ AIA Gold Medal winner Charles Moore designed my childhood home. This house sparked a fascination with physical space and its impact on our family, but I had little understanding of the profession of architecture. Although my high school included a drafting class, I instead focused on college preparatory courses. With a passion for literature, I applied to college as a writing major and was accepted into an intensive writing program at Washington University in St. Louis. To fulfill my curiosity for architecture, I enrolled in a few courses in the architecture school during my first semester. By my sophomore year, I was a full-fledged architecture student and spent the following five years dedicated to learning what it takes to become an architect.

Why and how did you decide on which school to attend for your architecture degree? What degree(s) do you possess?

❯ I was lucky that my school of choice included an architecture program since I applied as a writing major and shifted majors in my sophomore year. I graduated with a bachelor degree one semester early, and decided to continue with graduate work at Washington University, where I obtained a master of architecture.

Lincoln Middle School, Schiller Park, Illinois. Architect: Amy Yurko, AIA/BrainSpaces.

What has been your greatest challenge as an architect?

❯ My greatest challenge as an architect was to recognize my own areas of skill and talent and narrow the focus of my career accordingly. My first 10 years were spent pretending that I enjoyed roof details and foundation plans. I suppose it was my general perception that architects must be really good at everything related to bringing a building into being. Once I let go of that perception, I was able to hone those skills that were enjoyable and productive for me. I could then surround myself with team members who were passionate about and talented at those skills I was missing, and collaboratively we made some very good buildings.

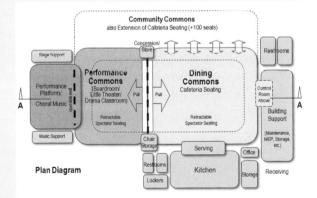

Plan Diagram

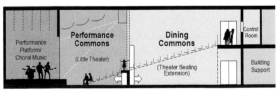

Section A-A

Marysville Getchell High School, Marysville, Washington. Architect: Amy Yurko, AIA/BrainSpaces with Craig Mason/DLR Group.

Marysville Getchell High School, Marysville, Washington. Architect: Amy Yurko, AIA/ BrainSpaces with Craig Mason/DLR Group.

What is BrainSpaces–Uniting Education and Architecture? How/why did your career progress to this connection?

❯ Along with working at various architecture firms, and primarily focusing on school planning and design, I developed a parallel career teaching archi-tecture. I have held teaching positions at the College of Architecture at Illinois Institute of Technology and the School of Architecture at the University of Southern California. Later, I taught architecture to middle school students at Drummond School, a magnet program of Chicago Public Schools.

Through these experiences, I found there to be a disconnect between students/educators and the architects who were responsible for designing their learning/teaching environments. I started my firm, BrainSpaces, as a link between my school planning and design experience and my passion for teaching—with the vision of becoming the missing connector. Understanding both educators and architects allows for an accurate translation of educational goals and needs into clear and effective direction for the project.

Therefore, BrainSpaces is a consulting practice promoting best practices and brain-based considerations in the planning and design of learning environments. Integrating architectural expertise and educational perspective is a unique strength of mine—to seamlessly assimilate both educational and physical components of this complex scope of work into a comprehensive, coordinated, and accurate set of tools for use and implementation by the design team of architects and engineers.

How is consulting different than working as an architect in a more traditional firm?

❭ At BrainSpaces I consult with school entities as well as with architects, depending on the individual project parameters. With either type of client, we offer the typical pre-design phase services of a more traditional firm. In general, the earliest portions of this phase emphasize client and stakeholder understanding, while the later portions collaborate with the architects to develop the conceptual design. In some cases, we are retained for the entire project to ensure the parameters established in pre-design are followed through in the built project.

This scope of services is quite similar to my roles in the more traditional firms with whom I was employed. This is to say that "traditional" firms and services often also offer "nontraditional" strategies for project development.

What are your primary responsibilities and duties?

❭ As leader of a small firm, I am responsible for all activities relating to the practice, including running the business, generating new work, and completing the work. I employ between two and five staff.

As an educational facility planner, I develop communication strategies and workflow processes for each client based on their specific characteristics. I facilitate stakeholder conversations which result in a thorough understanding of their needs. I show a range of carefully selected case studies to stakeholders with the intention of illuminating design possibilities. This understanding is then translated into space programs, adjacency diagrams, space attributes, and a written summary report. I often provide or collaborate in the generation of conceptual floor plans and massing diagrams.

What is the most/least satisfying part of a career as an architect?

❭ It is an overwhelming feeling to help facilitate the vision of students, educators, parents, and school leadership. The gratitude is palatable, and I always learn something new from each of them.

Perhaps the least satisfying work is financial management of the practice, particularly paying taxes!

Who or what experience has been a major influence on your career?

❭ Teaching has had a major influence on my career; thinking about thinking is a fascinating endeavor. In addition, planning and designing schools in southeast Asia has widened my perspective and increased my appreciation for all that I have. My son has allowed me to recognize my priorities and the value of time.

Environmental Design Excellence

NATHAN KIPNIS, AIA

Principal

Nathan Kipnis Architects, Inc.

Evanston, Illinois

Why and how did you become an architect?

⟩ Near where I grew up, along the North Shore of Chicago, there are amazing homes designed by everyone from David Adler to Frank Lloyd Wright. The residences in the area were built starting in the late 1800s, with construction peaking between 1910 and the late 1920s. Many of the homes located right along the lake on Sheridan Road are textbook examples of great European homes mixed in with the very first Prairie homes designed by Wright. In addition, there are also various contemporary designs, though not as numerous.

My parents would drive into Chicago and we would occasionally travel along Sheridan Road to get there. I would be glued to the window watching these great homes.

Later, the 1973 Arab-Israeli war and ensuing Middle East oil embargo opened my eyes about America's dependence on foreign oil. I felt that designing energy-efficient buildings would help decrease our reliance on that volatile energy source.

Why and how did you decide on which school to attend for your architecture degree? What degree(s) do you possess?

⟩ I applied to several schools, but chose the University of Colorado. I wanted to attend a school that offered an architecture program but also was not a very large university. University of Colorado

had a pre-architecture program and was not an overly large school.

At the time, I misunderstood the implications of a pre-architecture program, which means that the degree I would receive, a bachelor of environmental design, was not a professional degree and would require that I obtain a master of architecture to complete my studies. (My well-meaning, career counselor in high school assured me that this was the same as either a bachelor of architecture or a bachelor of arts in architectural studies.)

I also chose Colorado because of its highly renowned solar architecture program. Located in Boulder, the university was a natural center of interest in solar design. The climate and location are nearly perfect for studying solar design, being up at 5,000 feet above sea level and having more than 300 sunny days a year. Boulder is known for its liberal thinking, which went along with alternative energy research.

For my graduate studies, I researched more on where to attend. Arizona State University (ASU) in Tempe, Arizona, was recognized internationally for its solar and energy-conscious architectural design. Along with University of California at Berkley and Massachusetts Institute of Technology, I felt that ASU was one of the best schools for this field of study in the country. I was provided a partial scholarship, which made the decision very simple. I enrolled at ASU and graduated in the master of architecture program with an emphasis in energy-conscious design.

What has been your greatest challenge as an architect/principal?

⟩ Originally, my greatest challenge was convincing clients to let me push the envelope with what

Moldan Corporation, Evanston, Illinois. Architect: Nathan Kipnis Architects, Inc. PHOTOGRAPHER. NATHAN KIPNIS, AIA.

I want to do with "green" design. I would try to nudge them into going to a higher level. With the recent explosion of interest in green design, I now actually have the opposite problem. I have people coming to me with so many green ideas for their projects that I have to spend time prioritizing their goals and selecting the ones that are most appropriate for the project location and budget.

Another major challenge is to be constantly bringing in high-quality projects in a timely manner. I have been very fortunate to have had a nearly constant increase demand for our services, while rarely running slow periods or periods of too much work. I have also been able to obtain commissions that allow me to do quality design that generates positive publicity, which in turn provides me with the ability to bring in work of that caliber or higher. This is the kind of cycle that feeds upon itself in a positive manner.

What are your primary responsibilities and duties as an architect?

❭ My specific responsibilities are threefold. The client comes first and foremost. It is very important that I carefully listen to their requests and make sure we achieve them, even reading "between the lines" occasionally. I let them know that is it is their project, but my name is also associated with it, which means that there are certain design and technical standards that I want to make sure are achieved.

The next responsibility revolves around my office. I have to make sure we are properly compensated for the work we do, make sure the contracts are correctly set up and be smart about how we market ourselves. Marketing is an ongoing commitment that requires constant attention to make sure we have new ongoing media material "in the pipeline."

And finally, I have significant responsibilities to the people in the office. They must feel that they are part of the team and that their input is important to me. I have them attend various "green" seminars or events to further their education. I also try to get them to sample a very wide range of experiences in the office, from CAD work, client meetings, and field administration to public presentations. It is mutually beneficial.

Your firm is strongly committed to integrating excellence in design with environmental awareness. Can you provide more detail to this statement and describe how it is accomplished?

❭ What my firm attempts to do with as many projects as possible is to incorporate "green" principles at as many stages as possible. The earlier in the process the better. We try to do this in an integrated

▶ Green Vacation Home, Sturgeon Bay, Wisconsin. Nathan Kipnis Architects, Inc. PHOTOGRAPHER: WAYNE CABLE PHOTOGRAPHY.

▼ Ford Calumet Competition, Chicago. Architect: Nathan Kipnis Architects, Inc. PHOTOGRAPHER: NATHAN KIPNIS, AIA.

way, as opposed to "tacking on" green technologies and materials.

At the beginning of the project, I try to see what design decisions make the most sense in terms of "green" design and in response to the project's specific goals. If there is a solution that I feel works to satisfy both, I pursue it in detail. There is usually a single overall theme that unifies a design. Finding it is really the challenge. If I can get that one big idea to solve the project's key problem and make it work

"green," it usually can be done in an economical way and helps the client support it. To me, designing a green project is an opportunity to make the pure design even better and have more meaning. It should not be a burden to design green.

Can you describe more about your work with the "Green Bungalow Initiative?"

▶ Begun at the request of Mayor Daley in 2001, the "Green Bungalow Initiative" (GBI) was a program to provide green design guidelines for those purchasing bungalows in the City of Chicago. Mayor Daley grew up in a bungalow and has a natural affinity for them. The city had already established Bungalow Design Guidelines for people renovating bungalows. The "Green Bungalow Initiative" was established to provide a "green" vision for bungalow renovations and additions.

There were four primary consultants for the GBI. One was for architectural design, another for technical issues (ranging from mechanical systems to the physics of insulation's systems); one was for green materials and methods and the last for health-related aspects.

I was chosen to work on the green materials and methods, principally because I had recently completed the "Green Homes for Chicago" program, which was an international design competition in which my firm was one of five selected to have their designs built. The house that I designed was the least expensive to build and used many "green" methods and materials.

The four consultants provided written and graphical information that was intended to used by owners of bungalows or those about to purchase them as a guideline for "green" principles specific to bungalows. The information could also be used for any home style, but the content of the material was geared towards bungalows.

Where do you see the field of green architecture heading in the future?

❯ I believe that in the short term green design will be integrated into local and national codes on such a level that the term "green design" will disappear and become ubiquitous. Beyond that, however, there will be significant challenges as natural resources become scarce enough that it impacts people's lives on a daily basis. The consequences of cheap oil's disappearance is becoming more and more evident.

This is not a political problem that can be solved by drilling for more oil to the corners of the earth, but requires a fundamental change in how society functions. Politics being what they are, this message will no doubt be twisted every which way, but in the end, the path away from a fossil-fuel-dependent society is critical for its very survival. Renewable energy and appropriately designed built environments are the only way to accomplish this. Because existing buildings use so much energy and generate such enormous amounts of CO_2 emissions, architects are in a unique position to lead this change by designing

Belmont Development, Lake Bluff, Illinois. Architect: Nathan Kipnis Architects, Inc. PHOTOGRAPHER: NATHAN KIPNIS, AIA.

super-efficient homes and communities. The difficult aspect for this is to make people understand that in fact life influenced by cheap and abundant power will need to be scaled back. Hybrid Escalades are not the answer; they are the problem.

How did your education help you prepare for these challenges?

❯ By their very training, architects are able to think outside the box and look for solutions where others see only problems. "Celebrate the Problem" we used to call it in school. A specific part of that training is the ability to look back at historical precedents to see how they could inform a current problem. I like to examine how homes functioned before cheap oil and see what can be gleaned from those time-tested designs and integrate them aesthetically into the twenty-first century.

Who or what experience has been a major influence on your career?

❯ As I mentioned, the single biggest influence in my career was the 1973 oil embargo and how I thought I could contribute to a solution to it. This event is what started my career in energy efficiency, which has grown into "green" design in all of its forms.

Professors Philip Tabb at the University of Colorado, and John Yellot and Jeffery Cook at Arizona State University influenced the way I practice environmental design by showing me the importance of integrating energy efficiency into architectural design and understanding where the historical roots of environmentally sensitive architectural design were derived from Amery Lovins, who taught a summer school class at Colorado, made a huge impression on me relative to how architecture, energy and national security can be interrelated.

I was also fortunate to have worked in two very good, though very different firms. At Porter Pang Deardorff and Weymiller in Mesa, Arizona, the design principal, Marley Porter, had a great outlook on how fun design should be. It was an infectious quality that spread through the office. The other partners were also very generous in sharing their skills. It was a great work environment.

At PHL of Chicago, it was much more production based and very serious. Once you were at the project manager level, you ran a project like it was your own firm. They really taught me how to run an office.

More Than I Ever Dreamed

DIANE BLAIR BLACK, AIA

Vice-President

RTKL Associates Inc.

Baltimore, Maryland

Why and how did you become an architect?

〉 I knew at an early age that I wanted to be an architect. My parents hired an architect to design two family homes, so I was introduced to this inspiring profession when I was five years old. My mother always encouraged creativity and found a summer camp across the street from Taliesin, at the home of an architect who apprenticed with Frank Lloyd Wright. I had several teachers who inspired me; Mr. Godding, my art teacher from first through sixth grade, and my high school physics teacher, Mr. Ellenbecker. They gave me the confidence to pursue architecture even though I was intimidated by the challenges of school.

Why and how did you decide on which school to attend for your architecture degree? What degree(s) do you possess?

〉 When I graduated from high school, there were no accredited architecture programs in Wisconsin. so I attended the University of Minnesota in Minneapolis, Minnesota. The great Ralph Rapson was dean of the School of Architecture and it was an exciting time to be there. In those days the professors were all practicing architects, and every student held a part-time job in a Twin Cities' firm. In fact, an internship was a prerequisite to one's thesis. I earned a bachelor of arts in urban studies and a bachelor of environmental design on the way to my bachelor of architecture. After passing the archi-

PHOTOGRAPHER: DAVE WHITCOMB.

tect registration exam, I studied business at Johns Hopkins University and earned a master's degree and the Stegman Award for Excellence in the Study of Administrative Science. Even now I am thinking about a pursuing a couple of other degrees.

What has been your greatest challenge as an architect?

〉 Our greatest challenge is dependence on the economy and our clients' ability to undertake inspiring projects.

Lobby, RTKL Offices, Bond Street Wharf, Baltimore, Maryland. Architect: RTKL Associates, Inc. PHOTOGRAPHER: DAVE WHITCOMB.

Within your firm, RTKL Associates, you are a vice president. As a vice president what are your primary responsibilities and duties?

❭ At RTKL, a vice president's essential responsibilities include: pursuing project excellence, providing leadership, and supporting cultural behavior, financial management, and revenue generation. Each vice president has expertise in a particular market or service—my passion is for public and corporate work in the earliest phases of project development, programming and predesign. I work very closely with clients to understand project objectives, to communicate their vision and develop a shared mission with the design team. As vice presidents we manage project teams and have ultimate responsibility for design, budgets, profitability, and production quality. We are expected to contribute to the firm's vision and uphold that vision in daily practice. We are also expected to lead beyond project responsibilities in our professional organizations and communities.

Interior Stair, RTKL Offices, Bond Street Wharf, Baltimore, Maryland, Architect: RTKL Associates, Inc. PHOTOGRAPHER: DAVE WHITCOMB.

Conference Room,
RTKL Offices, Bond
Street Wharf, Baltimore,
Maryland. Architect:
RTKL Associates, Inc.
PHOTOGRAPHER: DAVE
WHITCOMB.

Briefly, how did you become a vice president within a well-respected firm?

❭ First off my interests and education gave me the right foundation for success at RTKL, not only had I earned a degree in architecture but also in urban studies—a fundamental tenet of all of the projects of RTKL. I spent my early years getting a broad range of experience so I could become a licensed architect. Then, I found the project phase that I excel at: programming and pre-design. Developing an area of excellence is important at RTKL because each vice president is responsible for bringing work into the firm, and our clients look for expertise. Eventually I earned another degree, a master in business, and consequently directed one of the largest offices of RTKL.

What is the most/least satisfying part of your job?

❭ The best part is the opportunity to work with clients who have the vision to pursue exciting projects and collaborating with the unbelievably talented experts in our office to make those dreams reality. Some of the professionals in our firm are so impressive that it is a privilege to accomplish things together.

The worst part of my job is facing the harsh realities of staff reductions when the economy fails. Losing wonderfully talented people who have contributed to our work and firm is excruciating.

Who or what experience has been a major influence on your career?

❭ One of my studio professors, James Stageberg, had a significant influence on my career. He offered me an internship at Hodne/Stageberg Partners, where he was a principal; I was honored to work with both great professionals and some of the most talented students at the university. James is always full of encouragement—a true mentor with zeal for life and architecture. He always had confidence in me, and he convinced me to take the position with RTKL and to go on to graduate school.

Creation of Genuine Community

WAYNE A. MORTENSEN, ASSOCIATE AIA, NASW

Project Manager/Urban Designer, H3 Studio

Lecturer

Washington University

St. Louis, Missouri

Why and how did you become an architect?

〉 I decided in the sixth grade to become an architect after an influential viewing of *Three Men and a Baby*. The vision of wearing my hard hat to the top floor of an uncompleted skyscraper with a roll of drawings was appealing. At first, it was skyscrapers, museums, and the other typical ivory towers that inspired and drove me.

Why and how did you decide on which school to attend for your architecture degree? What degree(s) do you possess?

〉 After looking around the country I found that I was most comfortable 90 minutes from home. I was thrilled with the foundation provided by the University of Nebraska and the myriad opportunities available within the large, public school context. One such opportunity led to my next stop, serving as president of the American Institute of Architecture Students (AIAS) in Washington, DC.

I left Lincoln, Nebraska, in May of 2003 with a bachelor of science in design (BSD). In August of 2004 I enrolled in graduate school and completed graduate master of architecture (M.Arch.), Urban Design (MUD), and Social Work (MSW).

Why did you pursue the additional credentials of a master of urban design and master of social work?

〉 Toward the end of my undergraduate education, I began to develop a deep cynicism regarding the failed social legacy of the architectural profession. Images of Pruitt Igoe's destruction and the utopian, though misdirected, visions from Le Corbusier and Frank Lloyd Wright convinced me that if I was to be an agent of social change I would have to learn about society from a different profession. Architecture, to me, was increasingly about much more than just bricks and sticks.

After looking around the country, there was only one place that would allow me to simultaneously pursue all three disciplines (architecture, urban design, and social work). At Washington University I began to stitch my disconnected thoughts into a cohesive thesis. Today, my research revolves around the connection between community design and social capital formation.

After your undergraduate degree, you had the opportunity to serve as president of AIAS. Please describe this experience and how it has informed your future as an architect.

〉 It was a life-changing experience and one that convinced me of the following. First, change is most easily attained from within the system. It does little good to throw stones as an outsider. I found this to be true for the collateral organizations (ACSA, AIA, AIAS, NAAB, and NCARB), the architectural profession as a whole, and our government—both at local and federal levels. Second, the value of serving others can be rewarding on many levels. There are myriad professional opportunities within our particular democracy that offer the chance to be both an idealist and wage earner.

Urban Coalescence by Wayne A. Mortensen at Washington University. PHOTOGRAPHER: WAYNE A. MORTENSEN.

The following text is on your "brief vitae"—To utilize the built environment as a tool to ameliorate societal ills through the creation of genuine community—communities in which civic engagement and social interaction can make a comeback. Can you provide further description as to what this statement means?

❯ For decades, America has been subsidizing the construction of communities that segregate, isolate, and homogenize entire groups of people. Public housing during the urban renewal period, for instance, separated society's most challenged citizens, marked them by placing them in monolithic towers, and surrounded them with no social support structure of any kind.

My professional goal is to investigate and create communities that integrate struggling citizens into socially normative contexts that foster the formation of bridging social capital and genuine civic engagement. Norms for millions of Americans— the ability to borrow a cup of flour from a neighbor to finish dinner for your family, obtain a ride to work if you are having car difficulties, or even obtain a lead on a new job—are not available

where they are needed most. Beyond this, how can we steer our suburban addiction toward communities that [re]connect and engage citizens?

What has been your greatest challenge as an intern thus far?

❯ I am an intern in only one facet of my life, when speaking with a representative of the National Council of Architecture Registration Boards (NCARB). Within this small sliver, however, the largest challenge, hands down, has been NCARB's stipulation that IDP supervisors be licensed in the jurisdiction where they practice. This has only a tangential connection with contemporary architectural practice and has kept me from earning IDP credit at a job I very much enjoy in a firm that has been very supportive of my licensure goals.

In a profession where large firms perform work in Dayton one day and Dubai the next this requirement places interns in a decidedly unfair situation—one where they have to challenge the professional approach of a firm much larger than them. This experience has vibrantly demonstrated why so many of our emerging professionals are forced to work at multiple firms if they wish to fulfill their requirements and attain licensure. Interns cannot be used as instruments of professional change.

Alternative career tracks compound these difficulties, despite their critically important (in many cases) role in the built environment. If architects are to become societal leaders—in all tracks of life—we must address these barriers and begin to catalog the value of practicing as an architect outside of "architecture."

What are your primary responsibilities and duties as an associate and as a faculty member?

❯ As an associate at my design firm, I work as a project manager and urban designer. I have the same level of responsibility—and accountability to our clients—as anyone else in the firm. As an associate lecturer, I teach courses at both the undergraduate and graduate levels that revolve around the social, political, and economic context in which American cities are built. I have a leadership role within the firm and have direct feedback into the workings of the design school.

▼ Social Sustainability by Wayne A. Mortensen at Washington University. PHOTOGRAPHER: WAYNE A. MORTENSEN.

How does teaching architecture differ from practicing?

❯ My courses are geared primarily toward urban design and the connection between teaching and practicing urban design is direct. I am constantly amused about how difficult it is to be on the other side of the podium and how, on any given day, I will practice exactly what I had presented earlier that day. Of course, you have to deal with the banal—endless call lists, emails, and coordination meetings—but the work is for and with real people, and that lack of abstraction produces a great amount of motivation.

What is accreditation and why is it important in architecture?

❯ Accreditation is the establishment of minimum criteria to assure baseline competence of graduates in a particular profession. Accreditation is a tool that allows the United States to assure a qualitative standard in all schools of architecture; effectively protecting vulnerable student populations from exploitation. Beyond the protection of students, accreditation allows the NCARB to accept the transcripts of thousands of architecture graduates each year without having to meticulously review their transcripts. Without the NAAB, architectural regis-

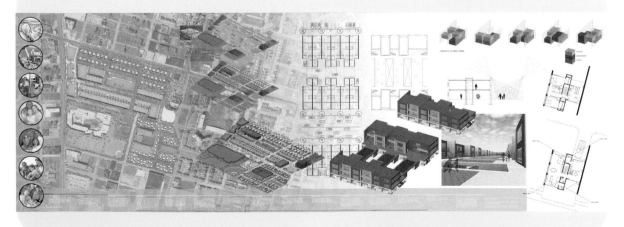

tration would be an even more tedious and process; licensure more elusive.

What are your 5-year and 10-year career goals relative to architecture?

❭ Within five years, I hope that I will be deeply involved in design projects that combine creative problem solving with community organizing and citizen empowerment. By then, I also aim to have published my first article in a peer-reviewed journal that will begin to explore the links between community success and community design—and to do it all as a licensed architect.

In 10 years I will be 38 and, thus, by a small margin, be eligible to run for president of the United States. Look for my yard signs: Mortensen for America; One Community at a Time.

Who or what experience has been a major influence on your career?

❭ Every day I interact with someone who has a lived an experience different than my own who impacts me in a tangible way. The more people I meet, the harder my resolve to create communities in which they will be able to thrive.

Integrating Practice with the Academy

CLARK E. LLEWELLYN, AIA, NCARB
Dean, School of Architecture
University of Hawaii at Manoa
Honolulu, Hawaii

Why and how did you become an architect?

❭ When I was in sixth grade, each student was asked to write on a piece of paper what they "wanted to be." I wanted to write "veterinarian," but I was not sure of the spelling, so I wrote down "architect." My decision was made.

Throughout junior high school I read the writings of Frank Lloyd Wright and managed to visit some of his buildings. Moving to Japan for my last two years of high school, I was amazed, awed, and inspired by traditional Japanese architecture. I would often escape from the dramatic collage of Tokyo and find refuge within rural shrines or temples.

While in Japan I attended the 1964 Olympics and, like many Olympics, architecture played an important role. It was through the works of Kenzo Tange that I generated an interest in contemporary architecture that extended beyond Wright. The subtly, power, and beauty of architecture entered my soul during those years in Japan.

However, my high school counselor was more objective. Because I had not taken any art classes, he did not believe architecture should be my major and "guided" me into engineering. I entered my first year of community college majoring in engineering. Within months I considered joining the military instead of being an engineer. I then contacted an architect inquiring if not having an art background should prevent me from being an architect. Based on his advice, I changed majors and followed my heart . . . something I still believe in.

Why and how did you decide on which school to attend for your architecture degree? What degree(s) do you possess?

❯ My father was in the United States Air Force, and I graduated from an American military high school near Tokyo. After graduation, I returned to my state of residence so I could afford an education. With two schools to choose from, I chose the one farthest away from family and overcast days (not necessarily good advice, but at 18 that was my rationale). Because of the remote location of Washington State University (WSU), upon arrival I planned to transfer after my first year. While disappointed upon my arrival, I grew to admire the location and found WSU to be an exciting program in a very special place. Though I had a relatively difficult start, I managed to graduate with the five-year bachelor of architecture with distinction.

Though I considered waiting until after I completed my professional internship to attend graduate school, I was "counseled" by numerous faculty at WSU to apply immediately after graduation. Unlike my high school counselor, they knew my heart and encouraged me to apply to programs that were previously out of reach (both financially and academically).

I considered graduate programs internationally (AA in London) and within the United States. With more forethought than five years earlier, I decided not to apply to any West Coast schools and narrowed my applications to Harvard and the University of Pennsylvania. I applied to Harvard because of the richness of resources, reputation, recommendations of WSU faculty, and a wide range of available ideologies and electives. Conversely, I applied to studio of master architect, educator, and philosopher Louis Kahn at the University of Pennsylvania. When I was accepted to both programs, I chose the Graduate

Whipple Ridge, Private Residence, Big Sky, Montana. Architect: Llewellyn Architects. PHOTOGRAPHER: CLARK E. LLEWELLYN, AIA.

School of Design at Harvard. Though I received multiple acceptances, Harvard was my first choice. The education was worth every dollar spent and the experience was priceless. I was in the first class to occupy Gund Hall. It was a very interesting year. I received my master of architecture from Harvard and, because of the education I received, I have never stopped learning.

Why did you choose to attend Harvard University to pursue your post-professional master of architecture? What was your particular focus or interest?

❯ I chose Harvard University because it did *not* have a particular focus or interest. It provided the most outstanding resources for learning within the world. With the combined resources of Harvard and MIT (two miles away), not one program could compete for quality of faculty, library, or breadth of programs. Gund Hall was a new building in 1972 and it was an exciting place to learn. It seemed to be a place where the student rather than the school or faculty could set the direction. I had already been through a structured undergraduate program and sought a resource. I was not disappointed. I tried to take advantage of the resources available. I took courses in development, structures, theory, and design at Harvard. I also took courses in building materials, construction law, and planning (with Kevin Lynch) at MIT. Werner Seligman and Shadrack Woods taught me the "why" of architecture that I had missed so much in my undergraduate education.

In retrospect, receiving my first professional degree from Washington State University and my master's degree at Harvard was ideal for my needs. I could not have asked for a better and more appropriate education.

What has been your greatest challenge as an architect/faculty member?

❯ As an architect my greatest challenge is the ability to create and build work that I feel capable of producing.

As a faculty member my greatest challenge is to eliminate student biases.

As an administrator, my greatest challenge is to provide support for our faculty, staff, and students.

How does teaching architecture differ from practicing architecture?

❯ Teaching is inspiring or guiding others to value learning. Therefore, I often do not consider myself a teacher. The knowledge I impart, in general, is past knowledge. It may within a journal or book, but it is still within our past. As an educator (versus teacher), I am responsible for inspiring students to look toward an unknown future. They must take risks that cannot take place in practice. They must imagine beyond what is historically possible.

My practice, on the other hand, must make the future part of our history. What I imagine must be built through construction means and tools that are usually historically based. Though I may attempt to create new techniques, forms, construction, processes, etc., they are all based on historical realms of possibility.

Whipple Ridge, Private Residence, Big Sky, Montana. Architect: Llewellyn Architects. PHOTOGRAPHER: CLARK E. LLEWELLYN, AIA.

Llewellyn Residence, Three Forks, Montana. Architect: Llewellyn Architects. PHOTOGRAPHER: CLARK E. LLEWELLYN, AIA.

Why did you make this career choice to become involved with education for your professional career?

❯ I became involved in education through of a series of events that were not fully planned.

After becoming a licensed architect in 1975 while practicing in Portland, Oregon, I decided to open my own firm. Because I had grown up in a military household and moved throughout my life, I did not have many connections from which to establish a client base. Therefore, I believed that if I returned to Washington State University and taught for a few years that I could move to an urban center, practice architecture, and teach part time to provide income while establishing an office. My mistake was underestimating how much I would like teaching. However, because I also enjoyed practice, I did both. Doing both full time requires much more than 40 hours a week.

My heart tells me that I am first an architect, second a university professor, and third an administrator. I may be a better administrator than either

of the two that reside within my soul, but that may be because I do value them so highly.

Throughout your career, you have been involved with the AIA. Why is this important for you as an architect?

❯ I have been an active member of the American Institute of Architects for about as long as I can remember. As a student I was active within the AIAS, after graduation I was an Associate member, and then I became a full member after gaining licensure in 1975.

There are a number of reasons for my involvement over the decades. The first reason is because I believe the profession should have a stronger and more effective voice. As much as one may find frustration with a professional organization because of its general promotion of "status quo," I believe the way to make effective and long-range change is through the American Institute of Architects. I have found the American Institute of Architects to be a place where one can actually make a difference if you get involved. Therefore, I am.

The second reason I am a member of the AIA is because of the people I have met over the years. I served seven years on the board of directors in Montana, driving almost 1,000 miles to meetings, so I met people who share a similar commitment to vision. They are valued allies and become valued friends.

The third reason is because I am an architect, educator, and administrator. Therefore, I work with students, faculty, and architects in training on a daily basis. These groups are part of our profession but have been historically underrepresented within the AIA community. Because I also practice architecture, I hope to help bridge the gap that often exists between the constituent groups.

The final reason I belong is because I feel a responsibility to be a member. I have used the AIA contracts for decades, benefited from their national and state lobbying efforts, handed AIA scholarships to students, benefited from their educational programs, and seen national advertising supporting the need for architects. Even if I had done nothing as an AIA member, I feel as though I have benefited from the organization and its volunteer membership. I have a sense of debt and obligation that must be paid in order for me to practice and teach within the profession I so much enjoy being a part of.

Who or what experience has been a major influence on your career?

❭ Robert M. Ford III, FAIA has had the greatest influence on my career. I first met him as a professor at Washington State University, where we had many discussions that lasted well into the night. We later taught together at WSU, at Mississippi State University, and at a private architecture program in Portland, Oregon. He mentored me through learning, teaching, and much of life. One other person who had a major influence upon my career is my wife, Beverly. She encouraged me to apply for tenure when I did not believe in such appointments and then to apply for director when I thought otherwise. She has supported my practice, both in times of growth and recession. People have had, by far, the greatest influence on my career.

However, I cannot leave this section without having noted the influences of places. I remember the very first time I walked into the Pantheon in Rome. I was awestruck. Since then other particular places have influenced me. These include the Alhambra, the ruins in Tikal, the Great Pyramids, and indigenous villages in Greece, Italy, Portugal, Turkey, Ecuador, the Middle East, and Asia. I have also been influenced and inspired by the rural West with the power of its landscape and architecture that has attempted to respond.

NOTES

1. NAAB (2009). "NAAB Conditions for Accreditation for Professional Degree Programs in Architecture." Washington, DC: National Architectural Accrediting Board.
2. NAAB (2009). Retrieved January 17, 2009 from http://www.naab.org.
3. AIAS (2009). Retrieved July 23, 2008 from http://www.aias.org.
4. American Institute of Architects (2008) Mentorship. Retrieved July 23, 2008 from http://www.aia.org/professionals/mentors/index.htm/.

③ The Experience of an Architect

"I hear and I forget. I see and I remember. I do and I understand."

CONFUCIUS (551 BC–479 BC)

EXPERIENCE IS THE SECOND MAJOR REQUIREMENT for becoming an architect. In most states, candidates satisfy the formal requirement for experience by participating in and completing the Intern Development Program (IDP), a program of the profession. However, early exposure to the profession through the experiential programs often offered through your institution is important. These programs may consist of shadowing an architect before you begin your formal education, a credit-bearing internship while in school, a career-related summer position in an architecture firm, or your first full-time position in an architecture firm. In all cases, you should seek opportunities for experience.

The authors of *Building Community: A New Future for Architecture Education and Practice*[1] recommend that schools, practitioners, and local and national architecture organizations collaborate to increase the availability, information about, and incentives for students to gain work experience during school. Clearly, because this report and study of architectural education was commissioned by the five collateral organizations, there is substantial consensus within the profession that gaining experience while an architecture student is valuable.

◄Armada Housing, s'Hertogenbosch, Netherlands. Architect: Building Design Partnership (BDP).
PHOTOGRAPHER: GRACE H. KIM, AIA.

But the question is *how*? How do you, as a student of architecture, obtain a position when you have no experience? This is a classic Catch-22; you need experience to gain a position and a position to gain experience.

What is experience? The dictionary defines *experience* as follows:

n. 1: the accumulation of knowledge or skill that results from direct participation in events or activities; 2: the content of direct observation or participation in an event[2]

Thus, to become an architect, it is important for you to participate directly in the profession—to observe or participate in architecture, an architectural firm, or your education. As you begin your studies, check with your school to determine if it has programs to assist you in gaining experience. Even if it does not, you still gain experience as you work in the design studio and other courses.

Gaining Experience as a Student

SHADOW

One way to learn about the profession is to shadow an architect through a typical day of activities. Obviously, this is a short-lived experience, but it should be easy to accomplish. Many architects are more than willing to help the next generation in this way. Also, some high schools have a career program involving shadowing to expose their students to career fields. Any opportunity to interact with an architect, however briefly, can help you understand the profession. For referrals to architects in your area, contact the local chapter of the American Institute of Architects (AIA).

VOLUNTEER

Volunteering is a common way to gain experience. After shadowing an architect, you could request an opportunity to volunteer in the firm for a short period. A number of nonprofit organizations have formal programs that can help you find a firm at which to volunteer.

RESEARCH WITH FACULTY

A wonderful opportunity for college students is a research experience with a faculty member. As for volunteering, approach a faculty member with teaching or research interests parallel to yours. Specifically, ask if you may assist in some manner with his or her research or writing efforts. This kind of experience may lead to further opportunities, both during college and after.

EXTERNSHIP

Sometimes considered a mini-internship, an externship provides students the opportunity to explore a specific career path, gain marketable experience, and make professional connections by working with professional alumni for an abbreviated period, usually a week during the winter or spring break. In many cases, schools match students with alumni, but they may also make connections with other area professionals.

The School of Architecture at the University of Virginia sponsors one of the largest externship programs in the country. Held during the winter break, the program provides students an opportunity to shadow an architect—typically an alumnus—in their workplace for a week. More than 125 students have this professional experience each year. The University of Michigan does a parallel program, Spring Break Internships, but it is held during the spring break. Through an unpaid weeklong internship, architecture students have an opportunity to learn more about the practice of architecture within a firm throughout the United States.

INTERNSHIP

The formal training required for licensure as an architect is typically referred to as an *internship,* but some institutions sponsor an internship program for students. The purpose of an internship is to provide the student with work experience for an extended period, usually a semester. In many cases, the internship earns academic credit. The position may be unpaid because it involves a large learning component.

Getty Center, Los Angeles. Architect: Richard Meier. PHOTOGRAPHER: R. LINDLEY VANN.

At Massachusetts Institute of Technology (MIT), the internship program helps students gain experience, improve practical skills, and be involved with real projects and practice during their Independent Activities Period, typically three weeks in January. Interns work full time for $3^{1}/_{2}$ weeks in small, medium, and large firms or in public or nonprofit agencies, and they receive six units of academic credit. In preparation for the program, students are expected to attend three meetings during the semester before the experience.

At the University of Texas at Austin, the Professional Residency Program allows students at the advanced levels of architectural design to serve an internship under the supervision of a registered architect in a selected architectural firm. The seven-month internship spans a semester and the preceding or following summer. Students can earn academic credit for the experience by extensive documentation of their work and may receive a modest stipend while in residency. Each year, the program involves approximately 50 students, both undergraduate and graduate students, in two sessions, January–July and June–December. Students are placed in firms in Texas and throughout the United States and other countries.

COOPERATIVE EDUCATION

This educational strategy combines classroom learning with productive work experience in a field related to a student's academic or career goals, achieved through a partnership of students, educational institutions, and employers. While details differ from school to school, some have established programs based on the idea of cooperative education.

The Boston Architectural College (BAC) has one of the most distinctive approaches to educating future architects in the entire country.

> The professional degree programs feature the model of concurrent learning: working in approved, paid, supervised positions in design firms during the day—the "practice" component of the curriculum—while studying several evenings a week at the BAC—the "academic" component of the curriculum. Although each component has a sequence of its own, the two are designed to be concurrent, allowing progress in one to facilitate learning in the other.
>
> BAC Catalog[3]

Required for all students in the School of Architecture and Interior Design at the University of Cincinnati, the Professional Practice Program gives students selected practical experience purposefully mingled with a gradually expanding academic background. The program consists of three months of carefully planned professional practice assignments alternating with three-month study periods. For students in architecture, the year-round schedule allows for eight quarters of experience while obtaining a six-year bachelor of architecture degree. Through the Professional Practice Program, students obtain firsthand knowledge of professional practices, expectancies, and opportunities. At the same time, they benefit from a realistic test of their career interests and aptitudes. Finally, as graduates, their experience makes them valuable to employers and increases their qualifications for responsible career opportunities.

Established in 1994, the cooperative education program for students in the School of Architecture at the University of Arkansas is designed to allow students to work for a full academic year (9 to 15 months) in an architecture firm after the third year. Initiated by the faculty, the program presently has students working throughout the state and the country.

CAREER-RELATED EXPERIENCE (PART-TIME/SUMMER)

Perhaps the most popular way to gain experience while in school is simply to obtain a position in a firm. While not a formal program like an internship or cooperative education, a career-related experience can be just as valuable, although perhaps more difficult to obtain. Most schools post positions with area firms, sponsor career fairs to connect students with firms, or host firms who interview on campus, but securing a position requires fulfilling a need of the employer.

Regardless of the type of program, gaining experience while in school makes you more marketable to prospective employers upon graduation. In addition, the experience may count toward IDP if it meets certain requirements (these have to do with the timing and length of the experience). For graduates of the BAC, completing the degree usually coincides with taking the Architect Registration Exam (ARE) because students work full-time while attending school. Note that in a recent survey of interns and young architects, almost half indicated that they had gained practical experience while in school.

FULL-TIME POSITIONS

Of course, the true challenge is securing your first full-time position with an employer. Searching for full-time work on your path to becoming an architect is important, but not easy.

When you graduate, you are *not* an architect. Remember, you must continue working under the supervision of an architect before being eligible to take the Architect Registration Examination (ARE).

What do you look for when hiring a new designer?

❯ I look for a strong portfolio of work.

Thomas Fowler, IV, AIA, Professor and Director, Collaborative Integrative-Interdisciplinary Digital-Design Studio (CIDS), California Polytechnic State University–San Luis Obispo

❯ I look for an excellent listener who has experience designing and planning buildings for the environment I work in.

H. Alan Brangman, AIA, University Architect, Georgetown University

❯ Our firm looks for graduate architects who have an inspiring portfolio, solid experience, and excellent references. We want to see an interest in the urban scale and the project types on which we thrive—large, complex, and important. We want to meet an engaging professional who can become part of our culture of creativity, collaboration, and communication.

Diane Blair Black, AIA, Vice-President, RTKL Associates, Inc.

❯ Initiative; a commitment to sustainability; ability to work well with others; comprehensive understanding of building methods and practices.

Lynn N. Simon, AIA, LEED AP, President, Simon & Associates, Inc.

❯ For me, all professional staff members must be designers. Therefore, all must be able to work together in a constructive and positive manner. Because of the size of my office and my inability to meet with everyone every day, all designers must be self-motivated and confident in making decisions and communicating with clients, contractors, public agencies, and suppliers. They should also know what they do not know—that is, they must know when to ask questions, do research, or seek an answer. Finally, designers must think creatively, responsibly, and with vision.

Clark E. Llewellyn, AIA, Dean, University of Hawaii

Borneo Island, Amsterdam, Netherlands. PHOTOGRAPHER: MICHAEL R. MARIANO, AIA.

❯ Talent and drive. The rest can be learned on the job.

Amy Yurko, AIA, Founder/Director, BrainSpaces

❯ I look for incredible talent and ambition.

William J. Carpenter, Ph.D., FAIA, Associate Professor, Southern Polytechnic State University; President, Lightroom

❯ I look for someone who is exceptionally skilled in design but who also is a very good listener who can hear, interpret, and deliver to the client what best addresses the their needs. The profession is in dire need of designers who are good leaders as well for their ability to integrate all of the complex and conflicting elements that go into the design. The designer is becoming less of a single source of creation and more of a conductor who leads the creative team, an orchestra if you will, that is comprised of all the individuals, groups, consultants and officials who have a say in how the structure will be used and what it will look like. As design moves "upstream" designers will need to know more about what goes on inside their buildings from an operational point of view as well as knowing every detail of the components that comprise their buildings as documented in the form of Building Information Modeling (BIM) technology.

Ambassador Richard N. Swett (r), FAIA, President, Swett Associates, Inc.

❯ First, and foremost, I look for people who think like an architect—that is, can solve problems architecturally. By this I mean they can look for unexpected solutions and solve them poetically. Many pragmatic concerns must be resolved in the design of a building.

In addition, I look for a good work ethic, good people, and leadership skills, commitment to excellence in architecture, creative problem-solving capabilities, and the potential to develop technical skills.

Edward J. Shannon, AIA, Director of Design, Benvenuti & Stein Design LLC

❯ A designer's communication skills—the ability to listen, speak, write, and represent ideas—provide insights into how well he or she can function within a professional practice. The last, representing ideas, is what distinguishes architects from others. In the final analysis, architecture is our ability to turn ideas into representations. Whether the representation is in the form of a diagram, sketch, rendering, or physical or digital model, the architect's ability to represent precedes the construction of reality. A young designer who impressed me the most and became a leader in our firm was expert at taking notes at meetings. This rapid method of communicating design ideas made him valuable as a designer and leader in our firm.

Robert M. Beckley, FAIA, Professor and Dean Emeritus, University of Michigan

❯ From a practical perspective, I look for someone who cares, who is interested in the world around him or her—someone who is aware and sensitive, who listens and asks questions, who moves forward with initiative even if backtracking is required to get it right. I look for someone who tunes into people, places, and things. From a philosophical perspective, a portfolio is not enough. I want people who speak of places they have visited that moved them in some way, and why. I want to know of specific life experiences that have shaped them personally and informed their design work.

Barbara Crisp, Principal, bcrisp llc

❯ I look for self-confidence, preparation, and a sense of humor. I look for people who know their strengths and weaknesses. I look for people who can be themselves.

F. Michael Ayles, AIA, Principal, Business Development, Antinozzi Associates

What do you look for when hiring a new designer? (Continued)

❭ A designer needs to have a thought process unlike the typical individual. A continuous reply of "what if we do this?" should be the ingrained attitude for any designer or design challenge. An individual that is a quick learner is ideal due to the rapidly changing technologies and products in the profession.

Kathy Denise Dixon, AIA, NOMA, Associate Principal, Arel Architects, Inc.

❭ Because young practitioners often have a considerable wealth of knowledge in technology that can be useful to the development of a practice, I recruit individuals with expertise in a range of digital tools who also have excellent visual, oral, and written communication skills because they add value to the firm.

Kathryn T. Prigmore, FAIA, Senior Project Manager, HDR Architecture, Inc.

❭ First, I look for the ability to conceptualize a problem, and second (immediately after the first), the ability to translate concepts into the physical world in the form of space, object, detail, etc.

Douglas Garofalo, FAIA, Professor, University of Illinois at Chicago; President, Garofalo Architects, Inc.

❭ I look for someone who is motivated, eager, not afraid to get their hands dirty and is also not afraid to ask questions. The best architects ask the best questions. They must be able to communicate well and speak to the power of their ideas. They need to have a vision, but still show humility. They need to be able to demonstrate that they can work with others in a positive and collaborative manner.

Robert D. Fox, AIA, IIDA, Principal, FOX Architects

❭ In interns, including those just out of school, we look for strong hand drawing and sketching skills, strong computer aptitude, a spark of design inspiration and understanding in the portfolio, and an eager enthusiasm and openness to a variety of experiences.

The ability to solve design problems through sketching solutions in real time with the client is a key differentiator in our services. Also, critically, our designers must have an aptitude for and willingness to use a computer.

Carolyn G. Jones, AIA, Director, Callison

❭ I generally look for skills not represented in a portfolio. We focus on evidence of basic technical capabilities and skill sets. I emphasize the basics, especially for entry-level staff, because we know people need time to develop more advanced skills. If someone has strong basic skills, we can add to and develop them over time.

Bibliothèque Nationale, Paris, France. Architect: Dominque Perrault. PHOTOGRAPHER: ISABELLE GOURNAY.

❭ I look for people who can learn and are willing to take on new challenges. Communication skills are also vitally important, including writing, speaking, sketching, drawing, and listening. Professional attitude and appearance, evidence of commitment or loyalty, and dedication also make a strong impression on me. I have always said that I can train for a lack of technical skills but I cannot correct character flaws of disloyalty, indifference, laziness, or untrustworthiness.

Randall J. Tharp, RA, Senior Vice-President, A. Epstein and Sons International, Inc.

❭ I look for passion and commitment to the profession when I interview young graduates. Their portfolios provide insight into their underlying talent, which is an essential ingredient, but architecture requires tenacity and perseverance, which can be just as important.

W. Stephen Saunders, AIA, Principal, Eckenhoff Saunders Architects, Inc.

❭ Someone who has strong personal skills to deal with other employees and clients and someone who possesses the fundamentals needed to be an architect such as drawing, drafting, and CAD but most importantly a well-rounded individual.

John W. Myefski, AIA, Principal, Myefski Cook Architects, Inc.

❭ I look for communication skills, both verbal and graphic. I look for confidence, a broad range of skills, and team spirit. I look for evidence of volunteerism.

Grace H. Kim, AIA, Principal, Schemata Workshop, Inc.

❭ Professionalism (organizational and communication skills), how do the individuals pursue their work, interest, design capability or potential, and computer literacy with hand sketching/drawing as a bonus. Broad design perspective. Level of artistry and craft in presentation.

Mary Kay Lanzillotta, FAIA, Partner, Hartman-Cox Architects

❭ We do not hire talent or seek out conscious individuals and nurture their talents. Instead, in our practice we seek out designers who are committed and passionate about becoming fully conscious of their world, humanity, and themselves rather than individuals who possess only narrowly focused disciplinary knowledge and skills. We nurture and develop designers who are alert, curious, question what they see, willing to collaborate, take risks, and provoke change within us.

Max Underwood, AIA, Professor, Arizona State University

❭ I look for great optimism. Most important, I look for people who are inquisitive and appear to possess a quest for analyzing, theorizing, and implementing their ideas regardless of obstacles or barriers.

Patricia Saldana Natke, AIA, Principal and President, Urban Works, Ltd.

Exploration Through Study Abroad

MARISA GOMEZ

Bachelor of Science Candidate

University of Maryland

College Park, Maryland

Why and how did you become an architect?

〉 I have always had interests in both mathematics and art. When I started looking for majors in college, architecture made the most sense. I was looking for a dynamic subject that I would not get bored of too quickly. An architecture class at Maryland Hall for the Creative Arts during my senior year of high school confirmed my interests. I loved the drawing, puzzles, and problem solving.

Why did you decide to choose the school that you did—University of Maryland?

〉 I was searching for a big institution with an NAAB-accredited architecture program, great study abroad opportunities, and a sailing team. Maryland was not my first choice but they provided me with the best financial support. The size of Maryland gave me alternative options if I decided against architecture. Being so close to DC provides me tons of resources at my fingertips. I am definitely pleased with my decision.

Why did you choose to pursue the four-year pre-professional Bachelor of Science degree?

〉 The four-year bachelor of science in architecture provides more flexibility than a five-year professional program. I like Maryland's adaptation of the

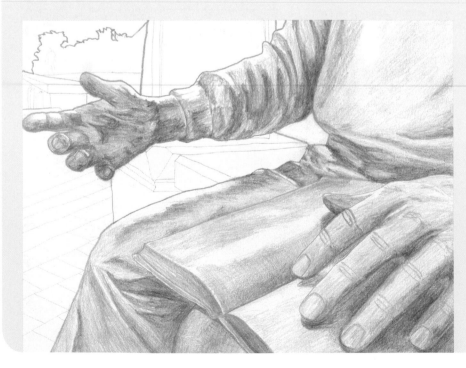

Kunta Kinte-Alex Haley Memorial by Marisa Gomez at University of Maryland.

program that focuses on liberal arts for the first two years and a studio sequence for the last two.

What has been your greatest challenge as an architecture student?

❯ Managing my time has definitely been difficult. I wish I had more time for activities like sailing, which I was very involved in before starting studio. Architecture is a never-ending experience. Your work is never finished; it could always be pushed further and done better.

You have had the opportunity to study abroad twice during your undergraduate studies prior to studio. How did these experiences prove valuable to your education?

❯ I spent a summer in ancient Stabiae with Professor Lindley Vann and a semester abroad at the American University of Rome. You can read as many books and study as many plans and sections as you would like, but nothing rivals the experience of standing inside the Pantheon, feeling your eyes soar through the dome. It is hard to explain the excitement of exploring Santa Maria del Priorato, Piranesi's church within the private Knights of Malta complex overlooking Rome and the Vatican dome. I will never forget the morning I spent discovering the hundreds of fountains in the gardens of Villa D'Este. Architecture is meant to be experienced, not just studied. Architecture is always better in person than in books and I had the unique opportunity to see some of the greatest in history. Most of the buildings I visited throughout my travels have principles that can be applied to any of my design projects in studio.

What is the most/least satisfying part of being an architecture student?

❯ The most satisfying aspect is the dynamic nature of architecture; it is always changing. There

Maryland State House by Marisa Gomez at University of Maryland.

is always more to learn. The least satisfying part of school is thinking about all the interests I have abandoned to pursue architecture.

What do you hope to be doing 5 to 10 years after graduation with regard to your career?

❯ Hopefully I will be traveling the world. I plan on attending grad school and becoming licensed. I have also considered teaching.

Who or what experience has been a major influence on your career?

❯ My travel has definitely been most influential on my career.

Introduction to Practice: Pure Excitement

ELIZABETH KALIN
Architectural Intern
Studio Gang Architects
Chicago, Illinois

Why and how did you become an architect?

> Somewhere around fifth grade I knew I wanted to be an architect. I took an exploratory class on architecture at my middle school that our art teacher led. My interest also developed because I grew up in a sprawling suburb of Minneapolis and that my father had an interest in architecture as well. On warm early evenings or weekends, we would often bike around new developments, walking through partially built wood-framed homes, trying to guess each the function of each room. I would select which bedroom would be mine in the event we would move when the home was finished. Our family also often walked through newly finished homes during the Parade of Homes, a biannual builders' showcase. I loved collecting floor plans from the real estate agents and bringing them home to compare what I liked best and least after experiencing them in person.

Shadowing real architects solidified my desire to become a professional architect. Both my middle and high school encouraged shadowing and gave students extra credit. During middle school I followed a friend's father who was an architect around for a morning and was fascinated with the scale models and large mock-ups on display in his office. Later in high school I was paired up with a woman who owned a small firm with her husband. I spent a full day with her and was itching to go to college by the end of it. So many aspects of the career appealed to me—the design challenges, the teamwork, the interactions with consultants and various user groups, the hands-on aspect of making models and most importantly, the variety of work.

▼ SOS Children's Villages Lavezzorio Community Center, Chicago, Illinois. Architect: Studio Gang Architects.
PHOTOGRAPHER: ELIZABETH KALIN, STUDIO GANG ARCHITECTS.

Sagrada Familia, Study Abroad Sketch by Elizabeth Kalin at Illinois Institute of Technology.

Why and how did you decide on which school to attend for your architecture degree? What degree(s) do you possess?

❯ I decided to pursue a school for architecture and began actively investigating options my junior year of high school. Immediately, the five-year bachelor of architecture seemed more suited to my interests as their coursework typically began with studio from the very first semester.

After several visits and interviews, and after receiving back information on scholarships at the schools to which I had applied, I decided to attend Illinois Institute of Technology (IIT) to obtain a five-year professional bachelor of architecture de-

gree. I graduated with high honors and a minor in Computers.

Why did you choose to study architecture at Illinois Institute of Technology (IIT)?

❯ My mother and I took a road trip around Midwest architecture schools in the late spring of junior year. We started off at North Dakota State, visited Iowa State next and finished in Chicago with visits to both IIT and UIC.

Many factors influenced my decision to attend IIT, but the biggest draw was Crown Hall. I had never heard of Ludwig Mies van der Rohe. I had no sense of the legacy of the school. I do remember the day was cool, cloudy, and damp. But the light in that building was incredible. So many of the other facilities I had seen were dismal, dark, and cramped. I tried to imagine myself somewhere for the next five years of my life, and there was simply no contest.

I was also drawn to Chicago itself. It was a larger city than I had grown up in, and I was looking forward to moving away from home, but Chicago was still close enough to Minneapolis.

Additionally, I had a wonderful interaction with the assistant dean from the College of Architecture. He gave us a tour, took us out to lunch, and was interested in my reasons for visiting the school and studying architecture. He was by the far the most receptive and encouraging administrator I met in my college search.

Paying for higher education is daunting no matter what schools a person is considering. Scholarships, both from the school and outside sources, had a large impact on my final decision to attend IIT. I recommend exploring as many options as possible— entering every essay contest and finishing every scholarship application you can get your hands on!

What impact did attending a pre-college architecture program at Pratt have on your decision to pursue architecture?

❭ Attending the pre-college summer intensive program at Pratt was an amazing experience. It was a great taste of the challenges of college ahead. It was an intense time where my boundaries were pushed in both sections of the program—foundation arts and architecture. It fostered personal growth in so many ways. I highly recommend the experience to anyone interested in pursuing an architecture education.

What has been your greatest challenge as an intern/architect thus far?

❭ Finding balance! I know many of my peers also wrestle with how much time to spend at work versus time to spend on your personal life, be it family, other interests/hobbies, competitions on the side, etc. There is so much for us to do as architects, I still find it difficult at times to draw the line between what must get done and what I want to get done to express our ideas.

The difference between being a full-time architecture student and being a full-time architectural intern is quite significant. I knew this adjustment was coming, and I felt I had prepared for it with my experiences working in offices over summer and winter breaks. It was something I struggled with most during my first full-time experience after graduation. The firm I worked for had a clear hierarchical system, and I clearly fell into the lowest level. Of course, everyone has to start somewhere, but at that firm in particular, I did not feel like I was asked to contribute anything personally design-wise and often felt I filled a role that so many know as the CAD monkey.

Enjoy every minute of being a student because it is such a personal, selfish, and indulgent time. You are the client as well as the architect. The constraints on projects are relatively small. You, as the head designer, are free to take design ideas and run with them. No budgets to agonize over!

Being in school is like testing the waters, and at work you have to dive right in. Many components of the realities of practice are never touched on in school, and I've felt a range of emotions while dealing with them on the job, from frustration to excitement. The learning never stops, which is part of the beauty of our profession. Don't let the vast abyss of things yet to learn/experience overwhelm you—you will take in what you need to as each project moves forward.

I also recommend being vocal about the experiences you want to obtain as in intern. When I started at Studio Gang, I made it clear that I needed construction administration experience to complete the Intern Development Program (IDP) and was put on a job that began construction a year later. Following a building from construction documents through completion and the grand opening celebration has by far been the most rewarding part of my career. It was an uphill battle at many points along the way, but we have been fortunate to receive a number of significant awards for the project and though completing the project alone was incredibly satisfying, the recognition is certainly an added bonus.

I recommend keeping up with the IDP paperwork as well. It only becomes more challenging as your responsibilities grow at work. If there is a third edition of this book I hope to be licensed by its production! I have procrastinated on that part of my journey, and I hope to make up for lost time soon.

SOS Children's Villages Lavezzorio Community Center, Chicago, Illinois. Architect: Studio Gang Architects. PHOTOGRAPHER: STEVE HALL, HEDRICH BLESSING.

What are your primary responsibilities and duties?

❯ I am incredibly fortunate to work at a firm where everyone does everything, literally. We draw by hand. We draw on the computer. We build models by hand. We build models in the computer. We render by hand. We render in the computer. We are constantly ordering samples and trying to investigate new materials. We also try to investigate new uses of very old and common materials.

Currently I am juggling two roles on two projects. On one, I am acting as the project architect and leading a team of consultants through the early stages of schematic design. I organize meetings, distribute agendas and meeting minutes, and organize site visits and mini-charettes. The owner has wanted to look at reducing the scope and budget, so we went through some value-engineering exercises with plans, sketches, and adjusted cost estimates.

On the other I am working with one of the principals on the lighting design—selecting light fixtures, getting reps to run calcs, ordering samples, and designing installation details and control plans with multiple daylight sensors and switching groups. I am also leading mechanical/electrical/plumbing/A/V coordination, working with the rest of our team in-house as well as numerous consultants. Coordination is such a key part of a successful project, and yet another example of something that can only really be learned in practice.

It is very important to find a firm that is a good fit for both you and the firm. At my very first summer job I heard encouragement from more than one person about switching majors "while it is still easy." Being an architect is not for everyone, and certainly every firm is a different little world of its own; part of the challenge is finding one that is a match for you.

Education Never Ends

DAVID R. GROFF

Master of Architecture Candidate

Virginia Tech–Washington Alexandria Architecture Center

Alexandria, Virginia

Why and how did you become an architect?

❯ I pursued a career in architecture because it allows me to use both my creativity and practical mindset in a complementary way.

Why and how did you decide on which school to attend for your architecture degree? What degree(s) do you possess?

❯ Presently, I am a graduate architecture student at Virginia Tech's Washington Alexandria Architecture Center. I worked in private practice for five years after earning a bachelor of science in architecture from the University of Maryland (2003). I started my college career in 1998 at Mount Saint Mary's College, going back and forth between majors in studio art, business, accounting, and marketing. After realizing that these fields were not a right fit for me, I decided to transfer to Maryland to study architecture.

You waited five years between your undergraduate pre-professional degree and your graduate studies. How will your time in practice impact your graduate studies?

❯ Stepping away from academics for five years has taught me the value of time away from studio. While many important lessons are learned in the studio environment, it is naïve to ignore the broader social context in which our buildings will reside. A well-rounded education and lifestyle is the key to creating good architecture.

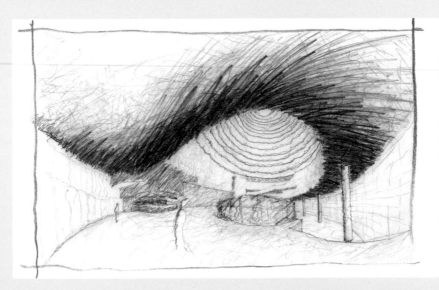

Study, National Museum of the American Indian by David R. Groff at Virginia Tech, Washington Alexandria Architecture Center.

What has been your greatest challenge as an architecture student?

❭ Time management and setting realistic expectations have been the most challenging aspects of my graduate career thus far. In contrast to professional practice, with tightly managed schedules and constant supervision, I am now in complete control of my time and education.

What is the most satisfying part of your education?

❭ Attending school in an urban setting, with direct access to great buildings, spaces, exhibitions, faculty and cultural amenities is the most satisfying part of my education. I am grateful for the opportunity to study significant historical and contemporary works and step away from the inevitable constraints of private practice.

Who or what experience has been a major influence on your career?

❭ There is not one single, seminal experience that has had a major impact on my career, rather each day serves to reinforce and strengthen my commitment to the profession.

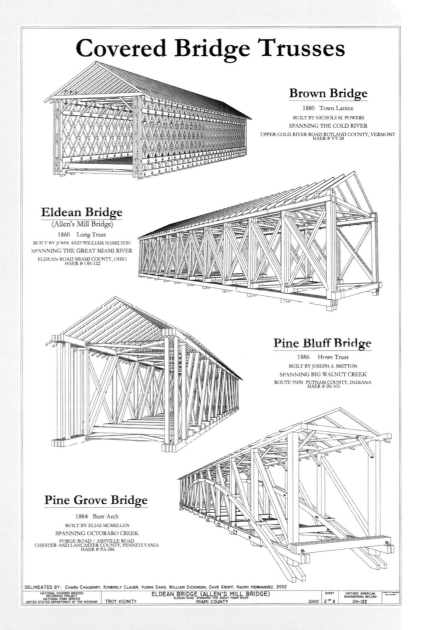

Covered Bridge Trusses, Historic American Buildings Survey (HABS), National Park Service. Delineators: Charu Chaudhry, Kimberly Clauer, Vuong Dong, William Dickinson, David R. Groff, and Naomi Hernandez. PHOTOGRAPHER: LIBRARY OF CONGRESS, PRINTS AND PHOTOGRAPH DIVISION, HISTORIC AMERICAN BUILDINGS SURVEY, HABS OH-122.

Bluebird, Maryland National Capital Park and Planning Commission. Prince George's County Department of Parks and Recreation Competition. Designer: David R. Groff.

Describe your experience with HABS/HAER.

❯ My summer internship with HABS/HAER was an invaluable one. I worked with a team of about 10 people, including architects, engineers, historians, and a photographer. Our team was assigned to study and document historic wooden covered bridges in the northeastern United States.

We spent about a week out in the field at each bridge documenting, drawing, measuring, and photographing every physical aspect of them. Each one that we studied utilized a different type of truss system and each was considered the best of its type. After gathering the information from the various

sites, we returned to Washington and spent the rest of the summer creating plans, sections, details, and three-dimensional models in the computer. Along with the engineers, historians, and photographers, we created a detailed biography of each bridge, that now rests in the Library of Congress.

During your senior year, you entered the Birds-I-View competition; your entry was selected and built for display. Describe the experience.

❯ The Maryland National-Capital Parks and Planning Commission; Department of Parks and Recreation, Prince George's County, Maryland sponsored "Birds-I-View," a public arts exhibition of over 50 fiberglass bluebirds created by artists from all over the county. The resulting designs were displayed at various sites throughout the county during the summer and fall of 2003.

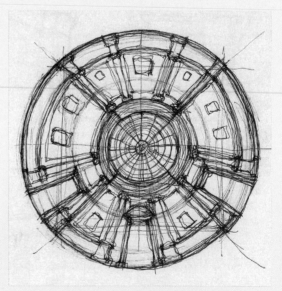

Study, National Gallery of Art, West Building by David R. Groff at Virginia Tech, Washington Alexandria Architecture Center.

We all started with a five-foot-tall fiberglass bluebird that we were to decorate in a creative and appealing way. My design incorporated lights that were attached to the outside of the shell, which then illuminated a multi-colored stained glass exoskeleton.

I had worked with stained glass before but I had never done anything close to this size or scale. It was particularly challenging because I had to figure out how it was going to be put together and then I actually had to build it. There were many times throughout the process when I was not sure whether it was going to work, but it finally came together after about two months, and I was pleased with the results. My creative design for the bluebird was featured in the *Washington Post*.

What are your 5-year and 10-year career goals relative to architecture?

❯ My main goal is to become licensed within the next five years. After that, I would like to start my own design-build firm, working on socially relevant projects.

From Teacher to Architect

TAMARA REDBURN, AIA, LEED AP

Project Architect

Fleming Associates Architects P.C.

Memphis, Tennessee

What has been your greatest challenge as an architect?

❯ The challenge has been learning and continuing to learn the many and varied aspects of constructing a building. I was surprised to learn that every project presents unique problems that require a custom solution. Learning how to coordinate the various disciplines within a project has also been a challenge for me, because it requires not only great attention to detail but also a clear understanding of all of the systems included within a building and how they interact with and impact one another.

What are your primary responsibilities and duties?

❯ I serve as the project architect, which means that I work under a designer (who designs the building) and a project manager (who manages the team and client). I am responsible for implementing the design and collaborating with other team members. I produce construction documents, coordinate with other disciplines, and meet with clients. I make decisions involving the design of the building, for example, designing doors and windows. A large part of my role is creating the details that make the design work. Details such as a special ceiling or a column reveal can be the difference between an ordinary building and an extraordinary place. I try to remember this quote from Charles Eames, "The details are not the details. They make the design."

I use Photoshop to show clients "before" and "after" photos of the effect renovations would have on the look of their building. I have also done extensive

Fishing Shack, Upper Michigan by Tamara Redburn, AIA, at University of Michigan.

presentation design to sell a client or a community on a building proposal. I use SketchUp to show clients how their building will interact with the site, creating fly-around movies to investigate the movement of the sun and shadows and show three-dimensional views of the building.

My unusual background as a teacher has come into play in my work. The firm I work for designs many schools and churches. Working there allows me to remain involved in education and to use my knowledge of schools and teaching in a new way. I have been fortunate to interact with teachers and other school personnel to create dynamic school buildings that will fulfill their particular needs.

What is the most/least satisfying part of your job?

❯ Three aspects of my position are equally satisfying. One is seeing and hearing the excitement of community members when we are discussing future improvements to their buildings. It is energizing to know that my work will have a positive impact on the community for many years to come.

Another is collaboration. I cherish being a part of a team, holding small charrettes to work out a design issue, interpreting the meaning of a building code, or debating the feasibility of various materials. The design is always richer from these interactions.

The third is seeing a project built. It is exhilarating to see the results of my work, to experience in three dimensions what was previously only on paper.

It is difficult for me to say what is least satisfying, because I love going to work every day. I enjoy each task for its potential to teach something new. I appreciate the need for attention to detail, the problem solving required, the interaction with other people both in my firm and outside of it.

Harding Academy, Lakeland, Tennessee. Architect: Fleming Associates Architects.

With a previous degree in secondary mathematics education and experience as a middle school math teacher for 16 years, what prompted you to become an architect?

❯ I participated in a summer program that enabled teachers to work at a business of their choice and incorporate that experience into their lesson plans. Because I was already teaching a house design project, I decided to go to an architecture firm to get ideas on how to expand the project. I very much enjoyed my time there and was fascinated with all that I observed.

The owner of the firm urged me to take classes at the local community college. The firm owner invited me back for the next summer and I took him up on it, doing basic drafting work and learning as much as I possibly could. I continued

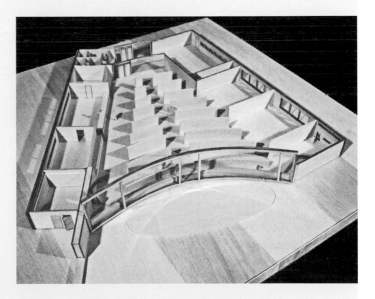

Branch Library by Tamara Redburn, AIA, at University of Michigan.

to teach during the day and took classes at night. He hired me again the following summer, when he hit me with a bombshell—when was I going to enroll in a master's degree program?

At the time I thought that was an impossible dream, but after visiting the design studio at the University of Michigan, I started to see a way to make it happen. With the generous and loving support of my husband (we had been married only two months at the time!), I quit my teaching job and went back to school full time. I have loved every day of it, and I have never looked back.

How has your previous background in education been helpful in the transition to becoming an architect?

❯ In teaching, I was always learning and trying new things. I developed a hands-on, interactive curriculum for eighth-grade math that did not incorporate a textbook. This background in experimentation has been helpful in architecture because I'm constantly learning new things and developing new strategies and design solutions.

Because of my previous work and life experiences, I have a maturity and outlook that most newly licensed architects do not possess. I think it makes me more reliable, more composed, and able to deal with various personalities and situations. I was very active in the governance of the school where I taught, which gave me valuable speaking and organizational skills, as well as experience in dealing with various factions that were sometimes at odds with one another. All of these talents are useful in architecture.

However, being a former teacher made me very critical of the architectural education. I had many amazing professors, but I also had my share who,

though they knew their subject matter very well, were unwilling and/or incapable of communicating it to their students. I was also bewildered and somewhat disillusioned by the studio culture. I had some wonderful studio professors and experiences, but I also experienced humiliation, anger, and frustration. Critiques were often haphazard and random and success or failure was sometimes dependent on which reviewer you happened to draw, not on clearly defined expectations.

Who or what experience has been a major influence on your career?

❯ Obviously, the employer at my first architecture firm, who urged me to get my master's degree, was the primary influence on my career. Without this influence, I would not be where I am today. I've also enjoyed the kind support of several wonderful mentors. I had a mentor while going through school who encouraged me, answered my many questions about the profession, allowed me to shadow her, and generally supported me. I also had a mentor and friend who served as my first supervisor, guiding me through the maze of completing a project well and on time. I continue to work with amazingly talented people who are generous with their time and knowledge. I believe that ideally everyone is both being mentored and mentoring others throughout their career.

Through the American Institute of Architects (AIA), I have met many wonderful influences, from my incredibly talented and dedicated peers on the first national committee I served on, the National Associates Committee (NAC), to the incredible architects on my local level, to the architects on the national stage who are working for real change. I have been influenced and inspired by all of these people to various degrees.

Finding a Place in Architecture

MICHELLE HUNTER

Project Architect/Project Manager

Mark Gould Architect

New York, New York

Why and how did you become an architect?

❯ Since the age of five, I have wanted to be an architect. A close family friend who is a builder sparked my initial interest in the profession, explaining to me the role of the architect in the building process. Ever since that point I have been intrigued by what an architect does and spent time as a child learning more about architecture. In school, I excelled in math and art classes, two subjects that are conveniently helpful in architectural education. The more my understanding of architecture evolved, the more interested I became in the subject and pursuing it as my career.

Why and how did you decide on which school to attend for your architecture degree? What degree(s) do you possess?

❯ I currently hold a bachelor of architecture degree from Carnegie Mellon University. After months of researching programs at various universities, I ultimately decided on attending a program that awarded a five-year professional degree. Some schools I was applying to offered only a four-year bachelor degree, which required students to go on further to obtain their master of architecture. The five-year architecture programs seemed to cover more material, and prepare the students better for a professional track. Additionally, after five years of undergraduate work, I could get a position at a firm and immediately participate in the Internship Development Program, and be that much closer to obtaining my license.

Mind Over Media Lobby, Pittsburgh, Pennsylvania. Architect: Studio D'Arc. PHOTOGRAPHER: NICHOLAS TAUB.

What has been your greatest challenge as a project manager thus far?

❯ My greatest challenge as a project manager thus far has been learning how to prioritize and maintain an understanding of the big picture. With the responsibility of overseeing projects, balancing all aspects is critical. I tend to be detail-oriented and want to problem solve, when all tasks may not necessarily require the same level of attention. Seeing the totality of the project is the key to successfully delegating work, being efficient, and generating profit.

Grand Pirouette by Michelle Hunter at Carnegie Mellon University.

What are your 5-year and 10-year career goals relative to architecture?

❭ In five years, I hope to be a licensed architect working on small-scale architecture and high-end residential interior projects. I would like to be working in a firm that promotes thoughtfulness in design and is constantly generating new and exciting ideas, a place where my education can continue and I can not only learn process but also design excellence. Within this time, I would love to begin exploring a practice of my own.

In 10 years, I hope to have my own small firm with a strong client base, beginning to address significant design issues and starting to make a name for myself in the architecture and interior design world.

Please describe your current position with Mark Gould Architect.

❭ My current position with Mark Gould Architect is that of project architect and project manager. As project architect, I work as part of a small team on multi-family or single-family residential projects doing concept design, design development, drafting, drawing set organization, and consultant coordination. My responsibilities as project manager include all that are listed above, plus the added tasks of writing client proposals, client correspondence, bid and contract negotiation with contractors, construction administration, and generally overseeing the project from start to finish.

What are your primary responsibilities and duties?

❭ Because I work in a small office, my responsibilities are not limited solely to those that directly relate to projects. I am often answering phones, doing administrative work, organizing the materials library, assisting with billing, and doing product research, in addition to my project duties.

What is the most/least satisfying part of your position?

❭ Without question, the most satisfying part of my job is seeing my clients happy with the final product. When a client tells me the difference my work has made in his/her life, I am completely fulfilled. Knowing that architecture can have such an impact on people's lives makes all the daily struggles worth

Private Residence, New York, New York. Architect: Mark Gould Architect. PHOTOGRAPHER: MARK GOULD ARCHITECT.

it, and reminds me why I wanted to pursue architecture as my career.

The least satisfying part of my job is putting a time limit on design. There is never long enough to do all the research, or explore as many design options, in as much depth as I would like. Having to balance profitability and billable hours with a creative endeavor is difficult, and can sometimes be unsatisfying. Fortunately I am gaining experience as I go, and with each completed project, I am able to bring that design knowledge to the next venture.

Who or what experience has been a major influence on your career?

❯ Many people and events have influenced my career thus far, in both positive and negative ways.

The most recent and profound influence has been one of my bosses, Charm Su. Like me, she also attended the Carnegie Mellon architecture program, so I immediately knew our understanding of design grew from the same place. As we began to work together, I felt excited collaborating with her and building on each other's ideas. Not only have I been able to work successfully with her, but I have learned a tremendous amount from her. Her innate understanding of design is so deep that it often seems like a reflex. Observing her process has made me reevaluate my own, seeing her design solutions have [sic] inspired me to think in new ways, and being exposed to her breadth resources has expanded my style and taken my design ability to a new level. Having the opportunity to work with her has truly made me a better designer.

Making an Unrelated Degree Count

LYNSEY JANE GEMMELL, AIA

Project Manager/Associate

Holabird & Root

Chicago, Illinois

Why and how did you become an architect?

❯ My undergraduate studies were art history and psychology. My emphasis was architectural history and my exposure to the theory and history of the practice of architecture led me to consider how I could continue my interest in the built environment. I no longer wanted to write about other people's buildings but to be involved in the design of buildings. In addition, I wish to teach in the future, and with architecture the possibility is open to teach both during and after practice.

▼ Parmer Hall, Dominican University, River Forest, Illinois. Architect: Holabird & Root. PHOTOGRAPHER: BALLOGG PHOTOGRAPHY.

Why and how did you decide on which school to attend for your architecture degree? What degree(s) do you possess?

❯ I chose a graduate program at an accredited school with a good, international reputation located in a large metropolitan setting. My undergraduate degree is a master of arts (First Class) and my graduate degree is a master of architecture.

Having recently become an architect, please provide details on your internship experience and taking the Architect Registration Exam (ARE)?

❯ Having worked at Holabird & Root part time during my last year of graduate school the transition to full-time employment was fairly painless. The hours spent as an intern are long but my experience was varied and my tasks were challenging. I was fortunate to be involved in a high-profile local job so was able to observe an active construction site and learn the process of construction. My level of client contact was probably more direct and ex-

Parmer Hall, Dominican University, River Forest, Illinois. Architect: Holabird & Root. PHOTOGRAPHER: BALLOGG PHOTOGRAPHY.

tensive than the normal intern experience and this definitely accelerated my career. At times I was certainly thrown in at the deep end but the constant challenges were rewarding.

Sitting for the ARE while working full time is arduous, and passing all sections is certainly a rite of passage. Some of the sections are a simple review of university course work, while others draw on work-related experience. I felt a sense of accomplishment at the end of the process but did not have a great appreciation of particular knowledge gained. The practice of architecture is a learning process every day and becoming licensed makes you no more knowledgeable than you were the day before.

What has been your greatest challenge as an architect thus far?

❭ I cannot identify a single greatest challenge but learning to accomplish as much as possible in the time available without working enormous amounts of overtime is a challenge. I continue to try and keep in mind the difference between professional responsibility and the end goal of the task at hand rather than one's ultimate design ambitions.

What are your 5-year and 10-year career goals relative to architecture?

❭ Being part of the firm's management structure has added further demands to the day-to-day tasks.

New Science Building, Wabash College, Crawfordsville, Indiana. Architect: Holabird & Root.

We have a very young and driven body of interns and young engineers; my goal is to support their career development while ensuring that the quality of our design and documents. We are challenging our processes with a goal to creating firm-wide consistency and stream lining our documents in order that we may have more time to focus on the design and execution of our buildings. Being a role model to younger architects and stimulating the intellectual discourse in the office so that we may continue to take pride in our practice.

What are your primary responsibilities and duties?

❯ As a project manager my responsibilities are client satisfaction, maintain project and internal budgets and schedules, and to ensure that my team have the resources and support they require. I still have a few projects in construction for which my role is project architect. I am responsible for translating and the design goals for the project, co-ordinating the work of any and all consultants, and the technical content of the documents. I manage a team of interns and mentor them as they are learning their craft.

What is involved in serving as project architect and what do you feel when you see a project completed?

❯ No matter your role in a project, the opening of a building that you helped create and hearing that a client is thrilled with their space makes all the hard work and painful experiences of coordinating projects large and small worthwhile.

Who or what experience has been a major influence on your career?

❯ In my undergraduate studies I had an art history professor, Professor Margaretta Lovell at the University of California at Berkeley, who pressed me to talk about what I wanted to do in the future. She encouraged me not to be afraid of the mathematics and physics that I thought would be involved in architecture (this has proved to be correct) and exposed me to the three-year master of architecture program for non-relevant degree holders.

Sustainable Residential Design

LISA A. SWAN

Residential Designer

Design Forward

Pasadena, California

Why and how did you decide on which school to attend for your architecture degree? What degree(s) do you possess?

❯ I was always told that Chicago was the birthplace of American modern architecture and the home to the first high rise. My initial interest in architecture was to build the tallest building in the world, so I began my search in Chicago. I happened upon the Illinois Institute of Technology (IIT) and their skyscraper studio. I spent a weekend visiting the school and was impressed with the students' work and the professors and even more impressed with the city of Chicago. It was an easy decision to move to Chicago and attend IIT.

▼ Hayes Residence, Window to View, Ocotillo Wells, California. Designer: Design Forward. PHOTOGRAPHER: GINA VAN VEEN.

I completed my bachelor of architecture from the Illinois Institute of Technology in 2001. In 2004, I returned to school to pursue my interest in business and received a master of business administration from Norwich University in 2006.

What has been your greatest challenge as an intern/architect thus far?

❯ I have found being in the "in-between" stage, out of architecture school, but not yet licensed to be a challenge. Being self-employed, I find myself explaining my status to clients. I use the term *designer* to market myself; however. it does not fully explain my skills.

Out of school less than five years, you founded the company Design Forward, focusing on sustainable residential design. What motivated you in this career decision?

❯ Architecture school and my peers taught me in order to be a successful architect you obtain an architecture degree, find a job as an intern, work for 5 to 10 years, acquire a license, and move on to open your own firm. Yet, when I found myself walking that path, I became discouraged. I did

not enjoy many of the aspects of my day-to-day work in a traditional architecture office, especially being at the bottom of the totem pole. I imagined myself working a drafting job for five years or more and decided it was simply not an option. I had reached point where I needed to either leave the profession of architecture or start challenging myself.

At this time, I had been out of school just under a year, living in San Diego working in a residential architecture firm. I had a strong interest in exploring straw bale design. There were only one or two firms in San Diego concentrating on sustainable architecture, and I found there was a high demand for design work. It was an opportunity to

take on chance on myself. It was March 2002 when I started Design Forward and began concentrating on sustainable and green architecture and most specifically straw bale homes.

You belong to the California Straw Building Association. What is "straw building?"

❯ *Straw building* refers to the use of straw as a building material. The most typical form is the use of straw bales as an insulation material. A common building form is non-load-bearing structure that is a post and beam frame with an infill of bales of wheat or rice straw. The result is a two-foot thick wall with substantially higher insulation value. Straw is gaining popularity in the green building industry, as it is a natural material in addition to an energy-efficient insulation.

What are your primary responsibilities and duties?

❯ As a single-person firm, I am responsible for *everything*. I spend most of my time design and drafting projects, this includes client meetings, design sessions, working with engineers and consultants, developing construction documents, creating material boards and working with the building department and cities. I devote nearly 10 hours a month to maintaining my websites, www.designforward.net and www.dfdrafting.com, and marketing my business to new clients, including attending home shows and green building events. Additionally, I spend a few hours billing and maintaining accounting records. One of my favorite parts of my job is working with the community. I have created and teach green building classes, straw bale workshops, and information sessions to get the word out about sustainable and energy-efficient building.

Hayes Residence, Niche, Ocotillo Wells, California. Designer: Design Forward. PHOTOGRAPHER: GINA VAN VEEN.

What are your 5-year and 10-year career goals relative to architecture?

❯ My five-year goal is to acquire my architecture license in the state of California. In the long-term future, I plan on taking a more active role in establishing building codes for green and alternative architecture. I often find building departments to be uneducated about alternative material and building systems, and it is difficult to acquire building permits without a fight. I hope to make the process easier for future projects.

What is the most/least satisfying part of your job?

❯ The most enjoyable part of my job is interacting with my clients and watching a project come together over a long conversation. I have found the most satisfying clients and projects are the ones in which the owners are involved in the process. On the flip side, it can be discouraging to watch a design change due to conflict with building departments or city design requirements. Sometimes the heart of the design is lost in red tape.

▲ Hayes Residence, Interior View, Ocotillo Wells, California. Designer: Design Forward. PHOTOGRAPHER: GINA VAN VEEN.

❱ Hayes Residence, Veranda, Ocotillo Wells, California. Designer: Design Forward. PHOTOGRAPHER: GINA VAN VEEN.

Who or what experience has been a major influence on your career?

❯ During my fifth year of architecture school at IIT, I studied under Professor Peter Land. Our semester design project was to create an energy-efficient environment. However, before we were allowed to place our pencil to paper, he required us to spend a few weeks researching sustainable systems. It was during this time I found straw bale construction and was instantly intrigued. The process was not appropriate for my design project for the semester, but I filed the information away, knowing it was something I wanted to use in the future.

A.R.C.H.I.T.E.C.T.

By applying your talents as an architecture student to gaining experience, you will be able to design your own career rather than just letting it happen. Be creative in organizing your search for prospective employers. While not guaranteed, the following ideas, spelling out the word *ARCHITECT,* may assist you in gaining experience more quickly.

ASSESSMENT

The first step in gaining experience involves assessing yourself. Assess what aspect of architecture inspires you: programming, design, interior architecture, construction management, and so on. What do you want to do in an architecture firm? What are you able to offer a prospective employer? Ask yourself, "Why should this firm hire me?" Constantly evaluate your interests, abilities, and values and how they match those of your current or a prospective employer.

RESEARCH

Research is critical. What positions in an architecture firm can best utilize your skills and knowledge? What employers have such positions? Do not limit your search to the architecture profession; the best employment opportunities may be with an interior design firm, a construction firm, a government agency, a corporation, or an engineering firm. Again, be creative in your search.

CONNECTIONS

Connections are crucial to success. Regardless of the discipline, over 60 percent of all positions are obtained through networking. Consider adding 5 to 10 names to your network monthly. Be sure to attend local AIA meetings, where you will meet architects in area firms. Listen. Learn. Talk. Remember, every conversation is a possible lead. The more ears and eyes you have looking out for the positions you want, the more likely it is that options will materialize.

The most effective method of learning of opportunities is networking, but most people, especially students, do not know what this is. Simply put, networking is informing people around you of your intent to gain experience and asking if they know of leads for you. In a school setting, you may network with classmates, professors, and staff. You may also approach guest lecturers or architects on your reviews. Ask if they hire students for the summer or for part-time positions. They may not be immediately responsive, so politely ask for a business card so you can follow up.

New sources available online to make connections include social media web sites Facebook (facebook.com) and Linkedin (linkedin.com). First, subscribe to these social media websites, but use them in strictly a professional business like manner. Once you have added your profile, you can search for individuals who have a connection to someone you are searching. With Linkedin, you can search on industry, school attended, or company to connect with future contacts.

HELP

You can get help with your search from a variety of sources. A good place to start is the university career center; a career counselor can help you target your job search. Along with the national AIA (careercenter.aia.org), many local AIA chapters post positions on the web or allow you to post your resume. Public libraries are another valuable resource. As well, you should seek support from others, especially family and friends; talking to them can be a big boost to your job search.

Most architecture programs post positions that announce regional employment opportunities on an online system. When seeking students to perform entry-level tasks, many firms send schools a position announcement outlining job duties and responsibilities, qualifications, and contact information. Do not limit yourself to your own institution, especially if you wish to relocate.

If you determine that you either need or want to work part time while in school, use these postings as a first step to learn of opportunities, but do not stop there. Contact the local AIA chapter to learn if they accept listings from area firms. Some local AIA chapters collect resumes from individuals seeking employment and allow firms to review them.

INTERIM POSITIONS

If you are unable to secure your ideal position for the summer or after graduation, consider an *interim* position. An interim position provides you with related experience, but is only a stop gap solution; you have no intention of staying permanently. Ideally, interim jobs allow you to continue your search, network with a wide variety of people, and build up your skills.

TOOLS

Your resume, ability to write cover letters, portfolio, and ability to interview are critical to the job search. They are important tools for communicating yourself to potential employers. Are your tools in top form? If not, practice your interviewing skills, rework your resume, or have someone critique your portfolio.

■ *Resume:* As in any discipline, a resume is essential when conducting a search for experience. While this book cannot fully cover the rigors of resume writing or other aspects of the job search, it can convey insights into this necessary tool. Keep your resume simple and straightforward. Provide information from your background and experiences that demonstrates your abilities. Do not be afraid to include skills learned from studio or other classroom projects under a section entitled "Course Projects." If you have not worked formally in an architectural office, promote your drawing, modeling or building, and design skills learned in studio.

You can add graphics to your resume. With the ease of scanning drawings and using graphic publishing software, placing an image on your resume can be powerful; however, exercise caution, as the image may make reading the resume difficult. Rather than including graphics on your resume, you could create a one-page portfolio, sometimes referred to as a "viewsheet."

■ *Cover Letters:* Just as critical and often treated as an afterthought, cover letters are in fact your introduction to the prospective employer. Most cover letters consist of three paragraphs: The first introduces you and explains the purpose of the letter; the second sells your skill set and makes the case that you are a match for the employer, and the third provides the terms of follow-up. Be sure to address the letter to an individual, not "Dear Sir/Madam." If you do not know the name of an individual, take the time to contact the firm and ask. Be persistent if the firm is reluctant to provide this information.

Finally, remember that the purpose of the resume and cover letter is to obtain an interview!

■ *Portfolio:* Just as important as the resume, and perhaps more important, is your portfolio. As architecture is a visual discipline, the portfolio is a direct link between the employer and your skills as an architect. For this reason, you should provide images that demonstrate all of your architectural skills—drafting, model building, drawing, design, and so on. As well, provide drawings from the beginning of one project's design process to the end. In other words, do not include only finished ink-on-Mylar drawings. The sequential drawings allow the employer to see your thought process as it relates to a design problem.

The portfolio is a creative act, showing your skills and imagination, but it is also an act of communication and a tool for self-promotion. Demonstrate originality and inventiveness, but also accept the restrictions and conventions of professionalism, and show that you can get your ideas across in terms that working architects and designers can understand.

HAROLD LINTON[4]

■ *Interviewing:* Good interviewing skills can make the difference between receiving an offer and not. Prepare for an interview by researching the firm. Think what questions might be asked of you and what questions you might ask of the interviewer. Ideally, practice prior to your interview with a roommate, colleague, or friend.

EXPERIENCE

At this point in your career, you may feel you have little experience. However, keep in mind that in many cases employers are hiring your *potential*. If you do not have adequate experience, consider trying one of the following to obtain the necessary experience: part-time work, volunteer work, informal experiences, or temporary work.

COMMITMENT

Searching for a position that will give you experience can be a full-time task. Although you are busy with school commitments, you should devote every possible minute to your search; doing so will pay off. However, as with any project, break your job search down into smaller manageable parts. Finalize your resume, research five firms, contact three colleagues, instead of being paralyzed by the scope of entire job search. If you have not already done so, start your search now! Do not wait until next week, next month, or until your last semester of school.

Johnson Wax Building, Racine, Wisconsin. Architect: Frank Lloyd Wright. PHOTOGRAPHER: R. LINDLEY VANN.

TRANSITION

Realize that you are going through a major life transition—that of entering the profession of architecture. Recognize that all aspects of your life will be affected. Summer vacations are a luxury of the past. Financial adjustments are necessary as you begin to receive a salary and acquire new expenses.

The job market may be tough; therefore, be assertive, learn the search process, and do not fear rejection. Searching for a position is a skill you will use throughout your life.

> The answer, in a nutshell, is:
> Thru your research
> And then thru your contacts.
> RICHARD N. BOLLES

Moving Toward Licensure

Transition: n. The process or an instance of changing from one form, state, activity, or place to another. Passage from one form, state, activity, or place to another.[5]

Entry into the real world should be a time of excitement, enthusiasm, and exploration. For the time being, school is over and it is finally time for you to apply the knowledge and insights you acquired during all those hours of studio. A yearly salary ensures financial independence. All kinds of doors are opening, presenting a world of opportunities.

This transition from the world of education to your first career position is dramatic and perhaps challenging. Most college graduates are not fully prepared for the magnitude of the transitions and adjustments that must be made on virtually all fronts, and are unaware of the consequences of not making these adjustments in a mature and speedy manner.

What a shock it can be when you, a new graduate, drop to the bottom rung of the career ladder. Just as a new college student has to learn the ropes of the new environment, the recent graduate starting a career position faces a whole new world. The challenges include maintaining a budget, dealing with your personal life, and adjusting to your first career position. The difficulty is that the real world is less tolerant of mistakes, offers less time and flexibility for adjustment, and demands performance for the pay it offers.

INTERN DEVELOPMENT PROGRAM (IDP)

Established jointly by the American Institute of Architects (AIA) and the National Council of Architectural Registration Boards (NCARB) in the late 1970s, Intern Development Program (IDP) eases the transition from academia to the profession. In becoming an architect, the IDP is an essential step. All jurisdictions require a structured internship for a period of time as their training requirement, and most have adopted the IDP as the training requirement necessary for licensure. It is in your best interest to become aware of the IDP early in your academic career (www.ncarb.org/idp).

> Intern Development Program (IDP) is a comprehensive training program created to ensure that interns in the architecture profession gain the knowledge and skills required for the independent practice of architecture.
>
> IDP GUIDELINES JANUARY 2009[6]

Effective January 2010, the NCARB is updating IDP requirements to more closely align with the current practice of architecture. Billed as IDP 2.0, these new program requirements will help ensure that interns acquire the comprehensive training that is essential for competent practice and will make reporting experience easier. For the most up-to-date information on IDP, visit the NCARB website (www.ncarb.org).

The program's foundation is the IDP training requirements. To satisfy them, you must complete specific periods of training in four major categories:

Category A: Design and Construction Documents

Category B: Construction Contract Administration

Category C: Management

Category D: Related Activities

Each of these training categories is subdivided into training areas (see the sidebar "Intern Development Program (IDP) Training Areas").

Training requirements are measured in training units equaling eight hours of acceptable experience. You earn training units for training acquired under the direct supervision of a qualified professional in one of two ways: participation or observation. Experience is gained by performing a particular task (pre-ferred) or by observing a professional with whom you work perform the task. The IDP Guidelines provides a detailed definition of each training requirement, core competencies that you should be able to perform at the completion of the internship phase of your career, and skills and application activities.

Just as critical are the work settings in which you can gain training requirements. The one work setting with no limit as to the number of training units is working under the direct supervision of a registered architect. Other settings with limits include working in an organization whose practice does not encompass the comprehensive practice of architecture, working for a firm outside the United States or Canada, gaining experience related to architecture under a registered engineer or registered landscape architect; for more details obtain the IDP Guidelines.

An integral part of the IDP is the mentorship system. Within the IDP, you have access to two individuals who assist you with your work experience and career plans. The supervisor is typically your immediate supervisor in your place of employment, while your mentor is an architect outside your firm with whom you meet periodically to discuss your career path.

As part of the IDP, the intern is solely responsible for maintaining a continuous record of experience in the training categories; however, in late 2008 the NCARB developed the electronic Experience Verification Reporting system (e-EVR) to enhance the delivery of reports by interns. The report identifies areas where training has been acquired and areas where deficiencies may still exist. For supervisors, it is an assessment and personnel management tool; for state registration boards, it is verified evidence of compliance with the IDP training requirements. Also learn the new six-month rule that requires interns to submit their training units in reporting periods of no longer than six months and within two months of completion of each period.

To ease the tracking process, the NCARB developed a nationally recognized recordkeeping system. You may develop your own recordkeeping resources or use your firm's time management system, which may accommodate the IDP training categories and areas. Because state registration boards may require the system developed by the NCARB, you are encouraged to contact your board regarding acceptable recordkeeping procedures.

Launched in 2004 by the AIA and NCARB, the Emerging Professional Companion (EPC)[7] (epcompanion.org) is an online professional development tool for interns on their path to licensure. Primarily intended as a means for interns to earn IDP credit, the EPC is broken into chapters that parallel the training areas of the IDP. Each chapter is structured with 10 sections designed to lead the user through an in-depth look at each training area. Other resources available to assist in you navigating the IDP are both the state and educator IDP coordinator. Depending on where you are in your education, both are available to answer questions on the program and connect you with possible mentors.

In a recent discussion with an intern-architect a few years out of school, she confessed that while architecture school prepared her to think and design, it did not sufficiently prepare her to work in an architectural office. She further admitted that the IDP, with its training areas, simply lists what you need to do. Asked for advice to give current students of architecture, she replied, "Take a chance, take a risk, and enroll in the IDP now while you are still in school."

Regardless of your academic level, take the first step to learning about the IDP by contacting the NCARB to request an information packet and apply online to being a NCARB Council Record. Begin the transition now; do not wait until graduation.

INTERN DEVELOPMENT PROGRAM (IDP) TRAINING AREAS

CATEGORY A: DESIGN AND CONSTRUCTION DOCUMENTS (350)*

Programming (10) is the process of discovering the owner/client's requirements and desires for a project and setting them down in written, numerical, and graphic form. For a project to be successful, all participants, including the owner/client, must understand and agree on a program at the outset.

Site and Environmental Analysis (10) involves research and evaluation of a project's context and may include environmental evaluation, land planning or design, and urban planning.

Schematic Design (15) is the development of graphic and written conceptual design solutions to the program for the owner/client's approval.

Engineering Systems Coordination (15) involves selecting and specifying structural, mechanical, electrical, and other systems, and integrating them into the building design. These systems are normally designed by consultants in accordance with the client's needs.

Building Cost Analysis (10) involves estimating the probable construction cost of a project.

Code Research (15) involves evaluating a specific project in the context of relevant local, state, and federal regulations that protect public health, safety, and welfare.

In *Design Development (40),* a project's schematic design is refined, including designing details and selecting materials. This step occurs after the owner/client approves the schematic design.

Construction Documents (135) are the written and graphic instructions used for construction of the project. These documents must be accurate, consistent, complete, and understandable.

Specifications and Materials Research (15) leads to analysis and selection of building materials and systems for a project. The materials specified for a particular project communicate the requirements and quality expected during construction. Specifications are included in a project manual that is used during bidding and construction.

Document Checking and Coordination (10) is the means by which quality assurance is established and maintained throughout the project.

CATEGORY B: CONSTRUCTION CONTRACT ADMINISTRATION (70)

Bidding and Contract Negotiation (10) involves the establishment and administration of the bidding process, issuing of addenda, evaluation of proposed substitutions, review of the bidder qualifications, analysis of bids, and selection of the contractor(s).

Construction Phase—Office (15): Construction contract administrative tasks carried out in the architect's office include facilitating project communication, maintaining project records, reviewing and certifying amounts due contractors, and preparing change orders.

Construction Phase—Observation (15): Construction contract administration tasks specifically carried out in the field include observing construction for conformity with drawings and specifications and reviewing and certifying amounts due to contractors.

CATEGORY C: MANAGEMENT (35)

Project Management (15) includes planning, organizing, and staffing; budgeting and scheduling; leading and managing the project team; documenting key project information; and monitoring quality assurance.

Office Management (10) involves the allocation and administration of office resources to support the goals of the firm.

CATEGORY D: RELATED ACTIVITIES (10)

Professional and Community Service (10): Interns find that voluntary participation in professional and community activities enhances their professional development. Such activities increase their understanding of the people and forces that shape society as well as augment professional knowledge and skills. Community service need not be limited to architecture-related activities for volunteers to accrue these benefits.

*Numbers in parentheses refer to minimum training units required; total IDP training units required equals 700.

National Council of Architectural Registration Boards[8]

ARCHITECT REGISTRATION EXAMINATION (ARE)

The last formal step in becoming an architect is taking and passing the Architect Registration Examination (ARE), administered by the NCARB (ncarb.org/are). The purpose of the ARE is "to determine if an applicant has the minimum knowledge, skills, and abilities to practice architecture independently while safeguarding the public health, safety, and welfare."

Its purpose is not glamorous, but glamor is not the intent of the ARE. It does not measure whether or not you are a good architect but rather your ability to practice architecture.

In February 1997, candidates began to take the ARE exclusively by computer in all divisions. In development since the mid-1980s, the new format generates a more comprehensive and efficient exam that more accurately measures a candidate's ability in a shorter period than traditional methods. In addition, the automated exam allows for more frequent and flexible testing opportunities, a more relaxed testing environment, faster score reporting, and greater testing security.

Another more recent development is that a handful of states now allow concurrent enrollment in the IDP and taking the ARE. What does this mean? Unlike in the past, interns enrolled in the IDP can now take divisions of the ARE prior to the completion of the IDP. Be sure to check with the NCARB or your state registration board for exact details, but such a development could reduce the time it takes to complete both the IDP and the ARE. However, note that you will not be licensed as an architect until both are completed.

Old South Church in Boston, Architects: Charles Amos Cummings and Willard T. Sears. PHOTOGRAPHER: LEE W. WALDREP, PH.D.

Also a new rule is the rolling clock. Under the terms of the rolling clock, which was implemented in 2006, candidates for the ARE must pass the divisions within five years. The five-year time limit begins on the date when the first passed division is administered. By virtue of this rule, candidates will need to be more diligent in scheduling the exam.

The ARE consists of seven divisions as listed below; six of the above divisions includes both multiple-choice questions and graphic vignettes. One division, Schematic Design only includes graphic vignettes:

Programming Planning and Practice

Site Planning and Design

Building Design and Construction Systems

Schematic Design (graphic vignettes only)

Structural Systems

Building Systems

Construction Documents and Services

To begin the process, learn more about the ARE from the NCARB's website; on the website are detailed study aids, including sample multiple-choice questions, one passing and one failing solution for each sample vignette, and a list of references for further study. As well, you are encouraged to download the practice software used by the ARE.

NCARB CERTIFICATE

Once licensed as an architect, you may wish to become licensed in additional states. To do so, consider obtaining a NCARB Certificate to facilitate licensure in other states, a process known as reciprocity. The first step is to establish an NCARB Council Record, which you would have done for initial registration. Once you complete the requirements for the NCARB Certificate—earning an NAAB- or CACB-accredited degree, fulfilling the requirements of the IDP, and passing the seven divisions of the ARE—you can apply for registration from other states as needed to practice architecture. Based on the most recent NCARB survey of registered architects, on average, architects are registered in two jurisdictions. There are 116,221 reciprocal (out-of-state) registrants and 220,347 total registrations in the United States.

Experience is a vital step in becoming an architect. Begin to gain experience in the profession as soon as possible by shadowing an architect in high school, completing an internship, or pursuing a summer position while in college. As well, your experience after you complete your professional degree will play an important role in your future career. Choose wisely.

Creating a Framework for Collaboration

GRACE H. KIM, AIA

Principal and Cofounder

Schemata Workshop, Inc.

Seattle, Washington

Why and how did you become an architect?

❯ My path to architecture was not a deliberate one. As a high school senior, life beyond graduation was far from my mind. I listed three "areas of interest" on my college application, one of which was architecture. My guess is that the admissions officer chose alphabetically and I was assigned to architecture for freshman advising.

From my first day of classes, I really enjoyed the architectural courses and I never looked back. The problem solving and ability to shape the built environment was fascinating and challenging.

Why and how did you decide on which school to attend for your architecture degree? What degree(s) do you possess?

❯ I have a bachelor of science in architectural studies and a bachelor of architecture from Washington State University, the only in-state school to which I applied. At the time I did not know I wanted to study architecture, so it worked out great that I ended up starting in a five-year bachelor of architecture program. The program structure provided the fundamentals to put me on a level playing field with my classmates in terms of skills and knowledge by the end of the first quarter.

After over a decade of practice, I completed a post-professional master of architecture program at the University of Washington (UW). I chose the UW program because I was a working professional managing a small practice and needed a program that would be adaptable to my educational goals (research in a specific topic).

Rainier View Senior Apartments, Fife, Washington. Architect: Schemata Workshop, Inc. PHOTOGRAPH COPYRIGHT: O'SHEA PHOTOGRAPHY.

Cosmetology Institute, Seattle, Washington. Architect: Schemata Workshop, Inc. PHOTOGRAPHER: SCHEMATA WORKSHOP, INC.

What has been your greatest challenge as an architect/principal?

❯ Maintaining balance in work and life.

Within the studio, it means balancing the time to draw, manage, and obtain new projects. This balance is achieved by the flat structure of the office. As the principal, it is not healthy to control everything. Our employees are privy to and accountable to the budgets of the office and projects.

In my life, it means balancing work with time for my husband and daughter, friends, and family. All are equally important, and despite the fact that my husband is my business partner, we make a conscientious effort not spend all our time talking about work or the firm. It is also about finding time to participate in the greater world through hobbies and philanthropy and seeing the world through the eyes of my one-year-old daughter.

How is being a principal of Schemata Workshop different from being an intern at Skidmore, Owings, and Merrill?

❯ As in intern at Skidmore, Owings, and Merrill (SOM), I felt like a cog in a large machine. I did my job and understood that others were also doing their part to make sure the project was successfully completed, but I never had a sense of the greater picture, not only architecturally but also from a management standpoint.

As a principal of a small firm, I have a comprehensive view of both the business, as well as the practice, of architecture. But I also want everyone else in the studio to be as aware of this as well. Open communication and a clear understanding of our business objectives ensure that we all satisfy the contractual requirements to our clients while helping the company make a profit, which ultimately translates to bonuses and profit sharing.

Roanoke Residence, Seattle, Washington. Architect: Schemata Workshop, Inc. PHOTOGRAPHER: SCHEMATA WORKSHOP, INC.

design phase to create a strong conceptual framework that is then carried throughout the detailing and construction of the project. The plural, *schemata*, is also a psychology term used to describe the way people perceive and organize environmental information. We paired schema with workshop to imply a more casual work environment as well as our hands-on design approach.

Our philosophy is dedicated to a collaborative design process that provides innovative and client-specific design solutions. Schemata Workshop will produce award-winning designs but as a secondary goal to client satisfaction.

As the first recipient of the Emerging Professionals Mentorship Award and the 2008 Young Architects Award, can you define "mentorship" and describe how an aspiring architect finds a suitable mentor?

❯ Mentoring is more about leadership than it is about satisfying Intern Development Program requirements. Mentoring is about being a role model, to give others the courage and confidence to tackle the situation themselves in the future. It is in this way that I think leadership is so integral to mentoring.

How did you arrive at the name Schemata Workshop and how does that describe the philosophy of your company?

❯ My partner and I did not want the name of our newly incorporated firm to be our last names, to be the "bosses" with our names on the door. Instead, we wanted to create a collegial studio environment, where everyone felt that they were integral to the team.

A *schema* is a framework or outline. It describes the overarching ideals of the studio and our design approach—to focus the design efforts of the entire design and construction team during the schematic

To find a suitable mentor, consider someone in your office, such as a supervisor to serve as a mentor, but be sure to seek out formal mentors outside your firm. This will help in the long term as you develop within the office and the "politics" begin to come into play.

Below are many avenues for finding a mentor:

Ask your professors about colleagues or alumni.

Consider asking the principal of that firm in which you interviewed, had a great conversation, but who had no available position to offer.

Attend AIA or other professional organization functions.

Ask a fellow young architect serving on a committee with you if they could recommend their supervisor or someone else from their firm that might be a good mentor.

If you work in a large firm, you could possibly consider finding a mentor from another studio within the firm.

Contact your state IDP coordinator and ask for help in locating a mentor.

What are your primary responsibilities and duties?

Vision: setting direction for the firm and helping the staff see their role in "steering the boat" towards that direction

Mentorship: leadership through actions

Marketing: securing new projects and potential client contacts

Design direction: working with the project team to establish a strong design concept and provide critiques/reviews as the design progresses

Technical oversight: ensuring that codes are adhered to and documents satisfy permit and constructability requirements

Client management: guiding the client through decisions and helping them identify opportunities that add value to their project

What is the most/least satisfying part of your job?

❯ Most satisfying is making a positive impact on people's lives through architecture. Least satisfying: expending countless hours on a Statement of Qualifications and an extensive public interview process only to receive a letter from the owner stating that the project was awarded to another firm but that we were a close second.

Who or what experience has been a major influence on your career?

❯ Donna Palicka, an interior designer at SOM, for whom I worked with for eight months on the programming for General Motors Global Headquarters. From her, I learned the importance of building relationships and that, as a woman architect, I could be feminine and still maintain a professional presence.

Mark Simpson, AIA and Jennie Sue Brown, FAIA are two principals of Bumgardner, a Seattle architectural firm that has seen its 50-year anniversary.

McDermott Place Apartments, Seattle, Washington. Architect: Schemata Workshop, Inc. RENDERING: SCHEMATA WORKSHOP, INC.

Both were instrumental in helping me develop skills that would eventually enable me to start my own architectural practice.

Most important, my husband and business partner, Mike Mariano, AIA, has played a critical role in my career development as a classmate, fellow intern, and now as a business partner. As a husband, Mike has supported me through difficult career decisions and has been patient with challenging work schedules.

Finally, I had the opportunity to attend Masonry Camp, an International Masonry Institute sponsored event in 1997. Spending the week with apprentice tradespeople and other young architects, I realized that the adversarial relationship between architect and contractor that is typically seen on jobsite could easily be avoided if all parties had a place at the table to discuss problems and arrive at consensual decisions.

Becoming a Positive Influence

JENNIFER JARAMILLO

Architectural Intern

Dekker/Perich/Sabatini, LLC

Albuquerque, New Mexico

Why and how did you become an architect?

❯ When I was in first grade playing with Legos with my brother, we were having so much fun I told him that I wished I could build when I grew up. He told me that it was called being an architect. From that moment on I was driven to become an architect. All through elementary school to high school my mom would tell me that architecture was a competitive field and I needed to earn good grades because my employer would look all the way back to my kindergarten report card. I laugh about it now, but I understand what she was trying to do. I am very thankful to have had this advantage growing up.

H.B. & Lucille Horn YMCA Central New Mexico, Albuquerque, New Mexico. Architect: Dekker/Perich/Sabatini, LLC. PHOTOGRAPHER: PATRICK COULIE.

Jefferson Green, Albuquerque, New Mexico. Architect: Dekker/Perich/ Sabatini, LLC. PHOTOGRAPHER: PATRICK COULIE.

Why and how did you decide on the University of New Mexico to attend for your architecture degree? What degree(s) do you possess?

❯ When deciding where to attend college, my decision was an easy choice. I lived in a suburb of Albuquerque, New Mexico, that has the only architecture program in the state. Also, my decision was easy because I was awarded the Legislative Lottery Scholarship, a state sponsored scholarship program funded by proceeds from the New Mexico Lottery.

What has been your greatest challenge as an architectural intern?

❯ As an intern my greatest challenge has been in understanding my role on an architectural project. I have the energy that wants to take on an entire project and run the show but my lack of experience prevents it. I can only gain experience from completing the mundane tasks and logging hours of time in all of the categories in the IDP. In other words, my greatest challenge has been the capacity for patience.

What are your primary responsibilities and duties?

❯ As an intern I have assisted on a range of project types and teams. I have been provided responsibili-

ties that range from the stereotypical bathroom and stair details to the more accountable role of running consultant coordination meetings. I have had the opportunity to submit projects for permit and negotiate with city zoning officials. I also serve as the assistant intern development coordinator at Dekker/Perich/Sabatini that is quite fulfilling; in this role I assist interns in their path to licensure by standing as a resource of information for all things intern.

What are your 5-year and 10-year career goals relative to architecture?

❯ My five-year goal is to become licensed by obtaining my professional degree, completing my internship requirement, and passing the ARE. My 10-year goal is to be promoted to associate within my firm and to always remain in a position that aids in the development of interns.

Presently, you serve as auxiliary IDP coordinator in your firm and associate director for the AIA New Mexico. How did you become involved with these experiences and how do they contribute to your career as an architect?

❯ I have had the good fortune of a spectacular mentor, Tina M. Reames of Cherry/See/Reames

Architects, LLP. She has been an active and positive influence in my life, and by her example I have developed a side of me that could have gone by uncultivated. She serves as the state IDP coordinator for New Mexico and therefore is always seeking avenues of getting intern information out to the architecture community. Because of her, I learned of the annual IDP Coordinators Conference being held in Chicago in 2007 that I attended on behalf of my firm. At the conference, I became an auxiliary coordinator, and after displaying my passion for helping fellow interns, I was invited to sit on the board of AIA New Mexico in the newly created position of associate director. I have taken these positions as opportunities to meet architects and professionals from around the country with a range of backgrounds in order to gain valuable insight on their takes and opinions on architecture.

What is the most/least satisfying part of your career as an architect?

❭ The most satisfying is being a part of such an exciting profession. The history of architecture goes back to the beginning of time, as man sought shelter from various environmental conditions, and developed over thousands of years to what we see and experience today. I am honored to be a part of such a historic and necessary profession.

The least satisfying part is my desire to know everything at once. I learn every day and the internship process adds to my library of knowledge. Architecture is a field where one learns over time and by experience. The frustrating part about this is that these lessons can only be taught and learned over the life of a career and not all at once.

Who or what experience has been a major influence on your career?

❭ During my senior year at the University of New Mexico (UNM), I was invited by the construction administration department at UNM to attend the Western Mountain Region ASC-AGC Deign/Build Competition. In this competition a team is presented with a project at 6 AM. The entire construction project, architectural design drawings are due

Jefferson Green, Albuquerque, New Mexico. Architect: Dekker/ Perich/Sabatini, LLC. PHOTOGRAPHER: PATRICK COULIE.

by midnight of the same day. I was the architect in charge of the design and construction documents.

This competition was a major influence on my career because I gained so much respect for my team members. Prior to the competition, I never knew the tasks a contractor has to perform for a project. During the competition, I was able to display the vital role an architect plays in the design process and gain the respect from each of my team members. Our team took second place, and up until that year UNM had never placed in the Design/Build Competition.

H.B. & Lucille Horn YMCA of Central New Mexico, Albuquerque, New Mexico. Architect: Dekker/Perich/Sabatini, LLC. PHOTOGRAPHER: TRAVIS LEWIS, DEKKER/PERICH/SABATINI, LLC

Realizing a Vision

JESSICA L. LEONARD, ASSOCIATE AIA, LEED AP

Campus Planner/Intern Architect

Ayers Saint Gross Architects and Planners (ASG)

Baltimore, Maryland

Why and how did you become an architect?

❯ Because my father is a landscape architect, I have always been surrounded by design. When I was a high school senior I was on a bus to a soccer game and looked out the window and saw a historic building with a beautiful courtyard—I decided that day that I wanted to create places like that. I now look at "becoming an architect" as a way to create beautiful, socially responsible places for people—architects are able to help people make their vision a reality. I believe we can be a voice and provide a vision for communities that otherwise would not be heard.

Why and how did you decide on the University of Maryland to attend for your architecture degrees? What degrees do you possess?

❯ I earned a bachelor of science in architecture and a master of architecture from the University of Maryland (UMD) in College Park, Maryland. When choosing a school to study architecture at, I knew I wanted to attend a four-year program

Glass Museum, Section Model by Jessica Leonard at the University of Maryland.

(4+2) in order to have a balanced liberal arts and architecture education. In addition to having a strong architecture program, it was important for me to be at a university that offered a wide variety of extra-curricular activities and programs. UMD had the benefit of being a large institution with a small architecture program. The intimate academic experience and one-on-one relationships with faculty provided the ideal learning environment. I stayed for my graduate studies at the University of Maryland because of the faculty relationships, focus on urban design, and the proximity of the school to Baltimore and DC (physical and professional).

During your graduate studies, you served as co-chair of the Studio Culture Task Force; what is "studio culture" and why is it important?

❯ Studio culture is a term used to describe the unique learning environment architectural education creates. The architecture curriculum is often seen as "studio and non-studio" courses. I believe

a better term is "academic/studio culture," where a balance is created between studio and non-studio courses. Architectural education should value the design studio experience and encourage an academic environment conducive to learning made through thoughtful connections between studio and non-studio courses. Studio learning encourages critical discourse based on collaboration, creativity, and learning through making. A healthy academic/studio culture engenders an environment where students and faculty come together to ask questions and make proposals, innovate with today's knowledge to address tomorrow's challenges. Studio education provides opportunities for students to develop their critical thinking skills and design process. The academic/studio culture must support and develop respect for the diverse backgrounds of the faculty and students' educational and professional experiences, and approaches to design. Fundamentally, academic studio culture is about balance (between studio, non-studio courses, and life), respect (for different ideas and backgrounds), and relationships/communication (between students, faculty, staff, and administration).

What led you to pursue an Urban Design certificate? How does your work with ASG incorporate urban design?

❯ It became clear to me by the end of my undergraduate education that my interest and skills were in large-scale design—understanding a site, transportation, access, program, and schematic design from a 20,000-feet view. Pursuing the urban design certificate allowed me to take focused classes outside of architecture to expand my knowledge of community design and understanding the relationship between people and architecture. Most of all taking an urban design seminar and working on my thesis gave me the technical skills and knowledge to design and plan in the urban environment.

Working in the Campus Planning studio at ASG requires me to understand a large site (campus) from 20,000 feet in the air. While the majority of the projects that I work on are not in an urban setting, the same principles of analysis and design apply. It is necessary to understand circulation patterns (both vehicular and pedestrian), the open space network, land use, constraints, and opportunities when you are designing in any environment or at any scale. The courses that I took at UMD for the certificate led me to focus on this level of analysis in greater detail, which has resulted in a natural transition into planning at ASG.

What are your primary responsibilities and duties?

❯ On a daily basis, I work on various aspects of campus planning, including area plans, land use studies, campus zoning, impact analysis, transportation, public/private development, and de-

▼ Reestablishing community: a renewed village center for Edmondson Village, Baltimore, Maryland. Thesis by Jessica Leonard at the University of Maryland.

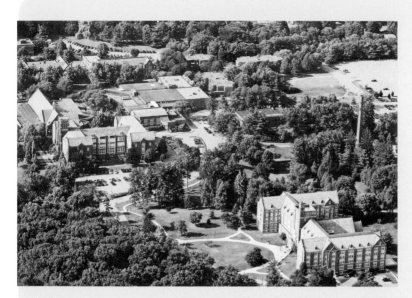

Nazareth College Master Plan, Nazareth College, Pittsford, New York.
Architects: Ayers Saint Gross Architects and Planners.

Nazareth College Master Plan, Proposed Campus Rendering Nazareth College,
Pittsford, New York. Architects: Ayers Saint Gross Architects and Planners.
RENDERING: MURALI RAMASWAMI.

mographic and economic studies. I conduct site analysis and mapping, participate in planning meetings, workshops, and design charrettes, and produce graphics and maps for campus sub-area plans, presentations, and a variety of informational handouts—often in a university administration support capacity, and develop pre-schematic architectural and site plans for proposed facilities.

What has been your greatest challenge as an intern thus far?

❯ Being patient. Out of school there is so much to learn, and so many aspects of a project, that I want to do everything right away. I have been fortunate to be involved in a lot of different projects at different phases—the challenge has been understanding the role of each person on a project—knowing that in time I will gain more and more experience and with that have more and more responsibility.

What are your 5-year and 10-year career goals relative to architecture?

❯ Becoming licensed in five years (or less) is the most pressing career goal. In the next 5 to 10 years I also hope to become an associate in a firm with more responsibility leading projects. Professionally, it is important for me to stay active in the Baltimore community and larger architecture community. Taking leadership roles in local design, transportation, and planning initiatives as well as mentoring future designers (high school and college students) are important goals for my career.

What is the most/least satisfying part of career as an architect?

❭ The most satisfying part of being an architect is helping people realize their vision. The least satisfying part of being an architect is nothing.

Working in campus planning allows me to travel to colleges and universities around the county—being around an intellectual environment and seeing some many diverse places is definitely a highlight of my job.

Who or what experience has been a major influence on your career?

❭ There have been many people and experiences that have influenced my career and help me reach my goals, but the major influences were the faculty, my assistantship, and my study abroad experience at Maryland.

Throughout my education I was fortunate to have faculty that encouraged me to explore my interests and highlighted my strengths (even when I did not realize them). I had an assistantship as an academic advisor and recruitment chair. Through that experience I had constant interaction with people, gave presentations to large and small groups, and helped create and pull together marketing materials for the school. I never realized until I started working how important that experience was. I developed communication skills and a comfort level for public speaking that has been a huge advantage in my career.

Studying abroad multiple times during my education was an irreplaceable experience. The ability to experience different cultures, have a city as your textbook, and draw constantly gave me a new passion for architecture and a love for travel that will stay with me throughout my career.

Encouraging Leadership in Future Architects

F. MICHAEL AYLES, AIA

Principal, Business Development

Antinozzi Associates

Bridgeport, Connecticut

Why and how did you become an architect?

❯ Realizing both my early ability to draw well and to build complicated structures with LEGOS, I intuitively knew that I was to become an architect. I enjoyed technical drawing through high school, especially in my advanced drafting classes where I learned computer-aided drafting (CAD) on some of the first versions of AutoCAD.

My guidance counselor looked at my strengths and interests and came up with some career suggestions as to what I might enjoy and succeed in—meteorology, astronomy . . . and *architecture*. None of

these seemed particularly lucrative in salary, but the thought of becoming an architect sounded not only important but unique too. I was told that there were many different careers I could go into once I did become an architect—so off I went to architecture school at a small private institution called Roger Williams College in Rhode Island.

I was not a great designer in college, nor did I have a high grade point average. In fact, I nearly dropped out midway through architecture school due to the continual criticism I received from one of my studio instructors—who said I had no creativity. When I found out that the instructor was not a practicing architect, but a theater arts set designer, I did not lose hope and persisted with my studies. I graduated in 1991 and landed an internship right out of college even with a poor economy. After one firm change, I completed the IDP in four years and passed the ARE, the very last time it was paper/pencil version

Antinozzi Associates Offices, Bridgeport, Connecticut. Architect: Antinozzi Associates PC. PHOTOGRAPHER: ANTINOZZI ASSOCIATES ARCHITECTURE AND INTERIORS.

Webster Bank, Prototype Bank Branch, Yonkers, New York; Bridgeport, Connecticut; Norwalk, Connecticut. Architect: Antinozzi Associates Architecture and Interiors. RENDERING: KEVIN MATIS.

in June 1996 . . . in one try. It happened . . . I became an architect 11 years after I first thought it possible.

Ultimately, I think the main reason I became an architect is the blend of so many disciplines and subjects—art, math, science, psychology, communications, marketing, history . . . and so many more. Becoming an architect can be as diverse as you want it to be—and I have certainly done that. I never thought about becoming anything but an architect.

Why and how did you decide on which school to attend for your architecture degree? What degree(s) do you possess?

❯ I applied to University of Virginia (UVA), Virginia Tech, University of Florida, Penn State, and, finally, my "safety" school, Roger Williams College. I really had no shot at getting into UVA (academically) or Florida (no state residency); Virginia Tech placed me on a waiting list, and Penn State accepted me—for my second choice major,

Meteorology. The last letter I received was my acceptance letter from Roger Williams, and I then realized I would not be watching clouds the rest of my life! It was also a benefit to be only two hours from home, so my "safety" school worked out pretty well.

Upon starting my freshman year, I learned that the school's architecture program was not accredited by NAAB. Fortunately, the program passed its initial accreditation that same year, meaning my degree would be accredited.

What has been your greatest challenge as an architect?

❯ No project, client or individual, has provided as big a challenge . . . than *me*. Without a doubt, balancing a professional career, community involvement, and a personal life has been my greatest challenge. Besides trying to find that balance, determining . . . and accepting . . . my strengths (collaboration) and weaknesses (technical detailing) as an architect has been both eye-opening and humbling.

As an architect by education and licensure, why did you move into a more "nontraditional" business development role? What are your primary responsibilities?

❯ After years of experience with my firm as a project architect, project manager, IT manager, and director of operations, I shifted into the role of director of business development in 2006. This opportunity and challenge became an avenue for me to advance myself in my firm, and I was elevated to managing partner in 2008. When asked by interns and young architects, I explain that I did not think of myself as a strong designer, but a more effective collaborator, communicator, and motivator. My skills migrated more from design to collaboration—client relationships, firm organization, team building, and resource management.

My primary responsibilities are simple—bring work into the office and oversee the marketing efforts of the entire firm. However, business development includes aspects that go beyond "marketing" or "public relations." You need to excel in a number of different fields—human resources, peacekeeper/ambassador, educator, psychologist, detective, etc. Many hats have to be worn, depending on the opportunities or situations that present themselves in developing the business strategy of an architecture firm.

What is the most/least satisfying part of your job?

❯ Most satisfying, especially now on the business development end, is receiving the phone call that we secured a major project based on a collective team effort, whether through a proposal, face-to-face interview, or recommendation from an existing client or consultant—or a combination of many efforts. It is nearly as rewarding to hear a client proudly state at a project's ribbon-cutting or grand opening that our firm produced a project

that exceeded every expectation they had, not just about our firm, but about the architect's "role" in general. In addition, mentoring an architectural intern or less experienced staff member is a huge reward for me since, as I get older, I realize there is much I have to share about the profession—just like those who mentored (and still mentor) me.

Least satisfying, without a doubt, is the letter, email, or phone conversation that indicates our firm was not short-listed or selected for a design project. There are times when hours, days, or even weeks can be expended to secure a project and, for no clear understanding or reason, the client and/or selection committee decides not to hire your firm. It takes a great deal of perseverance, patience, constructive criticism, firm/self-assessment . . . and antacids . . . to accept the sometimes disappointing results.

You have served as the Chair of the AIA's Young Architects Forum (YAF) and Committee on Leadership Education (CLE). What have you taken from those experiences and why is it important in your professional career?

❯ The YAF promotes both individual and program development, and addresses relevant issues faced by Young Architect members locally, regionally and nationally. The overriding goals of the YAF are to encourage **leadership**, **mentorship**, and **fellowship**.

It seemed natural for me to help create the CLE after my YAF involvement, especially after participating in the 2003 AIA Leadership Institute. Along with other Institute "graduates," we believed that the ideal of promoting and educating architects to be leaders in our society should be highly encouraged. The CLE is simply an AIA Knowledge Community that acts as a resource, and a motivator, for architects to get more involved in their firm, community, society, and even government.

Proposed Addition to Chatfield Elementary School, Seymour, Connecticut. Architect: Antinozzi Associates Architecture and Interiors. RENDERING: RYOUNG H. CHOI.

This AIA involvement allowed me to learn, hands-on, and lead more than I ever possibly imagined. I have become a more valuable architect (and business developer) and leader in the communities I live in and work with. The activities, travel opportunities, educational resources, networking, and, most of all, the people I have collaborated with, have had a dramatic impact in my development, not just as an architect, but as a leader in my firm and community. Many individuals mentored me as an up-and-coming architect and leader, and I believe it is now my duty to take what I have learned and pass my abilities and experiences on to the next generation of architects.

It took you five years from graduation from Roger Williams to becoming licensed. Can you describe your internship years?

❯ After graduation, I was fortunate to obtain an intern position with a well-known, 100-person architecture firm in the Hartford area. The economy was slow, I had no practical experience working in an office, and I did not have the strongest portfolio. So, when provided this opportunity, I jumped at every chance to exceed expectation. I also volunteered and participated in as many challenging project tasks as possible so that I could learn from the more experienced staff.

After being with this firm for two years, I was gaining experience but I feared that I might never be looked at as anything but an "intern" in an office this size. Starting to feel a bit "pigeonholed" and knowing that the workload was dropping substantially due to a lagging economy, I had a chance to leave and join a smaller firm—the same one I am with now.

As the only intern in the office, I was able to work at a more challenging level and had the opportunity to work on several different types of projects. I was not necessarily told what to do or how to perform the tasks on these projects—I listened and observed as much I could from each person in the office.

I looked up information if I did not know it and asked questions only when absolutely necessary.

During my five years of internship, IDP played a major part. As soon as completed by studies, I initiated my NCARB Council Record and recorded my experience—and I did not find it all cumbersome. Based on my experience, start the IDP process immediately. It will not be as intimidating!

Who or what experience has been a major influence on your career?

❭ Over the past six years, I have been integrally involved in the ACE Mentor Program of Connecticut—both as a chapter advisory board member and a state board of director. The mission of this program is to enlighten and motivate high school students toward architecture, construction, or engineering-related careers. In addition, ACE provides mentoring opportunities for professionals in design and construction fields, as well as the ability for firms to recruit minority and female students and increase their representation in the industry. By encouraging the implementation of this program in our office in 2002, I have observed nearly 150 high school students come through our office doors and develop an appreciation, understanding, and, for some, a passion for the design and construction industry. Our office encourages younger professionals to become the ACE mentors, and the influence these young mentors have had on these students has, in turn, influenced my outlook on the future of the architecture profession.

The Forgotten Middle

EDWARD J. SHANNON, AIA

Director of Design

Benvenuti & Stein Design, LLC

Winnetka, Illinois

Why and how did you become an architect?

❭ I grew up in the Chicago suburbs of River Forest and Oak Park, Illinois. So, at an early age I was exposed to the work of Frank Lloyd Wright and his disciples. As well, my father's business is closely related to the construction industry. Through these influences I developed an early appreciation and interest in the built environment. I took drafting in high school and was blessed with a very inspirational teacher (who was trained as an architect). He taught our class the difference between architecture and building. As high school students we were exposed to all the noted Chicago architects, past and present. My teacher instilled in me a sense of confidence. He told us that any of us could become architects if we wanted it badly enough. To a great degree, I believe this to be true.

Why and how did you decide on which school to attend for your architecture degree? What degree(s) do you possess?

❭ Although there are two reputable architecture schools in Chicago, I chose to go to Iowa State University to obtain the bachelor of arts in architecture because I wanted to experience campus life at a large Midwestern university. Leaving home enabled me to mature in many ways. There I learned many valuable skills that have enhanced my career greatly.

Pearson Residence Addition, Glen Ellyn, Illinois. Architect: Edward J. Shannon, AIA. PHOTOGRAPHER: DENNIS JOURDAN.

Shumway Residence Addition, Palatine, Illinois. Architect: Edward J. Shannon, AIA. PHOTOGRAPHER: DENNIS JOURDAN.

I chose Virginia Polytechnic Institute and State University for the master of architecture because I was interested in the design-centered teaching methodologies of the school. It was at Virginia Tech that I truly learned the difference between architecture and building. I also learned that in order for a building to become architecture, architecture must be present at the early stages.

▲ Private Residence, Exterior, Sister Bay, Wisconsin.
Architects: Edward J. Shannon, AIA, and Lane Allen, AIA.
PHOTOGRAPHER: DOUG SNOWER PHOTOGRAPHY.

▶ Private Residence, Interior, Sister Bay, Wisconsin.
Architects: Edward J. Shannon, AIA, and Lane Allen, AIA.
PHOTOGRAPHER: DOUG SNOWER PHOTOGRAPHY.

What has been your greatest challenge as an architect?

❭ Practicing architecture in suburbia. I consider myself a part of the "forgotten middle," the middle class/suburbia. However, it is often challenging to enlighten the middle class sector as to what is quality architecture/urban design, why it is worth paying more for, and why it can cost more to design.

Previously, you taught as a faculty member. How did that work inform your architectural practice and vice versa?

❭ My mantra had been that I teach better because I practice and that I practice better because I teach.

More specifically, I tended to bring a sense of pragmatism and reality into my teaching. I taught design studio, professional practice, and materials and methods. In the design studio I assisted in the students' awareness of the various forces (code, zoning, program, budget) that inform the design of a project. I am able to share my successes and failures in the materials and practice courses I teach.

Because I was a faculty member, there were always a lot of eyes on me in terms of practice. Not just in terms of the work I produce but also in terms of my practice ethics. Teaching is built-in accountability.

What is the most/least satisfying part of your position?

❯ Most satisfying is walking through a completed building project and sharing in the joy of that project with my clients.

Least satisfying is that some projects tend to drag on with many iterations and changes.

Who or what experience has been a major influence on your career?

❯ As mentioned earlier, my upbringing in the Chicago area was an influence. I am also grateful for many of my teachers, especially my drafting teacher at Oak Park-River Forest High School, Mr. Urbanick. More than a drafting teacher, Mr. U had a passionate love of architecture. He was trained as an architect at IIT, and he could have practiced architecture or taught at the university level. Yet he chose to teach high school and instill a passion for the art of building in many young adults.

Architect Harry Weese, amongst others, stands out as a model architect. Mr. Weese did not have a signature style; instead he let the client and site influence the building's form. Instead of trying to be different with his designs, he simply tried to be good. He could design simultaneously in many scales—intimate, human, and monumental. Instead of designing bold buildings that screamed out for attention, he was more concerned with making buildings humane. He had a very diverse practice that included single-family homes, high rises, schools, and subway systems. Although he was a modernist, he embraced historic structures and was a pioneer in preserving old buildings.

Empowering Environments

BARBARA CRISP

Principal

bcrisp llc

Tempe, Arizona

Why and how did you become an architect?

⟩ I never considered architecture as a profession until I enrolled in an architectural drafting class at night after receiving a degree in English. Through the course, I learned that I really loved visualizing space and had a strong desire to express myself creatively. The drafting course rekindled early desires for art and expression. Afterwards, I was able to secure a position in a wonderful firm that gave me a lot of opportunities to grow and learn and ultimately encouraged me to go back to school. So, I began slowly with the prerequisites and ultimately made an application and was accepted. This decision changed my life.

Why and how did you decide on which school to attend for your architecture degree? What degree(s) do you possess?

⟩ Being an older student, married, and with an undergraduate degree in a non-related area, I did not have the flexibility to go wherever I might have wanted. I would have attended a three + year master of architecture, but there was none in close proximity. I was fortunate that there was a good nationally ranked four + two program where I was living, and I entered the undergraduate program and first obtained a bachelor of science in design and ultimately received a master of architecture from the same institution.

What has been your greatest challenge as an architect?

⟩ The challenge of the bottom line, meaning money, as it relates to the value of design, is looming large more and more. It is a constant challenge to educate clients about the effects that quality design has on our world, on their world.

In addition, I strive to imbue the work I do with meaning, no matter how small the project. If I am unable to be true to my values and beliefs, I do not want the work. This is a voice I have grown and evolved over time—to follow my intuition and speak with my intellect as well as my heart. This is something that is not always easily understood by my clients, but over time, and with trust, it has allowed for some little design gems to surface that have both delighted and surprised the client.

The focus of your design work addresses sensory experience and perception that support and sustain well-being. Can you elaborate on this statement and what led you to this work?

⟩ On family vacations/road trips, when we stopped to eat my father would always tell us to close our eyes and ask us questions about our surroundings—what color are the walls, are there windows, how many tables, what do you smell?—which probably set up the framework for how I observe the world around me. I am very tuned in to the subtleties of my surroundings and sensitive to how they make me feel.

We have all been in places that we just cannot wait to get out of, and it is important to know why. Look a little deeper, tune in with all your senses to better understand what is going on that zaps your energy

When we are fully present, we not only live well, we live well for others.
Terry Tempest Williams

The simple act of writing meaningful words on paper
- a single word or a phrase in the form of a thought,
a wish, a promise or a prayer- makes them a message
in the larger world, to mix with the great wondrous
universe and all that holds meaning to the giver.

una promesa

We welcome you to partake in this simple act, knowing that
the messages will be blessed at the change of each season
by our Spiritual Care department.

a thought

Blessing Wall, Banner Good Samaritan Medical Center Expansion, Phoenix, Arizona. Designer: Barbara Crisp, Underwood + Crisp w/Thinking Caps. PHOTOGRAPHER: BILL TIMMERMAN.

or fosters this discomfort. Such environments do not support and sustain well-being; architects and designers need to make this connection. As well, environments that feel right need to be analyzed in a similar way. One must have a clear understanding of what allows for both types of environments to manifest. And this investigative understanding must go on within the larger global context as well as one's local culture.

Define "life-enhancing environments, sacred spaces."

❯ In *Human Spaces*, the book I authored in 1998, I defined the concept of life-enhancing environments as a place built or created to support and sustain the well-being of a particular occupant of time, place, and culture, where the body as a whole, both inner and outer, is regarded as essential to how the space is experienced. I would say that this definition still works, but what is more important is that there is a recognition that everything we create—our actions, thoughts, and the words we speak—all hold meaning and the potential to effect and change the world—mentally, physically, emotionally, and spiritually—so one must be conscious of that in the work they do, in what they create. All space is sacred if we do our work in a sacred manner.

What are your primary responsibilities and duties?

❯ My firm is small so I do almost everything depending on the project. And I have great resources too. My strengths are in working with clients and establishing those relationships, developing the design concept, and seeing it through the design process, with less involvement in the CD phase. Because my business is a small operation, I expand opportunity and abilities by collaborating with like-minded professionals to create a holistic offering to the client. This has brought both great joy and continued learning. Over time I have discovered that the front end is truly where I have passion and bring the most to a project—client relationships, programming, concept, design—although I know all

phases and do enjoy working through details and field administration.

What is the most/least satisfying part of your job?

❭ What I find most satisfying is helping clients envision and manifest their ideas and wishes in two and three dimensions—places, spaces, objects, surfaces—what they only have words for.

What I find least satisfying is when the work does not have meaning. I make an effort to be conscious of what I do and don't take on so that the sometimes not so pleasant reality of doing business does not overtake my core beliefs. However, day-to-day, it is the paperwork and billing and that I most dislike.

Who or what experience has been a major influence on your career?

❭ There are three influences that stand out:

■ Having my mentor, Bob Sexton, in the first architecture firm that I worked in, do me the valuable service of strongly advising that I return to school for a degree in architecture, knowing that I would never be happy otherwise. At the time, he saw something in me that I could not.

■ Becoming involved in AIAS as a student, and ultimately being selected to serve on the national AIA Architects in Education committee for three years. During that time I worked alongside of a number of deans

Place to Pause, Banner Good Samaritan Medical Center Expansion, Phoenix, Arizona. Designer: Barbara Crisp, Underwood + Crisp w/Thinking Caps. PHOTOGRAPHER: BILL TIMMERMAN.

Logos Textile Collection, Banner Good Samaritan Medical Center Expansion, Phoenix, Arizona. Designer: Barbara Crisp, Underwood + Crisp w/DesignTex. PHOTOGRAPHER: MAX UNDERWOOD, AIA.

from major institutions and made lifelong friends, traveled to campuses around the country, and was part of interesting and challenging dialogue on the interface between the practice of architecture and architecture education. This experience opened other unexpected doors.

■ Being the successful recipient of a travel fellowship to Europe in graduate school was significant because I became more aware that travel is invaluable and a must to anyone who wants to grow and evolve and understand the world as a living, breathing, non-static opportunity. You never see things the same way again.

Creating Positive Change

JOSEPH BILELLO, Ph.D., AIA

Professor and Former Dean

College of Architecture and Planning

Ball State University

Muncie, Indiana

Why and how did you become an architect?

❯ My family values linked a college education to becoming a professional of some kind—doctor, lawyer, priest, or engineer. I merged those expectations with strong abilities in mathematics and interests in art (primarily drawing; I have always doodled). A junior high art teacher recognized strong design and artistic ability in my work. Then, in high school, I became interested specifically in architecture after seeing the work of Frank Lloyd Wright in the library.

Impressed by the campus, I chose a university with exceptional architecture, the University of Pennsylvania. I went to college as a mathematics major, took a course in art and civilization as a

▼ Brooklyn, New York, Aerial View. PHOTOGRAPHER: JOSEPH BILELLO, Ph.D., AIA.

freshman, and had a dorm room across from the Richards Medical Center by Louis Kahn. I started drawing and architectural courses in sophomore year (in Frank Furness' Fine Arts Building) concurrent with thoughts about a major in English literature. I decided on architecture alone mid-junior year based on encouraging feedback and some very influential teachers—landscape architect Ian McHarg (and his visiting scholar/friends), structural engineer Peter McCleary, architect Louis Kahn, architectural historian James O'Gorman, architect Stasha Novitski (and a drawing teacher, Frank Kawasaki, whose words of encouragement, "when you are an architect" helped create the confidence that I could do it).

Graduation was concurrent with the army draft (Vietnam War). I got a graduate school deferment, attended a first year of graduate school, suspended studies, went to Europe and galvanized my architectural passion, returned to the U.S. to work in practice. I returned to graduate school re-energized and concluded studies enthusiastically as a result of the formative travel/work year.

I interned in public and private practices in the Santa Fe, Denver, and San Francisco. At that time, internships were not structured to expeditiously help professional preparation. I became a registered architect concurrent with my efforts to establish my own practice in San Francisco. Other urges for independence and a fruition of professional efforts eventually led me to teach and practice at the same time in New Mexico.

Why and how did you decide on which school to attend for your architecture degree? What degrees do you possess?

❭ I hold degrees from the University of Pennsylvania (bachelor of art, major in architectural studies), Washington University (master of architecture), and the University of Maryland (Ph.D.).

I decided to attend Washington University for my professional degree for a number of reasons. First, some of the best graduate students at Penn had come from undergraduate school at Washington University. Though I wanted to stay at Penn, at that time, the school took students from other schools, almost entirely. Washington University also represented pioneering—my first move away from the East Coast. The faculty was interesting (including Buckminster Fuller's former partner, James Fitzgibbons, and "young Turks" like Mike Pyatok and Charlie Brown). I played four years of intercollegiate soccer at Penn and had soccer colleagues who were from St. Louis, had good things to say about it as a place, and returned there after graduation.

What has been your greatest challenge as an architect/faculty/dean?

❭ As an architect, my greatest challenge is getting good design built. As a faculty member, it is balancing excellence in teaching with attempting to generate new knowledge (scholarly inquiry). And finally as a dean, the challenge is creating positive change and closure; staying focused on the dynamic "high ground" of excellence in design and planning education amidst constant challenges with the myriad of administrative, paperwork, and personnel management duties that are never finished.

Can you describe the differences between being a professor and dean?

❭ At my present institution, architecture professors teach students primarily. Most engage in additional scholarly pursuits. A few are deeply committed to the production of new knowledge. Some engage

Keet Seel Ruins Stabilization, National Park Service, Navajo National Monument, Arizona. Architect: Southwest Cultural Resources Center. PHOTOGRAPHER: JOSEPH BILELLO, PH.D., AIA.

budget management, strategic planning, implementation, and reporting to constituents of all stripes, primarily upper-level administration. It is a largely nonstop around-the-clock, 7-days-a-week, 52-weeks-a-year, notwithstanding delegation of duties.

What is the most/least satisfying part of your job?

❯ Most satisfying are the incredible moments when groups and individuals—students, faculty, staff, and visitors—are at their best—breakthroughs, thinking globally/acting locally—realizing that things larger than us are happening as a result of what we are doing.

Least satisfying is knowing what we are capable of and seeing what we do. An absence of closure, resource politics of public higher education administration, and the need to appeal to constituents that know little of what a dean does and/or how higher education operates today are great challenges.

You served as the associate dean for research at Texas Tech University and on the board of directors for the Architectural Research Centers Consortium. In the context of that part of your background, what is the importance of research in architecture?

❯ Research is the way in which new knowledge can most readily enter the profession and professional education. It is also the way that all professions recharge themselves (their knowledge bases) and ultimately justify why they need to remain a profession in a world where knowledge can be rapidly disseminated and put into use. Regrettably, most architects and many architectural educators have little understanding of architectural research—the rigors of methodically

in community-based projects as service activities. Some maintain small practices. Faculty maintains a 30-week academic year commitment with comparatively high levels of discretionary time for inquiry.

In contrast, the deanship carries a comparatively minor teaching responsibility but does have significant leadership and fundraising dimension and a huge administrative responsibility—personnel and

producing it, how to effectively integrate it into design, and how it accelerates rates of learning/practice possibilities. This is a huge challenge ahead for our schools and profession.

Who/what experience has been a major influence on your career?

❯ Those who have had a major influence include Buckminster Fuller, Ian McHarg, and my children. Experiences that have been most influential include global travels and teaching, exhibitions of paintings inspired by architecture, professional practice triumphs and failures, and time spent in a myriad of projects and conversations with many remarkable people.

The Temple de la Sagrada Família, Barcelona, Spain. Architect: Antonio Gaudi. PHOTOGRAPHER: JOSEPH BILELLO, PH.D., AIA.

NOTES

1. Boyer, Ernest L., and Mitgang, Lee D. (1996). *Building community: A new future for architecture education and practice.* Princeton, NJ: Carnegie Foundation for the Advancement of Teaching, p. 117.
2. *The American Heritage Dictionary.* (2000). Boston: Houghton Mifflin.
3. Boston Architectural Center, www.the-bac.edu. Accessed June 28, 2008.
4. Linton, Harold. (2004). *Portfolio Design, Third Edition.* New York: W. W. Norton.
5. *The American Heritage Dictionary.* (2000). Boston: Houghton Mifflin.
6. NCARB. (2009). Intern Development Program Guidelines, Washington, DC, p. 5.
7. Emerging Professional Companions, www.epcompanion.org. Retrieved September 21, 2008.
8. NCARB. (2009). Intern Development Program Guidelines. p. 38–53.

❹ The Careers of an Architect

The building of a career is quite as difficult a problem as the building of a house, yet few ever sit down with pencil and paper, with expert information and counsel, to plan a working career and deal with the life problem scientifically, as they would deal with the problem of building a house, taking the advice of an architect to help them.

FRANK PARSONS[1]

AS PARSONS STATES IN THE PRECEDING QUOTATION, the building of a career—the process of career development—is a difficult, but important task, yet he also notes that few individuals prepare for their careers in a thoughtful, careful, and deliberate manner. Instead, many often fall into a career, while others make random career choices that show little commitment to their occupation, often leading to dissatisfaction.

Career Designing

Regardless of where you are along the path to becoming an architect—completing your architectural education, gaining experience in an architecture firm or in the process of taking the Architect Registration Exam (ARE), you should pursue deliberate career designing to maximize career success.

◀ VOB BMW, Rockville, Maryland. Architect: DNC Architects. PHOTOGRAPHER: ERIC TAYLOR, ASSOCIATE AIA. PHOTO © ERICTAYLORPHOTO.COM.[1]

You may argue that a career is not something you create or plan, that it just happens. However, like architectural projects, careers should be carefully planned. In many ways, designing a career is parallel to designing a building. Programming, schematic design, design development, working drawings, and construction are replaced in the career development process with assessing, exploring, decision making, and planning.

ASSESSING

> Know thyself.
>
> INSCRIPTION OVER THE ORACLE AT DELPHI, GREECE

When an architect designs a project, what is typically the first step in the process? Most likely, programming. As William Pena points out in *Problem Seeking,*[2] the main idea behind programming is the search for sufficient information, to clarify, understand, and state the problem. In a similar manner, when designing your career, the process begins with assessing.

Assessing is learning about yourself. Assess where you want to be; analyze what is important to you, your abilities, the work you would like to do, and your strengths and weaknesses. Just as programming assists the architect in understanding a particular design problem, assessment helps determine what you want from your career. This ongoing process must be reiterated throughout your entire career. The details of assessment include values, interests, and skills. But what exactly are values, interests, and skills, and how do you determine them?

Values

Values are feelings, attitudes, and beliefs you hold close to your heart. They reflect what is important to you; they tell you what you should or should not do. Work values are the enduring dimensions or aspects of our work that you regard as important sources of satisfaction. Values traditionally held in high esteem by architects include creativity, recognition, variety, independence, and responsibility.

As a quick inventory, circle which of the following you value in the work you do:

Helping others

Improving society

Creativity

Excitement

Working alone/with others

Monetary reward

Competition

Change and variety

Independence

Intellectual challenge

Physical challenge

Fast pace

Security

Responsibility

Making decisions

Power and authority

Gaining knowledge

Recognition

Interests

Interests are those ideas, events, and activities that stimulate your enthusiasm; they are reflected in choices you make about how you spend your time. In simplest terms, interests are activities you enjoy doing. Typically, architects have a breadth of interests because the field of architecture encompasses artistic, scientific, and technical aspects. Architects enjoy being involved in all phases of the creative process—from original conceptualization to a tangible finished product.[3]

To determine your interests, for an entire month, note what you most and least enjoy doing each day. At the end of the month, summarize and categorize the preferences you have recorded. Here is another method; in 10 minutes of continuous writing, never removing your pen from the paper or your fingers from the keyboard, answer the question: What do I like to do when I am not working?

Skills

Unlike interests, skills or abilities can be learned. The three types of skills are functional, self-management, and special knowledge. Having a functional skill means that you are able to perform some specific type of activity, action, or operation with a good deal of proficiency. In contrast, self-management skills are your specific behavioral responses or character traits such as eagerness, initiative, or dependability. Last, special knowledge skills are what you have learned and what you know.

The importance of knowing your skills is echoed by Richard Bolles in his book, *The Quick Job-Hunting Map*[4]: "You must know, for now and all the future, not only what skills you have, but more importantly, what skills you have and enjoy." With respect to skills, think back over the past five years. What were your five most satisfying accomplishments? Next to each, list the skills or abilities that enabled you to succeed. Similarly, review your failures to determine traits or deficiencies you want to overcome.

A variety of techniques may be used to conduct an assessment. The few listed here are simply to get you started; others include writing an autobiography and undertaking empirical inventories or a psychological assessment with the assistance of a career counselor. Regardless of the method you choose, only you can best determine what skills you have acquired and enjoy using; the issues, ideas, problems, organizations that interest you; and the values that you care about for your life and career.

EXPLORING

Students spend four or more years learning how to dig data out of the library and other sources, but it rarely occurs to them that they should also apply some of the same new-found research skill to their own benefit — to looking up information on companies, types of professions, sections of the country that might interest them.

ALBERT SHAPERO

Schematic design is the phase of the design process that follows programming. Schematic design generates alternative solutions; its goal is to establish general characteristics of the design, including scale, form, estimated costs, and the general image of the building, the size, and organization of spaces. According to the AIA *Architect's Handbook of Professional Practice*,[5] the goal of schematic design is to establish general characteristics of the building design, such as the scale used to satisfy the basic program requirements and estimated costs. Additionally, schematic design identifies major issues and makes initial decisions that serve as the basis of subsequent stages.

In career development, exploring is parallel to schematic design. It develops alternatives or career choices. Career exploration is the process of accumulating information about the world of work. Its goal is to obtain career information on a plethora of careers or specializations within a particular career. Even if you already have chosen architecture as a career, it is still necessary. Instead of exploring careers, you can explore firms, possible career paths within architecture, and other areas that impact your architectural path.

How do you explore? In *Career Planning Today*,[6] the author describes a systematic process that includes collecting, evaluating, integrating, and deciding. Following these four steps guarantees the highest possible level of career awareness.

Where do you begin? First, you must collect career information from a variety of sources, both people and publications. With respect to people, the most popular tool is called *information interviewing*. What you do is interview someone to obtain information. You could interview with one of

HSB Twisting Torso, Malmo, Sweden.
Architect: Santiago Calatrava.
PHOTOGRAPHER: GRACE H. KIM, AIA.

the senior partners in a local firm, a faculty member, a classmate or colleague, or your mentor. Other ways to explore include attending lectures sponsored by the local AIA chapter or your university, volunteering your time through local AIA committee or other organizations of interest, becoming involved with a mentor program, and observing or shadowing someone for a day.

As Shapero says, you should use your research skills to access any and all information you need on a career. Visit your university career center or local public library and inquire about the following publications: *The Dictionary of Occupational Titles* (*DOT*), *Occupational Outlook Handbook* (*OOH*), *Guide to Occupational Exploration* (*GOE*), *What Color Is Your Parachute?* Ask a reference librarian to identify other resources that you might find valuable. In addition, investigate resources at your local AIA chapter or the library/resource center at area architecture program. Other resources to access include the Internet and professional associations (see Appendix A).

After completing the exploring process, your next step is the decision-making process.

DECISION MAKING

What most people want out of life, more than anything else, is the opportunity to make choices.

DAVID P. CAMPBELL

The heart of the design process is design development. Similarly decision making is the heart of the career development process. Design development describes the specific character and intent of the entire project; it further refines the schematic design and defines the alternatives. Decision making means selecting alternatives and evaluating them against a predetermined set of criteria.

How do you make decisions? Do you let others decide for you? Do you rely on gut-level reactions? Or do you follow a planned strategy of weighing alternatives? Whatever your method of deciding, you should to be aware of it. While some decisions can be made at the drop of a hat, others, including career designing, require more thought.

For demonstration purposes, review the following architectural application of the decision-making process.

Decision-making

Decision-making Model	Architectural Application
(1) Identify the decision to be made.	Need or desire for new space or building.
(2) Gather information.	Develop a building program (budget, style, size, room, specification, layout).
(3) Identify alternatives.	Develop alternative schematic designs, incorporating the program.
(4) Weigh evidence.	Evaluate schematic designs as they meet determined needs, preferences.
(5) Choose among the alternatives.	Select the design which best captures ideals.
(6) Take action.	Draw construction documents; develop time table; break ground, begin construction activity; architectural "punch list."
(7) Review decision and consequences.	Long range evaluation may identify need for major building renovation for re-use.

Decision making can be difficult and time-consuming, but knowing that the quality of decisions is affected by the information used to make them, you will quickly realize that making informed decisions is an important skill to learn.

As you can see, both exploring and decision making are critical steps in successful career designing. Do not wait to begin this important process; instead, take this information and build your future with career designing.

PLANNING

If you do not have plans for your life, someone else does.
— ANTHONY ROBBINS

Planning is bringing the future into the present so that we can do something about it now.
— ALAN LAKEIN

"Cheshire-Puss," … said Alice, "would you tell me, please which way I ought to go from here?"

"That depends a good deal on where you want to get to," said the Cat.

"I don't much care where …." said Alice.

"Then it doesn't matter which way you go," said the Cat.
— LEWIS CARROLL, *ALICE IN WONDERLAND*

You may wonder why a quote from a popular children's book. If you look closer, you realize that half of reaching your destination is to knowing the direction in which you wish to head. Planning is key to fulfilling your career goals.

After the owner/client and architect decide upon a design for a potential building, the next step is the development of plans. These plans —construction documents, specifications, and schedules—all play an important role in realizing the design. In a similar way, planning, as part of the career development process, ensures that a successful career will be realized.

In its simplest form, planning is the bridge from dreams to action; it is merely an intention to take an action by a certain time. At its fullest, planning is creating a mission statement, developing career goals, and preparing action plans.

But what are mission statement, goals, or action plans?

In his book, *Seven Habits of Highly Effective People*,[7] author Stephen Covey states that a mission statement focuses on what you want to be (character) and to do (contributions and achievements) and on the values or principles on which being and doing are based. To start the planning process, draft your mission statement by asking yourself: "What do I want to be? What do I want to do? What are my career aspirations?" Review the following example.

After you have crafted your mission statement, the next step is to develop goals that will lead to its fulfillment. Goals are future-oriented statements of purpose and direction to be accomplished within a specified time frame. They are steppingstones in achieving long-range aims and should be specific and measurable. Write down your goals. It has been said that the difference between a wish and a goal is that a goal is written down.

I desire to act in a manner that brings out the best in me and those important to me — especially when it might be most justifiable to act otherwise.

Once you establish your goals, you are ready to develop the action plan that will help you accomplish them. Action plans are steps on the path toward your goals; they are steppingstones in achieving related short-range intentions. Look at your accomplished goals. What steps must you take to accomplish them? As with career goals, write down your action plan, including specific completion dates.

Petajavesi Old Church, Petajavesi, Finland. PHOTOGRAPHER: TED SHELTON, AIA.

The final step in planning is to review your action plans and goals regularly. Cross out the goals you have accomplished and revise, add to, or delete others. Be honest with yourself. Are you still committed to achieving your goals? You can change them, but remember that the magic road to achievement is *persistence*. Abandon goals only if they have lost meaning for you—not because they are tough or you have suffered a setback.

Now, you have read about the entire career/designing process: assessing, exploring, decision making, and planning. As you progress through your professional career, you will realize that this process is never-ending and cyclical. As soon as you have secured an ideal position in a firm, you will wish to assess your new life situation and make adjustments to your career design accordingly. As well, consider the following:

You know the story of the three brick masons. When the first man was asked what he was building, he answered gruffly, without even raising his eyes from his work, "I am laying bricks." The second man replied, "I am building a wall." But the third man said enthusiastically and with obvious pride, "I am building a cathedral."

MARGARET STEVENS

In your future career, will you lay bricks, build a wall, or build a cathedral? Regardless of your answer, designing your career is one of the most important tasks during your lifetime. Yet if career designing is so important, why do most people spend such little time on it? Think about it!

Career Paths

Pursuing architecture prepares you for a vast array of career possibilities. Many of these are within traditional architectural practice, but many are also available in related career fields.

Within the traditional architecture firm, you may obtain a beginning position as an intern and progress to junior designer, project architect, and, eventually, associate or principal. This does not happen overnight; it can take a lifetime. You may pursue your career in a traditional firm regardless of its size—small, medium, or large—or you may choose to work in a different setting such as a private corporation or company; a local, state, or federal government agency; or a university—or, after obtaining your architectural license, you may start your own firm. You must consider which path is best suited for you.

ARCHITECT POSITIONS

Senior Principal/Partner	Architect/Designer II
Mid-Level Principal/Partner	Architect/Designer I
Junior Principal/Partner	Third-Year Intern
Department Head/Senior Manager	Second-Year Intern
Project Manager	Entry-Level Intern
Senior Architect/Designer	Student
Architect/Designer III	

AIA Definition of Architect Positions[8]

Nontraditional career paths tap into the creative thinking and problem-solving skills you develop during your architectural education. These opportunities also are growing in popularity; in a survey of interns and young architects, nearly one-quarter of the respondents indicated that they do not plan on pursuing a traditional career in architecture although they still plan to obtain their license. Further, respondents working in nontraditional settings reported better salaries, benefits, and advancement opportunities. These results are not shared to encourage you to pursue a nontraditional career path, but rather to demonstrate that an architectural education is excellent preparation for many sorts of positions. In fact, the career possibilities with an architectural education are limitless.

Milwaukee Art Center, Milwaukee, Wisconsin. Architect: Santiago Calatrave. PHOTOGRAPHER: LEE W. WALDREP, Ph.D.

Compiled is a beginning list of traditional and nontraditional career paths (see the sidebar "The Careers of an Architect"). Katherine S. Proctor, former director of student services at the University of Tennessee, shares her perspective:

> For an individual interested in the career of architecture, the possibilities
> are endless. I have seen students graduate and become registered
> architects, professional photographers, lawyers, bankers, business
> owners, interior designers, contractors and artists. The education is so
> broad with a strong liberal arts base, that it provides a firm foundation
> for a wide array of exploration. This comes from the content of the
> curriculums, but also from the methodology. The design studio, which is
> the core of the curriculum, provides a method to take pieces of intellectual
> information and apply it within the design process. The movement from
> thinking to doing is powerful. The ability to integrate hundreds of pieces
> of information, issues, influences and form and find a solution is a skill
> that any professional needs to solve problems, whether they are building
> issues or life issues.
>
> KATHERINE S. PROCTOR, FCSI, CDT, AIA

THE CAREERS OF AN ARCHITECT

TRADITIONAL FIRM

Draftsperson
Intern
Junior Designer
Model Maker
Principal
Project Architect
Senior Designer
Staff Architect

OTHER EMPLOYMENT SETTINGS

Architectural Illustrator
Corporate Architect
Facilities Architect
Public Architect
University Architect

ARCHITECTURAL EDUCATION

Academic Dean/Administrator
Architectural Historian
Professor
Researcher

ART AND DESIGN

Architectural Photographer
Art/Creative Director
Artist
Clothing Designer
Exhibit Designer
Filmmaker

Furniture Designer
Graphic Artist/Designer
Industrial/Product Designer
Interior Designer
Landscape Architect
Lighting Designer
Museum Curator
Set Designer
Toy Designer
Web Designer

SCIENCE AND TECHNICAL

Building Pathologist
Cartographer
Civil Engineer
Computer System Analyst
Construction/Building Inspector
Illuminating Engineer
Marine Architect
Structural Engineer

CONSTRUCTION

Carpenter
Construction Manager
Construction Software Designer
Contractor
Estimator
Fire Protection Designer
Land Surveyor
Project Manager
Real Estate Developer

RELATED PROFESSIONAL

Architectural Critic

City Manager

Environmental Planner

Golf Course Architect

Lawyer

Preservationist

Product Manufacturer Representative

Property Assessor

Public Official

Real Estate Agent

Urban Planner

Writer

Design-Build Teaming

RANDALL J. THARP, R.A.

Senior Vice-President and Director of Construction

A. Epstein and Sons International, Inc.

Chicago, Illinois

Why and how did you become an architect?

❭ In my late elementary years, I took several art classes outside of school and became very interested in drawing. When I was in middle school my family moved to England, where I took technical drawing classes that I really enjoyed and excelled in. We often had projects in which we would draft plans and then build the design in our wood shop or metal shop classes.

During my time in Europe, I had the opportunity to visit and see many great buildings and places of architectural history, including the Hagia Sophia, the Parthenon, Pompeii, and ancient Roman sites in England. All of these experiences set the background for an interest in architecture that was encouraged by an architect in our neighborhood. I took all of the architectural design and drawing classes in high

school and made the decision to pursue a career in architecture when I went into college.

Why and how did you decide on which school to attend for your architecture degree? What degree(s) do you possess?

❭ During high school I lived in suburban Detroit, Michigan. In talking with neighbors and teachers, I kept hearing that the University of Michigan was one of the best schools in the country. I also learned from a neighbor architect that Michigan was the only college in the state that offered a master of architecture program. While a sophomore in high school I decided to attend the University of Michigan to obtain a degree in architecture and become an architect. I applied to Michigan only and earned my bachelor of science (architecture), master of architecture and master of business administration degrees.

What has been your greatest challenge as an architect?

❭ My greatest challenge has been to bridge the gap between two sides of the building industry where those involved have traditional adversarial roles: architect and contractors. Having spent my entire

Alberto Culver R&D Facility, Melrose Park, Illinois. Architect: A. Epstein and Sons International, Inc. PHOTOGRAPHER: JEFF GUERRANT, JEFF GUERRANT PHOTOGRAPHY.

career in design-build I am both and thus break down other preconceived notions about these two. Some see me as an architect that does construction, while others want to view me as a contractor who tries to do design. Although I am a licensed architect, I really am neither architect nor contractor. I view my role as an integration of both that creates a synergistic result.

Why did you pursue the dual degree—master of architecture/master of business administration during your graduate studies?

❯ In my last year as an undergraduate in the architecture program at Michigan I really began to understand the many facets to being an architect and that not all architects were the same. I also realized I was not going to be a designer.

From knowing architects that had different responsibilities, I realized that if I added business skills to my strong technical skills that I could really be an asset to another architect that was more focused

on design. At the same time Michigan began offering a formal joint M.Arch./M.B.A. program. I took the GMAT and applied to both the business and architecture graduate programs and was accepted.

I was completely surprised to see how my architectural skills applied to business, especially in the areas of marketing and strategic planning. The problem seeking, programming, and solution development skills I had learned in architecture school fit right in and I soon found out that I was a very good designer of marketing plans and business plans. I really believe that my business education helped me both find my niche and give me unique skills that have provided many opportunities in my career.

How and why did you pursue a career path more related to construction than traditional architecture?

❯ The salary is better.

Also, I felt that my skills, especially my business skills, were much more valued within a construc-

Iscar/Ingersoll Manufacturing/ Office Building, Cherry Valley, Illinois. Architect: A. Epstein and Sons International, Inc. PHOTOGRAPHER: STEINKAMP-BALLOGG PHOTOGRAPHY.

tion environment than in a traditional architectural practice. Within a construction organization my design and architectural technical skills were more unique and the more business orientation of the construction industry offered me greater opportunity to use these talents from day one. Compared to architecture firms, construction and development firms were much more forward thinking and immediately saw opportunities to put me in the front line with clients and leading projects because of my unique skill set.

What is design-build teaming?

❯ Design-build is an integration of the design and construction process that breaks away from the traditional design-bid-build process.

Design-build involves the collaboration of all parties from the onset of the project. The construction professionals, the designers, engineers, and the architects all participate in jointly understanding the client requirements for quality, cost, and schedule and the impact of design decisions and solution alternates are evaluated by all parties, using their combined expertise and skills to arrive at a final solution that best meets all three of these basis client requirements as well as the specific details of the project.

What are your primary responsibilities and duties?

❯ My primary responsibility is as the leader of Epstein's Construction Group, where I work with 35 construction professionals in our home office and at project jobsite locations around the country. In this capacity I am focused on participating with others to secure new business, maintain client relationships, identify new talent, and develop current staff, overseeing administration for the group and reviewing project and group financial performance on a continuing basis.

For several clients, I am the project executive or principal in charge. In these cases I assure that our project execution plans are being implemented and our clients' requirements are being met.

I also serve on Epstein's management committee and am a member of the corporate board of directors. In these roles my primary responsibilities are to develop and plan strategic and tactical corporate plans to implement and manage across the firm.

What is the most/least satisfying part of your job?

❭ I love the opportunity to hire young graduates out of architecture and engineering programs or early in their careers. It is rewarding to see them succeed and to know that I have played a role in teaching them, providing them opportunities, and enhancing their work experience. I also find it exciting and rewarding to be involved from the initial stages of meeting a prospective client and following the process from proposal through sale, project kick-off, design, documents completion,

groundbreaking, and on through construction and occupancy.

The least satisfying is the administrative work necessary within a larger organization. All of it is critically necessary but generating and reviewing reports, sitting in update meetings, and handling bureaucratic issues is simply not stimulating.

Who or what experience has been a major influence on your career?

❭ When I was at the University of Michigan as a student I had the opportunity to have a work-study position at the University Planner and University Architect handling a variety of responsibilities. I gained a better understanding of the interaction of all the parties around the table and learned how the process of getting a project from needs assessment through program, concept and to a final design was much more valuable than most of what I was learning in the classroom or studio. I was an outside observer of the process and could see it for what it was.

Albertsons Freezer Expansion, Franklin Park, Maryland. Architect: A. Epstein and Sons International, Inc. PHOTOGRAPHER: STEINKAMP-BALLOGG PHOTOGRAPHY.

Green Building Pioneer

LYNN N. SIMON, AIA, LEED AP

President, Simon & Associates, Inc. – Green Building Consultant

San Francisco, California

Why and how did you become an architect?

❭ I became an architect because I believe that architects can effect positive change in the built environment. The universities where I studied embraced philosophies that emphasized environmental issues.

Why and how did you decide on which school to attend for your architecture degree? What degree(s) do you possess?

❭ I hold a bachelor of arts in architecture from University of California at Berkeley. I had always wanted to attend UC Berkeley since I was a small child. Both the beauty of northern California and the liberal university setting were appealing. I attended graduate school at the University of Washington in Seattle because of my interest in healthcare architecture. Seattle and University of Washington were a good match for my own personal values. The program offered the academic support and flexibility I was looking for while earning my master of architecture.

What has been your greatest challenge as an architect?

❭ As an architect, my greatest challenge is continually running a thriving business.

What is a "green building consultant" and how did you become involved?

❭ A green building consultant is one who uses a practical and collaborative approach to advance sustainable and healthy building design and construction practices.

▼ Kolligan Library, University of California, Merced, Merced, California. Architect: Skidmore, Owings, & Merrill LLP. PHOTOGRAPHER: MARK MAXWELL.

Aerial view, University of California—Merced Campus, Merced, California. PHOTOGRAPHER: MARK MAXWELL.

I was committed to exploring how architects can change society for the better, initially focusing on healthcare architecture. As a graduate student I wrote my thesis on "healthy buildings." Through my graduate studies, I realized my true interest in environmentally responsible buildings that are healthy for both humans and the planet. The most formative experience for me was serving as the national president of the American Institute of Architecture Students. For my platform, I chose "Sustainability."

As a consultant, what are your primary responsibilities and duties?

❯ My primary responsibilities and duties include strategic planning, workshop facilitation, design consultation, LEED project management, specifications review and materials research, guidelines and educational resource development, and presentations and trainings.

What is a LEED Accredited Professional (AP) and why is it important?

❯ A LEED accredited professional (AP) means one has the fundamental knowledge of green building and the LEED rating system developed by the U.S. Green Building Council. A LEED accredited professional will demonstrate experience in the following areas:

- Tenure in green building and construction industry knowledge

- Familiarity with documentation process for LEED certified project

- Knowledge of LEED credit intents, requirements, submittals technologies, and strategies within their discipline

- Practical experience working with multiple design disciplines

- Understanding of life cycle cost and benefits of LEED

- Familiarity with LEED resources and processes

The accreditation provides recognition for those who have made a commitment to work in green building.

What is the most important quality or skill as a consultant?

❯ The most important qualities or skills required for a consultant is communication and the ability to work well with others.

Who or what experience has been a major influence on your career?

❯ Thus far in my career, major influences include serving as national president of the American Institute of Architecture Students (AIAS) and working for and in association with the U.S. Green Building Council. As well, I have been influenced by the commitment and passion of the many people I have met and worked with through the years in the Green Building arena.

A Creative Career Transformation

ERIC TAYLOR, ASSOCIATE AIA

Photographer

Taylor Design & Photography, Inc.

Fairfax Station, Virginia

Why and how did you become an architect?

❯ I decided on an architectural career to combine my visual/creative side with technical aptitudes. I went to college, worked in intern positions in high school and college to learn about the work world of architecture; during my architectural career I worked in variety of firms—a 3-person design firm to 150-person (A&E) firm.

Why and how did you decide on which school to attend for your architecture degree? What degree(s) do you possess?

❯ I looked for a school that combined a strong design direction with the practical side. I wanted to graduate with practical skills along with

Corporate Interior, Fairfax, Virginia. PHOTOGRAPHER: ERIC TAYLOR, ASSOCIATE AIA. PHOTO © ERICTAYLORPHOTO.COM.

Potomac Tower, Fairfax, Virginia. Architect: I. M. Pei. PHOTOGRAPHER. ERIC TAYLOR, ASSOCIATE AIA. PHOTO © ERICTAYLORPHOTO.COM.

design sensibilities. I chose Syracuse University and graduated with a bachelor of architecture degree. I also studied photography as a sideline.

Why and how did you transition from being an architect to an architectural photographer?

❭ I had 17 successful years in architecture, many as a senior project architect and designer. My work included office buildings; commercial, municipal, and educational buildings; and interior design. But I came to a crossroads in my career—I could join another firm, start my own firm, or try something new. I chose something new.

I had always loved photography and had coordinated the photo programs at the firms where I had worked. I realized I could bring something to architectural photography that was unique: a true understanding of architecture from inside the profession. So my new direction was set. Because I lacked some of the technical expertise, I attended photography school to learn about professional lighting and camera systems. I built up a photo portfolio by shooting projects on specification and by photographing the projects of architect friends. Then I got serious about marketing and launched my new career.

How are the two disciplines the same? Different?

❭ The skills needed for success in architecture are parallel to those needed for success in architectural photography—ability to communicate visually and verbally, ability to visualize three-dimensionally, ability to distill a set of requirements to their essence, ability to arrive at solutions that answer these requirements, ability to entertain others.

Both disciplines require an attention to detail and the ability to visualize what does not yet exist. The goal of architecture is to arrive at a three-dimensional solution to a complex set of criteria. The goal of architectural photography is to analyze that three-dimensional solution and find a compelling two-dimensional representation of it that explains the three-dimensional reality. While architectural design deals with form, volume, color, texture, perspective, etc., the essence of photography is light and its effect on the rendering of those design elements. I believe an understanding of design concepts, design elements, and construction methods enhances architectural photography.

When provided a commission, how do you approach the assignment?

❯ First, I meet with client to discuss the scope of the assignment—exteriors, interiors, and/or aerials, quantity of images expected, and so on. Next, we discuss the intended uses of the photography—display prints, award submissions, in-house newsletters, website, etc., the design concept that the designer wants to be sure is expressed in the photos, the logistics of access to the space, scheduling, budget. From there, I scout the location to assess the equipment needs. Finally, I schedule assistants and do the photography.

What has been your greatest challenge as a photographer?

❯ Predicting the weather! It is difficult to schedule exterior shoots very far in the future since it is weather dependent. Other than that, it has the same challenge as starting any new business, developing a client base. On the technical side, photographing interiors under mixed lighting—day-lighting, fluorescent, incandescent—was a new challenge. But on the creative side, I feel like I have been preparing for this my whole life.

What is most/least satisfying about your work as a photographer?

❯ Most satisfying is creating dynamic images and having clients excited about them; being involved with a wide diversity of building types, design, and construction; in addition, I no longer have to wait a year or two to see the results of my efforts!

I do miss the complexity of the design problem-solving process, but it is outweighed by the satisfaction I gain from photography.

Do you still consider yourself to be an architect?

Yes, but more now as it influences my photography and my understanding of the buildings and construction that I photograph.

Who or what experience has been a major influence on your career?

❯ In college, I became aware of the value of strong visual presentation. Good design professors required it, and I learned that dynamic graphics and

Fredericksburg Academy, Fredericksburg, Virginia. Architect: Cooper Carry & Associates. PHOTOGRAPHER: ERIC TAYLOR, ASSOCIATE AIA. PHOTO © ERICTAYLORPHOTO.COM.

photography were essential tools to explain and ultimately gain the support of others for a design solution. As an architectural photographer, I see myself as an aid to others in their marketing efforts, by providing dynamic images of their design work.

Why still photography vs. video or interactive images?

❯ While video allows a broad-sweep understanding of a building or space, I see architectural still photography as visual editing. In this way, still compositions present the built environment in an edited version, so others will see the inherent concept, form, composition, texture, color, balance, and beauty that I see.

Ronald Reagan Washington National Airport, Washington, DC. Architect: Cesar Pelli & Associates. PHOTOGRAPHER: ERIC TAYLOR, ASSOCIATE AIA. PHOTO © ERICTAYLORPHOTO.COM.

More Than Just Architecture

CASIUS PEALER, J.D.

Assistant General Counsel (Real Estate)

District of Columbia Housing Authority

Washington, DC

Cofounder/Co-Editor

ArchVoices

Why and how did you become an architect?

❯ I chose to go to architecture school because it was the most challenging, mind-expanding, and creative experience I could find as an undergraduate. When I graduated from school, I used those same criteria to select a variety of jobs and experiences—representing architecture students nationally, driving a taxi, working construction, volunteering for the Peace Corps, going to law school, and helping to develop mixed-income communities. All of those positions allowed me to be creative, and some actually required it. They were all challenging, and I learned a great deal about myself and about the world around me. As long as I can continue in those situations, I will always be becoming an architect.

Why and how did you decide on which school to attend for your architecture degree? What degree(s) do you possess? Why did you pursue an additional degree in law?

❯ I received a five-year bachelor of architecture from Tulane University, meaning that I started my professional degree program as a 17-year old, right out of high school. While I treasure the intensity of the five-year programs, I think that a great many individuals would be better served by obtaining

PHOTOGRAPHER: KEITH WASHINGTON. PHOTO © D.C. HOUSING AUTHORITY.

a liberal arts undergraduate degree followed by a true professional master degree.

I was fortunate in that I pursued a double major in philosophy, which gave me more experience reading and writing than my architectural education. As for my school choice, I was fortunate to receive a scholarship to attend what was otherwise my last choice school. Tulane University and New Orleans were both excellent places to study architecture and life; I could not have chosen a better place to study.

Regarding my decision to go to law school upon my return from the Peace Corps I looked at working in architecture firms. But I would have had to do entry level work in order to get licensed, which would not immediately recognize my other skills and experiences. So I decided that I could perhaps serve the profession better by working on public policy regarding design and construction. When I spoke to professionals who had gone to public policy school, they often said that they wished they had gone to law school either instead or in addition to policy school. So, I sought out joint degree programs in law and public policy, preferably with a focus on affordable housing and community development. The University of Michigan Law School has a unique legal clinic where students work with neighborhood nonprofit organizations in Detroit to develop affordable housing. I was fortunate to be accepted, and found positive opportunities that drew me into the private sector, representing public agencies, before completing the policy degree.

You recently completed a law degree from the University of Michigan Law School. Why law? How will you combine your law degree with your previous architecture degree?

❯ The most interesting questions in both architecture and law are the difficult and complex ones.

In architecture, we often have to resolve the intersection of conflicting systems, whether technical systems or important design elements. This resolution has to happen in a way that fits with and ideally reinforces the underlying structure of each system as a whole. The same is true of the most complex issues in law. Typically, there are at least two competing interests, but each carries with it larger concerns about policy and justice and they must be resolved in a way that aligns with and ideally reinforces the underlying concerns. We also want legal decisions to inform and help others to predict the outcomes of future situations and conflicts. Although my work is transactional—meaning primarily that I do not go to court or have an adversarial relationship with my clients' business partners—there are still competing interests and larger public policies to consider as they affect specific development projects. In the end though, I see my formal legal career as a piece of a larger puzzle that will eventually more directly engage design and environmental concerns on a daily basis, supported by my knowledge and understanding of the law and legislative process.

How is architecture and law the same? different?

❯ The obvious similarity is that both are licensed professions, with important duties to the public regarding public safety and welfare, a rigorous licensure process, and ongoing ethical obligations. Both professions have significant challenges from other fields, such as construction managers for architect and accountants and accounting firms for lawyers. Both have concerns about specialty licensing, though the legal profession has found a way to coexist and even co-opt some of these efforts, while the architecture profession strongly resists efforts by healthcare architects for a recognized specialty credential. Both

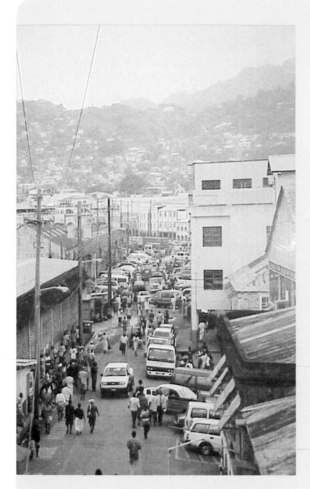

Typical Street in the Capital City, Kingstown, St. Vincent, West Indies. PHOTOGRAPHER: CASIUS PEALER, J.D.

professions also have challenges increasing their racial and ethnic diversity in the ranks of practitioners as well as in visible leadership positions, though the legal profession's licensing requirements mean that far more diverse graduates go on to become licensed than in architecture.

One important difference, though, is the extent to which professionals in each field have become ubiquitous and are relied on for advice beyond the specific issues on which they are experts. There are a variety of possible reasons for this, and I certainly believe that architects could be at least as good counselors as lawyers are. But an underlying challenge for architecture's relevance is the view that architects are best served by being a small group of elite practitioners rather than a large corps of professionals. Architects take pride in repeating statistics about how just half of all students who start in architecture graduate, and how just half of graduates go on to become licensed. However, as a result of these statistics, the Washington, DC, chapter of the American Bar Association is larger than the entire national membership of the American Institute of Architects. There are many small and medium-sized cities in the country with just one or two architects, while even the smallest small towns have a local country lawyer, even in a world with increasingly global law firms. I believe that the breadth and expanse of the legal profession is the main source of its power. As long as architects individually want to be big fish in a small pond, the profession as a whole will continue to be a small pond on a large planet.

What has been your greatest challenge during your professional career?

❯ Finding purpose and community within an entirely different culture and in unfamiliar surroundings has been my greatest challenge since (or before) my graduation from Tulane. Living in a rural agricultural village in a developing country as a volunteer with the Peace Corps, I often felt there was so much that they needed that anything I did would be helpful. Other times, I felt there was so much they needed that nothing I could do would ever matter at all.

Earlier in your career you served as a volunteer with the U.S. Peace Corps in the West Indies. Why did you choose to volunteer? and please provide details of your experience.

❯ I volunteered for the Peace Corps and was assigned to an island in the West Indies to teach carpentry to teenagers who did not get into the equivalent of high school. I also worked with another volunteer teaching small business skills to a group of artists and craftspeople on the island, forming a professional association of sorts. We helped this association to create the first e-commerce website on the island, selling products directly to consumers as far away as Japan. Additionally, I helped coordinate a SAT prep class for students hoping to attend colleges in the U.S., UK, and Canada. Finally, I made a number of good friends in, and learned a lot from, the Rastafarian community on the island. I continue to perform Peace Corps service here at home, by sharing my experiences and deepening Americans' understanding of the Caribbean islands.

I feel that service to your country is important, whether you do it abroad through the military or Peace Corps, or in the United States through AmeriCorps, Teach for America, or some other organization. I wanted to learn a lot about another culture and to have to question—and thus solidify—my own values and personality. Also, I wanted to make lifelong friends of people with different interests and perspectives, but a similar commitment to and faith in the world.

Where do you work now and what are your responsibilities?

❯ The DC Housing Authority provides affordable housing and community development to some of the neediest families in the city. I work as a real estate attorney for the housing authority, drafting documents and structuring financing for some of the most complex development deals in the country resulting in mixed-income communities. In addition, I have taken on the

Typical Street in the Capital City, Kingstown, St. Vincent, West Indies.
PHOTOGRAPHER: CASIUS PEALER, J.D.

role of helping the housing authority to improve the energy efficiency of its developments and to increase the health of our residents. In 2006, the City Council passed legislation that made DC among the first cities in the U.S. to require private developers to meet green building standards. Because of the mixed-income nature of many of our development projects, we have to ensure that private developers building public housing comply with the requirements and overall intent of this innovative law. Additionally, our agency has taken the initiative to finance $26 million in energy efficiency improvements for our existing buildings, which will pay for themselves over approximately 12 years. Doing this work in particular has helped keep me close to design and construction issues, at the same time as I continue to learn about the development and financing process necessary to enable architects to design affordable housing.

What is the most/least satisfying part of your career?

❯ The most satisfying part of my career has been the year I worked as a taxi cab driver in New Orleans. While being a cab driver might sound like a ridiculous job, I was interested in understanding more about how the general public talks about architecture, the built environment, and cities in general. This position allowed me access to a wide variety of people. I spent all day driving through the city with my windows down, I had a company car, and I frankly made more money than any of my classmates were making at the time.

It turns out that people of all types and backgrounds really do talk about architecture and the built environment all the time. It took me a while to understand this because I was used to hearing architects talk about architecture. I had thought that I might need to ask specific questions or to have a questionnaire perhaps—but I finally realized that all I needed to do was to learn to listen better.

What I learned was that people most appreciate things like material and color and symbolism, and usually in quite sophisticated ways—though architects are often uncomfortable with symbolism, color, and material, in approximately that order. My cab fares' appreciation of the built environment was also much more holistic than many architects' simply because we have learned to work within defined professional boundaries and to focus on a client's project at the inevitable expense of context. But the people I talked with didn't make a distinction between the street and the street lighting and the landscaping and the handrail and the building itself.

Who or what experience has been a major influence on your career?

❯ Working full time for 10 months in an architecture firm while taking a semester off early during my professional degree was quite influential. Because the firm experienced incredible growth while I was there, I participated in more meaningful roles than a typical second-year student. When I went back to school, I looked at architecture and at my education very differently. In some ways, I realized that there was much we were not being taught or even told about. I became very involved in the AIAS as a means of seeking more direct professional contact for my classmates and me. I also realized that school was a unique opportunity to explore the full boundaries of design and my design work became much less constrained.

Vincentian Family, Mesopotamia, St. Vincent, West Indies. PHOTOGRAPHER: CASIUS PEALER, J.D.

Like many people, I encourage students to integrate practical knowledge into their educational experience. This encouragement often takes the form of exhortations to get out in the "real world," contrasted with the cloistered academic environment of colleges and universities. But there is a "real world" apart from the open-plan offices of most design firms as well. The vast majority of the world lives outside the developed world and in significant states of poverty. Having some personal experience traveling and ideally living in a community where the entire academic versus practitioner dichotomy is itself quite academic—in other words, the real world—will have a significant influence on your career.

What are your 5-year and 10-year career goals?

❭ I want to be doing work that, if I were not doing it, would not be getting done. That is a paraphrase of an anonymous quote about success that I heard years ago. I want to be surrounded by good and creative people, working hard to implement big ideas. I want my work to profoundly affect at least a few other people, and I want there to be a tangible, physical element to the result. I want the freedom to write for others, either as part of my salaried job or as an extracurricular activity. And I want to be open to new opportunities and challenges as they present themselves. Incidentally, these are life goals, but I see my career as in service to fulfilling my life.

Conscientious Real Estate Developer

AHKILAH Z. JOHNSON

Chief of Staff Investment Services

Cherokee Investment Partners

East Rutherford, New Jersey

Why and how did you become an architect?

❯ I thought I wanted to be an engineer for most of my adolescent years, a result of my strong mathematical skills and my mother's lobbying. My high school, a polytechnic high school, placed a strong emphasis on engineering and calculus, and differential equations. There was a creative side in me that grew tired of math and its equations. I stumbled upon architecture as it masqueraded in an elective AutoCAD class I took. Immediately I fell in love. I can honestly say architecture was my high school and college sweetheart.

▼ Camden Redevelopment Project, Camden, New Jersey. Developer: Cherokee Northeast, LLC. ILLUSTRATION COURTESY OF ERNEST BURDEN III, OSSINING, NY.

Why and how did you decide on which school to attend for your architecture degree? What degree(s) do you possess?

❯ When I graduated from high school, I wanted to attend a historically black college and university (HBCU). There are very few architecture schools throughout the United States, let alone architecture schools at a HBCU. I really did not have many options.

I chose the bachelor of architecture at Howard University because of its strong reputation for excellence, its location in a major city, and its record for graduating black architects. I also relished its proximity to my mother's house in Baltimore.

I chose to pursue a master of science in real estate development and finance because I felt like developers had more control over the built environment than architects. I wanted to possess the control that developers had so that I could create conscientious developments that respected social and

Meadowlands Golf Redevelopment Project, Bergen County, New Jersey. Developer: Cherokee Northeast, LLC. ILLUSTRATION COURTESY OF TOM SHALLER, ROBERT A. M. STERN ARCHITECTS.

environmental communities. I selected Columbia University because of its location in the great laboratory known as New York City and because it offered a superior master's program.

What has been your greatest challenge during your professional career?

❯ The biggest challenge in my professional career has been my being. As a double-minority in a white male dominated profession, I am constantly subject to challenges and difficulties. The absence of role models and mentors who look like me and understand my background has truly had an adverse affect on my career development.

Certainly, many of my challenges have not all been direct derivatives of my gender and racial composite. However, professional careers are cultivated by three distinct functions: skill, knowledge, and relationships. It is my opinion that of these three functions, the relationships component has a significant and disproportionate affect on career development. As the saying goes, "it's not what you know, it's who you know."

Nonetheless, I think I have and will continue to adapt to the absence of role models and mentors as I continue my career. As I have in the past, I will encounter individuals who will have some positive significance on my career. I will continue to learn and strive for excellence. I hope one day to fill the void in my career by mentoring a young African American female who aspires to a career in architecture or finance.

Why did you pursue the additional degree—master of science in real estate development?

❯ I enjoyed my career as an architect, but I did not feel like I knew how to put together a building from a construction standpoint. I understood construction documents and building systems, but I did not truly understood how buildings are put together. I chose to pursue a career in construction management because I thought it would make me a better architect. I enjoyed my time in construction management and I certainly feel like it helped me to better hone my skill set in the built environment. Yet I wanted more.

Meadowlands Golf Redevelopment Project, Bergen County, New Jersey. Developer: Cherokee Northeast, LLC. ILLUSTRATION COURTESY OF TOM SHALLER, ROBERT A. M. STERN ARCHITECTS.

As a real estate developer I am able to address all of my passions for creating built environments. I am now able to have a commanding impact on the type of developments that are created, while being true to the idealistic architect in my soul. I can create environments that are examples of sensitive and good design and planning.

How and why did you pursue a career path more related to development than traditional architecture?

❯ As an architect I felt like developers and development companies had control and ultimate say on what was to be built. However, I did not think that these individuals understood nor appreciated the impact development has on our society.

What is real estate development?

❯ Real estate development is the creation of communities and the repositioning of land or buildings into a higher or better use. Real estate development intends to capitalize on underutilized land by developing new land uses that are marketable and profitable. Real estate development is a long process that commingles multiple disciplines (engineering, architecture, planning finance, marketing, law, and environmental impact) to create an end product.

What are your primary responsibilities and duties? What are "deal analysis, due diligence, and asset management"?

❯ Cherokee Northeast is the capital disbursement arm for a major private equity firm called Cherokee Investment Partners. Cherokee Investment Partners raises funds from large groups, mainly pension and insurance funds, to invest in the redevelopment of brownfield sites throughout the United States and Western Europe.

As an employee of Cherokee Northeast my primary focuses are deal analysis, due diligence, and asset management. A *deal* is development project that is in conceptual or schematic stages. *Deal analysis* is the process of reviewing deals that are in the pipeline. As developers we are constantly chasing new deals and preparing for placement of capital investments. Thus, we are constantly reviewing the feasibility and positioning of prospective deals.

Due diligence is the internal review process of a site or a potential deal prior to the act of acquiring land and developing it as a project.

Asset management consists of managing the ongoing development of projects we currently have in our portfolio.

What is the most/least satisfying part of your job?

❭ The least satisfying part of my job is having to sacrifice ideals for budget purposes. It seems like there is always a case for value engineering in the building industry. As an architect I noticed that designs and building materials were constantly being changed to accommodate needs and wants for smaller budgets. It seems we cut and skim all kinds of important elements, be they functional or aesthetic, to save a buck or two.

Nonetheless, when faced with the reason why I choose a career in development over a career in architecture, I sometimes reason that the practice of architecture differs so greatly from the study of architecture. Architecture when studied is a mixture of practical and theoretical ideals—emphasis is placed on design and function as a couple. In contrast, the practice of architecture is dictated by money and a developer's pro forma bottom line.

Who or what experience has been a major influence on your career?

❭ Of course, the experience of attending undergraduate school and graduate school had a major influence on my career. The influence came from the many professors and professionals I encountered. However, I think the majority of the influence on my career came from the peers I encountered while I was in the different university settings. The abundance and wealth of knowledge available to me while I was in university was key in my career development.

Meadowlands Golf Redevelopment Project, Bergen County, New Jersey. Developer: Cherokee Northeast, LLC. ILLUSTRATION COURTESY OF TOM SHALLER, ROBERT A. M. STERN ARCHITECTS.

Affecting Design Through Policy

LOIS THIBAULT, R.A.

Coordinator of Research

U.S. Architectural and Transportation Barriers Compliance Board (Access Board)

Washington, DC

Why and how did you become an architect?

❯ I started in anthropology, moved to pre-Colombian archaeology, and then transferred into art history. A great teacher on the history of architecture opened my eyes to the built environment and its history as expressed in the city of Boston and environs. As I began to appreciate good design, I began to wonder if I could produce it myself. When my children entered grade school, I decided to try. The experience was terribly difficult for all of us, but somehow it worked out.

Why and how did you decide on which school to attend for your architecture degree? What degree(s) do you possess?

❯ I have a bachelor of architecture; it was the only degree possible at the time/school. The architecture program at Maryland was new and seemed interesting and innovative, and it was affordable for us, as we were Maryland residents.

What has been your greatest challenge as an architect?

❯ Dealing with the dawning realization that I was not a very good designer.

How and why did you pursue a career path in the federal government after a career in private practice? How are the two career paths the same? different?

❯ I spent almost 15 years in commercial and residential practices and found I liked the sub-specialties: historic preservation, accessibility, code compliance. These are undervalued in many offices, which limited my ability to progress, succeed, and advocate for what I believe is important.

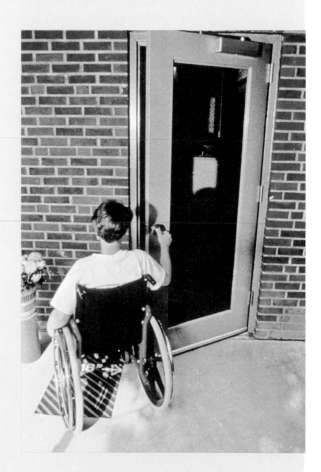

Door opening showing approach space needed for wheelchair.
COURTESY: FAIR HOUSING ACT DESIGN MANUAL (HUD).

Administrative and regulatory skills are more useful in government. Additionally, government benefits and security beat those in practice.

Earlier in your career, you were on staff with the American Institute of Architects (AIA). What did you do for the AIA and how did this experience contribute to your career?

❯ I worked on education issues, both professional development and architecture education, and spent some fascinating time in support of our convention planning (where I met the famous and future-famous). I am proudest of the library of career advisement materials I developed for students considering architecture and of my work—with many others—polishing the IDP. I also did a brief stint with the long-range planning initiative of the AIA.

All of this exposure enabled me to develop a big-picture view of the profession and its members; this, in turn, helped me focus on my own strengths and interests and led me to an opportunity opened up by the passage of the Americans with Disabilities Act (ADA) in 1990.

What are your primary responsibilities and duties with the Access Board?

❯ I oversee my agency's research activities, planning, developing, and commissioning the work that underpins our development of accessible design standards for buildings and facilities. I am also responsible for our rulemaking work on pedestrian facilities in the public right-of-way, and an early interest in acoustics fed by an adjunct professor in the School of Architecture at Maryland has led to an agency initiative aimed at improving listening conditions in classrooms for kids who have hearing loss and related disabilities.

Public Payphone TTY M120.

What is the most/least satisfying part of your position?

❯ Most satisfying is being able to have a substantial effect on my own profession's ability to design accessible buildings and facilities; least satisfying is coping with the effects of political change on our agency's mission.

Who or what experience has been a major influence on your career?

❯ Opportunity knocking . . . I must say, I never planned any of it but I was lucky enough to have been prepared so that I could take advantage of interesting opportunities when they arose. I have had a career of great range and satisfaction, with lots of autonomy. International travel has also influenced my thinking in many ways.

Association Executive

CHRISTOPHER J. GRIBBS, ASSOCIATE AIA

Senior Director, Convention

The American Institute of Architects

Washington, DC

Why and how did you become an architect?

❯ Why? It was a natural outcome of my interests and skills in art, building, and problem solving. How? By going to school, traveling, taking summer jobs related to construction and historic building documentation, and interning for a small firm.

▼ College of Fellows, Salk Institute Laboratory Complex–2003 AIA Convention, La Jolla, California. Architect: Louis I. Kahn. PHOTOGRAPHER: REBECCA LAWSON PHOTOGRAPHY.

Why and how did you decide on which school to attend for your architecture degree? What degree(s) do you possess?

❯ After floundering for a few years following high school, I went to an architecture school with a strong design-focused program. One of several architecture schools in my area, the University of Detroit, Mercy, offered small classes, solid academics, and extensive studio work. I especially enjoyed the learning opportunity afforded each semester to travel and tour architecture in other cities—a short trip each fall to nearby cities, and longer spring trips to more distant locations, including exploration of ancient ruins in Central America. I have a bachelor of architecture, a five-year degree.

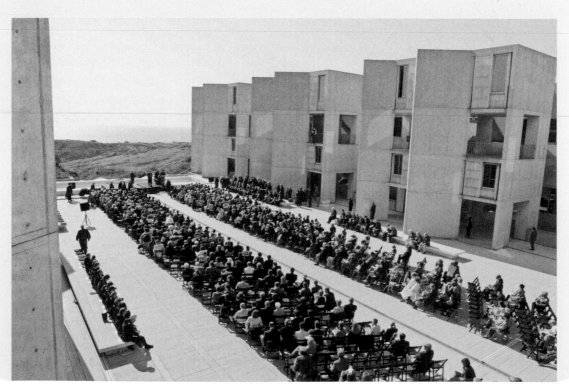

Why and how did you transition from working in architecture to working in an association?

❯ Moving from traditional architectural practice to documentation of historic buildings to association management was very natural, following opportunities as they were presented. Simply stated, moving out of the practice of architecture happened when I was in Washington, DC, between jobs for a one-day educational seminar on historic preservation. I was an active volunteer in the AIA Detroit Chapter as the associate member director, and heard about a position at AIA national headquarters prior to my trip to Washington for the seminar.

I inquired about the position and was offered a quick interview on the day of the seminar. They apparently liked what I had to say and asked if I could return the next day for a more extensive interview. I did and left to return home that afternoon. I returned to Detroit, started a new job in a small, upbeat firm, only to receive a call from the AIA on my third day on the job offering me the position. To say the least, this was very clumsy as

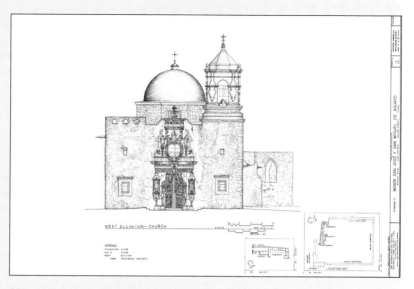

Mission San Jose y San Miguel de Aguayo. Historic American Buildings Survey (HABS), National Park Service, San Antonio, Texas. PHOTOGRAPHER: CHRISTOPHER J. GRIBBS, LIBRARY OF CONGRESS, PRINTS AND PHOTOGRAPH DIVISION, HISTORIC AMERICAN BUILDINGS SURVEY, HABS TX-333.

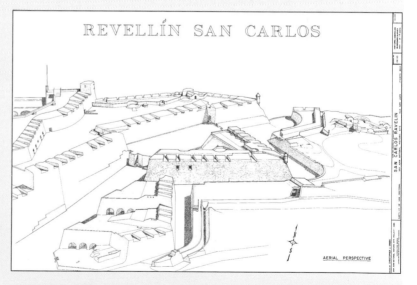

Castillo de San Cristobal, San Carlos Ravelin. Historic American Buildings Survey (HABS), National Park Service, San Juan, Puerto Rico. PHOTOGRAPHER: CHRISTOPHER J. GRIBBS, LIBRARY OF CONGRESS, PRINTS AND PHOTOGRAPH DIVISION, HISTORIC AMERICAN BUILDINGS SURVEY, HABS TX-333.

I had just started the new job and had to immediately tell them I was leaving. Of course, they completely understood the value of the opportunity and wished me the very best of luck.

After graduation, you worked as an architectural technician and supervisory architect with Historic American Buildings Survey (HABS); can you provide details on these experiences and what skills they developed?

❯ The absolute best experiences in my early years were two summers spent working for the HABS. It was a thrill and tremendous challenge to have the opportunity to travel for the summer (and get paid) to measure and draw cool historic buildings. I had the opportunity to travel to San Antonio, Texas, and San Juan, Puerto Rico, to pursue the mission of HABS: preservation through documentation. I feel this was a terrific way to contribute to the lasting memory of America's built environment.

Even today, the thrill is to know the product of those summers will always be part of the permanent collection in the Library of Congress (LOC), information open freely to the public. The drawings my teams produced are now free to download in high-resolution formats from the LOC website. Search on "Mission San Jose y San Miguel de Aguayo, San Antonio, Texas" and "Castillo de San Cristobal, San Carlos Ravelin, San Juan, Puerto Rico" at http://memory.loc.gov/ammem/collections/habs_haer/.

During your tenure with the American Institute of Architects (AIA), you have held a few different positions. Please detail those projects that have been the most worthwhile.

❯ First and foremost, the various positions have afforded me the opportunity to constantly be challenged and to grow. I would not have stayed at the Institute if the work had not been both challenging and rewarding. I have had the great fortune to advance, position to position, within a large organization that affords many opportunities.

Currently I serve as the senior director with chief responsibility for the annual AIA national convention, driving the vision, development, and leadership for all convention initiatives.

For five years I was a director in the Professional Practice Department. I managed partnerships with over 25 allied organizations to develop design tools and award programs, disseminate information, and identify subject matter experts.

For nearly two years I was the managing director of the Professional Practice Department, responsible for 18 staff operating the 23 national committees, the organization's principal source of practice information, expertise, research, and education in architectural practice fields.

What is most/least satisfying about your position?

❯ Actually, in my role today—convention planning for a very large annual event—much of what I do is like live television. Creating all from scratch, we are given a budget and a location (a convention center) in which to hold a performance. A date is set and we have 8 months to assemble on a live 4-day show for 20,000 people. The difference from live television is that we organize nearly 480 events, ranging in size from 25 people to assemblies as large as 3,500 people. The joy comes when I can watch the people walk in, the lights go down, and the speaker takes the stage on cue and delivers a strong and valuable presentation. Even more gratifying is to hear the concluding remarks, applause, and then to see the audience depart in earnest stride to get to their next event.

Do you consider yourself to be an architect?

❯ Yes, in an indirect way, but I often have to catch myself, being introduced as a "trained architect" working for the architects association. Somehow people seem to understand that I do not design anything . . . until I tell them about convention.

Each year the event is held in a different city, so the problem is renewed, the challenge is altered, and the solution unique.

Who or what experience has been a major influence on your career?

❯ Supportive mentors have been the key to my professional success. Seeking and retaining a strong mentor has been absolutely critical to give me the confidence to continue and succeed even in the most difficult of times.

Places and Environments

COURTNEY MILLER-BELLAIRS

Assistant Director/Senior Lecturer

Architecture Program, University of Maryland

College Park, Maryland

Why and how did you become an architect?

❯ Studying architecture seemed like it was the right discipline for me. I excelled at academics and was strong in art; my family encouraged me to obtain a "university education" rather than attending art school. Architecture seemed like a discipline that would be academic and artistic. For me, it was not a question of becoming an architect, but gaining the education of an architect was important. I still do not know what I want to be when I grow up.

Rendezvous Point, watercolor on paper, 17½ × 10½ inches. Location: Cornwall, United Kingdom. ARTIST: COURTNEY MILLER-BELLAIRS.

Gallery, oil on canvas, 24
× 36 inches. Location:
Annapolis, Maryland.
ARTIST: COURTNEY MILLER-
BELLAIRS.

Why and how did you decide on which schools to attend for your architecture degrees? What degree(s) do you possess?

❯ I graduated with a bachelor of science from the University of Maryland. This was my state school and I attended not knowing what my major would be. I was an education major, a graphic design major, and then a drawing/drafting teacher recommended architecture. I thought this might be a good fit. I was delighted to have some direction and worked toward applying to the architecture school as a sophomore. I was admitted to the major and thought this was a good indicator that it was right for me.

For my graduate studies, I was seeking something that was totally different than my undergraduate experience; I graduated with my master of architecture from Yale University. I also knew that Yale was artistic and that there was a "building project" in the first year. I also had a few mentors educated at Yale like Marion Weiss (Weiss/Mandfredi) and Charles Gwathmey.

Having spent 10 years in the United Kingdom, what are differences/similarities in architecture that exist between the United States and United Kingdom?

❯ The architectural education in the UK has a foundation in the arts. Many students study in foundation programs, allowing them to explore for a year (post-secondary-education) in fine art, sculpture, jewelry, product design, ceramics, spatial design, fashion design, etc. Afterwards, they apply to bachelor of arts programs in architecture with an artistic foundation and are able to excel in the discipline. The BA focus in the UK is often conceptual and related to cultural and physical contexts. Without really knowing it, the foundation I was receiving in the first seven years of teaching (post-teaching-fellow as a graduate student) was a mixture of architecture and visual arts/communication.

With respect to practicing architecture, the biggest difference is in the U.S., an architect is responsible for managing consultants who are directly contracted to the architect. In the UK, the clients hire the consultants.

What are your primary responsibilities and duties?

❱ Currently, I coordinate the first design studio (junior level) at the University of Maryland with 54 students, 6 teaching assistants, and a first-time lecturer. I consider the mentoring and strategic roles I play in this position the most important.

As assistant director of the architecture program, I mentor the undergraduate advisors, two additional teaching assistants, and two work scholar students. In addition, I serve as the liaison of the architecture program to various undergraduate university committees. My responsibilities also include orientation and admissions at the undergraduate level.

What is the most/least satisfying part of your career as an artist/lecturer?

❱ As a teacher, most rewarding is both displaying my own creative work in a successful exhibition and seeing my students display their artistic work related to architecture in the design studio or through one of the elective courses I teach. As an artist, knowing that what I am doing is what I am meant to do is extremely satisfying.

As a teacher, in the United States, I feel there has been a tremendous shift since I was a student. The informal boundaries between student and professor have blurred the distinction or the clear boundaries of respect and expectation of student and teacher. In the history of architectural education, the dynamics have at times been extreme. I think students should be willing to take what their teachers say and present, and try it out. Students need to trust that the outcome will be good and that something will be learned in the process. There is a

humbleness associated with being a "lifelong learner." This can be useful for student and teacher.

Why and how did you pursue your art career?

❱ I was awarded a prize for "art and architecture" when I graduated from Yale. With the prize, came a letter from the Andrus family that had provided the award, inviting me to display my paintings in Norfolk, Connecticut. After being in the UK for one year, I took a two-month sabbatical from Koetter Kim and Associates in London to work on the exhibition. I felt what it was like to work as an artist. This felt so right for me that, ever since that

Chapel View, oil on canvas, 48 × 36 inches. ARTIST: COURTNEY MILLER-BELLAIRS.

first exhibition in 1997, I have made it my goal to find a way to paint.

Pursuing a career in art has meant balancing my creative work (painting) with teaching. At times this balance is difficult and overwhelming when there is an exhibition looming. I am always ambitious and like to have new work with each new opportunity.

What has been your greatest challenge as an architect?

❭ Struggling with the idea that the right role for me might not be as an architect in traditional practice.

Do you consider yourself an architect?

❭ I have worked hard to consider myself an artist because my background and preparation to be a "traditional architect" was so strong. I consider myself an artist who cannot separate from my background in architecture.

Who or what experience has been a major influence on your career?

❭ Moving abroad and having more of a chance to do things that were not expected of me has been an influence. In other words, it has taken a lot out of me to try to do something that was not architecture. Because I spent so much of my life studying architecture and providing service to the AIAS, it has been very hard to say to myself, my family, and others that "traditional architecture" has not been for me until now. I do not know what the future holds, but I hope that I make the right choices along a path that is not in my control. The choices are never easy.

I had a drawing professor at Yale, Kelly Wilson, who said to me once, "Courtney, never miss an opportunity to show your work." This comment has lingered and I often repeat it to my students.

What makes you a good teacher/advisor?

❭ I like to tell students about my personal experience as an artist. It is especially valuable to speak about the hard times, when resources, energy, and inspiration seem to be lacking. These are the experiences that are good to speak to students about . . . the ones that let students know you too have been there. Other directives inspire students to go beyond their boundaries and to work until they find the best way forward. These are totally different kinds of conversations. Either way, this kind of interaction with students is a calling.

Exploring the World of Architecture

MARGARET DELEEUW

Marketing Director

Celli-Flynn Brennan Architects & Planners

Pittsburgh, Pennsylvania

Why and how did you become an architect?

❯ I am not an architect! I am the marketing director at an architecture firm. It is important for anyone considering architecture to understand that an architectural degree opens doors across the board. Architecture is truly a multidisciplinary profession, encompassing a wide range of skills and disciplines that can be applied to many fields. As marketing director, I promote the firm's architectural and planning experience in attempt to secure new projects. I have to be knowledgeable about our project history, aware of market conditions, and responsive to specific needs of each of our clients.

Why did you decide to choose the school that you did – University of Maryland?

❯ The University of Maryland is a top-ranking public university. In addition to your GPA, your school's reputation carries a lot of weight for employers. Upon graduation, interviewers were impressed with my degree from Maryland. It was also important to me to attend a large university with a number of other disciplines to explore. I appreciated the course structure that enabled me to gain a strong liberal arts background in addition to studying architecture. Maryland's location is ideal; being close to Washington, DC, and Baltimore, traveling to these cities was easy and convenient. Maryland felt like home with a bustling student body, beautiful campus,

Lightbox Study, Charcoal Rendering by Margaret DeLeeuw at University of Maryland.

and outstanding facilities. Since high school, I had my heart set on studying in Italy, so I was hooked with Maryland's summer abroad program.

My curriculum of the bachelor of science in architecture gave me the flexibility to take classes in many areas during my freshman and sophomore years and then to focus strongly on architecture during the

Junker Center for Student Recreation, Penn State Erie, The Behrend College, Erie, Pennsylvania. Architect: Celli-Flynn Brennan Architects & Planners.

two-year studio sequence. It gave me a strong liberal arts education that is a solid base on any resume.

You have had the opportunity to study abroad to Italy twice during your undergraduate studies. How were these experiences valuable to your education?

❭ Study abroad opened my eyes and mind to the world. Both experiences gave me exposure to different cultures, languages, people, and places and sparked my passion to learn and to travel, which for me will be lifelong pursuits. Architecturally speaking, studying buildings on-site brought lessons I had learned in studio full circle. Travel is a journey that will give anyone a fuller perspective of the world.

Upon graduation, you worked as an architectural intern at RTKL-UK in London, England. Why work abroad? How was in different from working in the United States?

❭ Working abroad was my version of studying abroad while no longer in school. I wanted to ex-

pand my horizons and I knew that immediately after graduation was the time to do it. London is a multinational city so working there meant meeting people from all over the world. It was also a lesson in being independent and resourceful. I went over with little money, no place to live and no friends and I ended up working for a great architectural firm, living happily in a trendy flat, and making many friends who I am still in touch with today.

Presently, you work at the Marketing Director for Celli-Flynn Brennan Architects & Planners, an architectural firm. What do you do and how has your architectural education prepared you?

❭ I am responsible for responding to requests for proposals (RFPs), preparing presentations and writing promotional materials, attending interviews with prospective clients, and managing relations with current clients. In this position I prepare PowerPoint presentations and firm portfolios; my drawing, design, and computer classes gave me strong graphic skills, which are critical for marketing. Because of my architectural education, I *speak the language* of architecture and understand the design process and building construction. My degree has also given me great credibility among architects.

What has been your greatest challenge in this new position?

❯ My greatest challenge is positioning myself in a place where I will be successful in securing leads for the principals of the firm to pursue. This is a matter of developing relationships with key players over time. Celli-Flynn Brennan specializes in education, religious, and historic restoration projects. I maintain a database of college and university administrators, school board members, religious leaders, and more. I also monitor the publications and activity of associations—always on the lookout for ways to get our foot in the door.

What has been the most/least satisfying part of your position?

❯ The most satisfying part of my job is the amount of responsibility I am provided. I see the process of developing a proposal through, from when we receive a letter to when the portfolio goes out the door. The principals then look to me to secure interviews and win jobs. This is challenging but very rewarding when we are successful. As marketing director, I am often the public face of the firm, so I always have to be on my toes, conveying a positive image of the firm.

What are your 5-year and 10-year career goals?

❯ I have come to learn that I am most interested in the "business side" of architecture. My five-year goal is to continue my career in marketing and new business development position in the field of architecture. I would like to attend graduate school to get my M.B.A. Perhaps I will work for a larger firm in the future, become a partner, work for a consulting firm.

Who or what experience has been a major influence on your education/career?

❯ My friends, professors, colleagues, and family have all influenced me. They have listened to my dreams as well as my concerns throughout all of my education and career decisions. Everyone has provided me with their own unique pieces of advice and has supported me along the way.

NOTES

1. Parsons, Frank. (1909). *Choosing a Vocation*. Boston, MA: Houghton Mifflin Company.
2. Pena, William. (1987). *Problem Seeking: An Architectural Programming Primer*. Washington, DC: AIA Press.
3. Beery, Richard. (1984). "Profile of the architect, A psychologist's view," *Review*. Summer 1984, p. 5.
4. Bolles, Richard. (1991). *The Quick Job-Hunting Map*. Berkeley, CA: Ten Speed Press.
5. American Institute of Architects (2008). *Architects Handbook of Professional Practice*. Washington, DC: American Institute of Architects.
6. Powell, C. Randall. (1990). *Career Planning Today*. Dubuque, IA: Kendall/Hunt Publishing Co., p. 42.
7. Covey, Stephen. (1989). *Seven Habits of Highly Effective People*. New York: Fireside.
8. AIA (2006) *Definition of Architect Positions*. Washington, DC: AIA.

5 The Future of the Architecture Profession

*The future is not a result of choices among alternative paths offered by the present, but a place that is **created**—created first in the mind and will, created next in activity. The future is not some place we are going to, but one we are creating. The paths are not to be found, but made, and the activity of making them, changes both the maker and the destination.*

JOHN SCHAAR, Futurist

HAVE YOU EVER TRIED TO PREDICT THE FUTURE? If not, you might determine that such an exercise is not worthwhile after reading the preceding quote. Instead, John Schaar suggests that the future is to be created. Chapter 4 discussed how career designing helps you in launching your career, but what is the future of the architecture profession? To what extent can you prepare for its future? How do you prepare for it? Or how do you create it?

Although it is not the intent of this publication to engage in prognostication, it will provide some topics currently emerging from the profession as it evolves.

◄ Beyeler Foundation Museum, Riehen (Basel), Switzerland. Architect: Renzo Piano. PHOTOGRAPHER: GRACE H. KIM, AIA.

Sustainability

Twenty or so years ago, it was called "energy-conscious design"—the use of natural systems to heat and cool buildings. Now, it is called "sustainability." Green architecture goes beyond the use of natural systems; it is changing the process of designing a building, for example, to eliminate the use of fossil fuels, being aware of the building materials we use, and understanding the impact of architecture on the environment. On your path to becoming an architect, you will want to learn more about sustainability.

To that end, you may wish to become a Leadership in Energy Efficient Design Accredited Professional (LEED AP). As outlined by the Green Building Certification Institute, those credentialed as LEED AP are building industry professionals who have demonstrated a thorough understanding of green building and the LEED® Green Building Rating System™ developed and maintained by the U.S. Green Building Council (USGBC).[1] More students prior to graduation and recent graduates upon graduation are pursuing LEED AP as a credential to help launch their professional careers.

Technology

Twitter, Facebook, email, iPhone, jumpdrive, laptop. You probably know these terms, but architects that have been in the profession for a number of years may not. Over the past 20 years, technology has played an increasing role within the architecture profession. Because of continued advancements, technology will continue to impact architects and the work they do. It is the guess of anybody as to what comes next, but be prepared.

To stay ahead of the technology curve, seek out opportunities to learn how to maximize the technology to your advantage. Certainly, most architecture programs have resources and courses that will assist you, but be proactive. All architecture programs have computer labs with the necessary software and output facilities, but more and more are adding digital fabrication facilities. Students can now plot three-dimensional models of their ideas. However, be cautious, as technology will not design buildings; remember, technology is only a tool.

BIM—Building Information Modeling

Over 30 years ago, it was thought that the advent of computer-aided design (CAD) would eliminate or reduce the need for architects. Of course, the exact opposite happened as CAD and computer technology actually created career opportunities for architects. The practice of architecture was revolutionized as construction drawings were done on the computer, but at the end of the design process. Now, building information modeling (BIM) is the new CAD.

BIM manages the components of building through its life cycle using a three-dimensional, real-time, modeling software. By doing so, it increases productivity during building design and construction. With CAD, the architect would draw a representation of the building on the computer; with BIM, the architect creates a "virtual model" of the building along with all of its components.

Firms are only beginning to use BIM as part of their architectural practice, but the trend is occurring. To be adequately prepared for it, challenge your architecture program to teach it as part of the curriculum. Take the time to learn the software: Autodesk Revit, Bentley Architecture, Graphisoft ArchiCAD, Tekla Structures, and Nemetschek N.A. VectorWorks Architect.

Collaboration

During your education, you may participate in a group design project, but this is rare. Instead, any group projects you have may be for non-design courses or simply to construct a site-context model for a studio project; you will complete most of the projects by yourself. In contrast, almost all projects in practice are the work of a team. Each individual contributes to the overall task.

In practice, teamwork becomes paramount. With respect to earlier topic of BIM and that of IPD, which follows, collaboration is even more important. Thus, to adequately prepare for your future as an architect, seek out opportunities that connect you with others in accomplishing a task. Even challenge a professor to assign a group design project. Or team up with a few studiomates to enter a design competition to develop teamwork or collaboration skills.

Integrated Project Delivery (IPD)

First, what is IPD? Not to be confused with IDP (chapter 3), IPD is Integrated Project Delivery. As outlined in the AIA/AIA California guide, IPD is a project delivery approach that integrates people, systems, and business structures and practices into a process that collaboratively harnesses the talents and insights of all participants to optimize project results, increase value to the owner, reduce waste, and maximize efficiency through all phases of design, fabrication, and construction.[2]

The traditional method has the architect work with the client through to construction documents (CDs). At that point, the CDs are put out to bid by general contractors. From there, the architect and client would select a contractor to build the project. In some cases, the bids would come back from the contractors too high for the project budget or errors might be found in the CDs. With IPD, there is collaboration between the architect and contractor; they team up much earlier in the design process to avoid any issues.

Diversity

Why is diversity important to the future of architecture? It is important because historically, the profession of architecture has lacked diversity especially in the areas of gender and ethnicity (see Chapter 1). More recently, the profession has sought means by which to increase the numbers of women and minorities, but much more still needs to be done. What can you do to encourage others to become architects?

Aside from demographics, diverse experiences, ideas, and lifestyles are also important. To become a true architect, you should be able to appreciate diversity and understand its meaning from the perspective of design. How can you, as an architect, design a project/building for a client with a viewpoint different from your own?

Globalization

Thanks to globalization, the world is shrinking. As a result, the practice of architecture is becoming more global. More U.S. firms are designing projects around the world; some have offices in Beijing, London, Paris, Dubai, and countries throughout the world.

More international students are studying architecture at U.S. institutions, while more students from the United States are studying abroad for a semester as part of their curriculum. In addition, U.S. students are obtaining their degrees from international institutions. Opportunities exist, but do due diligence in learning licensure requirements when your education is from another country.

This trend of globalization will continue. If interested, participate in a study abroad program, learn architecture from around the world, and seek possible employment positions in other countries. Working abroad may quite worthwhile but may prove to be more difficult.

Agent of Social Change

Many current architecture students have a strong desire to pursue a career in architecture not for stature or money but rather to serve as an agent of social change; they specifically state that their career goal is to improve neighborhoods, communities, and cities through design. Why? Does it truly matter? What is important is that these aspiring architects want to change the status quo. They want to give back.

Further proof of such a movement is the popularity of organizations such as Habitat for Humanity International, Architecture for Humanity, Design Corps, and Freedom by Design™, a new community service program of the American Institute of Architecture Students (AIAS). Do you wish to be an agent of social change? If so, become involved with an issue that impacts our society. Change the world.

Distance Education/Learning

Aside from the preceding subjects, another topic worthy of consideration is distance education/learning; it is a current form of pedagogy becoming more prevalent in all forms of education. The Boston Architectural College launched the first online, low-residency distance master of architecture, allowing students in the program to work full-time where they live and work while studying through online courses; students need not relocate but need to come to Boston for intensive study days each semester.

As an architect, you may need continuing education to maintain licensure or AIA membership. Instead of attending in-person conferences, you can participate in online webinars or listen to available podcasts. Some architecture programs also provide certain continuing education courses online.

Undoubtedly, terms or issues related to the future have been omitted. If so, it was not done intentionally, but rather because no one can truly predict the future. And finally, to adequately prepare for the future of architecture, consider reading *The New Architect: A New Twist on the Future of Design* by James P. Cramer and Scott Simpson.

Aside from the trends listed in the sidebar, Cramer and Simpson state the *Next Architect* must develop excellent "clientship" skills, the ability to deal effectively with multiple decision makers simultaneously, many of whom have conflicting goals. But how do you develop this new set of workplace skills? Listen!

THE NEXT ARCHITECT: A NEW TWIST ON THE FUTURE OF DESIGN [3]

James P. Cramer and Scott Simpson

TRANSFORMING TRENDS

Integrated, Collaborative Design
Design-Build Dominates
Globalization Comes Home
Talent Shortage
BIM Technology Sets a New Standard
Demographics Are Destiny

Productivity and Performance
The Power of Branding
Fast Architecture
Designing the "Design Experience"
Going Green
Life Cycle Design
High Definition Value
Strategic Optimism

What do you see as the future for the architecture profession?

❯ I see a strong future for the profession of architecture as long as architects listen to the needs of clients and to the voices of people trained in architecture who do not necessarily practice architecture.

H. Alan Brangman, AIA, University Architect, Georgetown University

❯ The architecture profession is being challenged in ways similar to other professions. The role of the professional is being questioned in modern society because the public has much greater access to information than before.

To maintain their role as professionals, architects must maintain their role as experts. This challenge grows as buildings and the activities that buildings house become more and more complex. Even in residential construction, new materials and technologies emerge every day. Architects must master the skills necessary to stay abreast of societal, cultural, and technological changes that are part of everyday contemporary life. This is the biggest challenge for architects and the profession today and in the future.

Robert M. Beckley, FAIA, Professor and Dean Emeritus, University of Michigan

❯ The profession will continue to move in an interdisciplinary direction. Architects will need to place themselves at the forefront of major political, environmental, and social issues and become integral in solving problems (through design and policy).

Jessica L. Leonard, Associate AIA, LEED AP, Campus Planner/Intern Architect, Ayers Saint Gross Architects and Planners

❯ Optimistically, I hope that design gains currency in certain areas, such as housing and urban planning; these areas now seem quite formulaic and static.

Douglas Garofalo, FAIA, Professor, University of Illinois at Chicago; President, Garofalo Architects, Inc.

❯ The computer is the single most important development in architecture since the widespread use of steel in construction. The ability to quickly modify plans, model them in accurate three-dimensional settings, and produce a highly integrated set of construction documents is a boon to architectural design and to the construction field.

The global pressures that are pushing green design to the forefront will increase, creating high demand for architects who base their practice on green principles. I feel that green design is not a passing style but essential for all design. There is no other choice.

Nathan Kipnis, AIA, Principal, Nathan Kipnis Architects, Inc.

❯ It is a guaranteed future; since the beginning of time we have constantly built and rebuilt—this will not change. The future five years is extremely strong for young architects because of the pent up demand for new buildings caused by the current economic recession.

John W. Myefski, AIA, Principal, Myefski Cook Architects, Inc.

❯ In broad terms, there are two possible futures for architecture: one where the profession is radically different than it is today and one where the profession does not exist at all. What this means is that this traditionally old man's profession desperately needs creative, articulate, and passionate young people. As a result, I think this is an exciting time to enter the profession, especially for creative, big-picture problem solvers with a serious work ethic.

In the future, the profession of architecture will formally encourage graduates to seek a variety of roles in society, much as the legal profession has done for over 50 years.

Casius Pealer, J.D., Assistant General Counsel (Real Estate), District of Columbia Housing Authority; Cofounder, ARCHVoices

〉 I see a mixed future for the profession, but also the potential for great opportunity. The profession as a whole recognizes that architects at one time had a much greater role in leading and directing the process of conceiving, planning, designing, and constructing the built environment than today and that they ceded much of that leadership to other professionals affiliated with the industry—such as developers, contractors, design-builders, real estate professionals, even business consultants and accounting firms. Most of these are not as well trained and well equipped as architects are with the skill set to lead effectively. Individual architects, firms, and the profession as a whole must be willing to promote their strengths as problem identifiers and problem solvers. If they focus on the products of what they do (drawings, specifications, and, ultimately, buildings) rather than the benefits their solutions provide to clients, then they will be viewed as a commodity. The willingness to take responsibility for the solutions and promoting the benefits of architectural skills can gain back leadership in the process. Architects must take professional responsibility for understanding and creating complete solutions that meet their customers' goals and objectives. For architects that do so, I think the future holds endless opportunity and greater financial rewards than for those who simply want to produce designs and drawings.

Randall J. Tharp, RA, Senior Vice-President, A. Epstein and Sons International, Inc.

〉 The future of the profession will be the insertion of architects into a range of hybrid forms of practice. We are starting to see a return of architects' direct involvement with the craft of building architecture, compared to the period in which they were mainly responsible for designing the drawings and models that a third party built. A number of emerging firms are directly involved in design through construction. The direct link of the computer to the manufacturing process will have dramatic effects on the profession in the future.

Thomas Fowler, IV, AIA, Professor and Director, Collaborative Integrative-Interdisciplinary Digital-Design Studio (CIDS), California Polytechnic State University–San Luis Obispo

〉 For decades, architects have been giving away their responsibilities to create other new professions—elevator, kitchen, code, and color consultants as well as owner's representatives and construction managers. This has whittled away at their role in the process and caused them to become highly specialized in fields such as healthcare or education. Some may argue that this is a result of our litigious society, but I think it also reflects the desire of some architects to create architecture with a capital *A*. Those architects relinquish their responsibilities for writing specifications and following through with construction documents. In some cases, foreign-based production firms are hired to crank out drawings overnight, allowing large firms to further relinquish this responsibility and deliver new buildings to their clients at breakneck speed. While these trends may yield greater profit for large architectural firms and their corporate clients, they seem to diminish the value and integrity architects can bring to a project by questioning the moral and ethical values of the triple bottom line.

I see young architects coming out of school with a renewed interest in craft and the tectonics of construction and with an ever-increasing interest in design-build as well as commercial development. I hope the architectural profession will realize the importance of being generalists and take back the roles and responsibilities that were once integral to doing good architecture.

Grace H. Kim, AIA, Principal, Schemata Workshop, Inc.

❭ The profession will grow more interdisciplinary. The architecture profession has come to encompass the need for greater knowledge of building technology with emphasis on the interconnectedness of building systems throughout the design process.

Ethics relates to the study of thought, reasoning, and judgment. Architects must look more closely at choices that affect their own well being and that of others. The most recent accolades to the Auburn Rural Studio set the path for a more technical, sustainable, yet humane design process. This has infiltrated into many architecture schools and minds of practicing architects.

Patricia Saldana Natke, AIA, Principal and President, Urban Works, Ltd.

❭ Architects must learn that collaboration with a diverse population will drive us into the next hundred years. To create the diversity we all hope for, the profession must continue to strongly reach out to children and young adults and express its own importance. Once the youngest generation begins to understand the role of architects, the more society will appreciate the breadth of our work and responsibility.

F. Michael Ayles, AIA, Principal, Business Development, Antinozzi Associates

❭ Within the foreseeable future, the traditional architect will always have a place. However, the profession as a whole must respond more quickly and responsibly to the needs of clients, society, environment, and global responsibilities. Architects must assume more responsibility and provide stronger leadership. The profession must invest heavily in lifelong learning, expanding and clarifying the role of architecture, and building a greater sense of respect and need for the profession within the public. Individual architects and the profession as a whole must demonstrate leadership and vision to build a better global community.

Clark E. Llewellyn, AIA, Dean, University of Hawaii

❭ In the future, the profession will see more restrictive building and energy codes as well as increased client demands. To meet these challenges, design professionals will need to explore and develop innovative building materials and systems, as well as faster and more efficient methods of documenting designs.

Robert D. Roubik, AIA, LEED AP, Project Architect, Antunovich Associates Architects and Planners

❭ The profession of architecture currently does not reflect the changing dynamics of society, particularly gender and race. The profession must increase the number and visibility of architects who are women and people of color; otherwise, it will become obsolete and irrelevant. It is the responsibility of both the architecture schools and the profession as a whole to promote and assist these underrepresented groups.

Further, the profession has a responsibility to make the role of architects known to society. Society must understand that we are a vibrant, well-trained, intelligent, creative group of individuals who can improve neighborhoods and catalyze change in communities.

Tamara Redburn, AIA, LEED AP, Project Architect, Fleming Associates Architects, P.C.

Harm Weber Academic Center, Judson University, Elgin, Illinois. Architect: Short and Associates. PHOTOGRAPHER: LEE W. WALDREP, Ph.D.

❯ Difficult to predict. My hope is that for a whole range of reasons, including technology and environmental responsibility, the profession and the public will develop a better appreciation of history.

Mary Kay Lanzillotta, FAIA, Partner, Hartman-Cox Architects

❯ I see a delightful, humane, quality built environment for the "forgotten middle." Right now architecture seems to serve the upper and lower classes of society most. The wealthy have always and will continue to hire architects for architectural solutions to their building needs. To an extent, the poor are often afforded good architecture through social programs. But then there is the forgotten middle, the suburban middle-class sector. This is where I see the greatest architectural mediocrity, particularly in single-family houses, which are often a

family's biggest material asset. The New Urbanist and Not-So-Big House movements are excellent efforts that are helping to turn things in a different direction. However, it's a huge ship that must be brought about. It may take generations to restore the middle-class built environment to humaneness.

Edward J. Shannon, AIA, Director of Design, Benvenuti & Stein Design, LLC

❯ The future is already here; the next generation of architects is studying in our schools today. These students are fully engaged with the complex realities of their evolving world, and they understand that a fundamental rethinking of architectural practice is necessary. They are investigating dynamic interpretations that continually adapt and respond to an open-ended and indeterminate future.

Max Underwood, AIA, Professor, Arizona State University

What do you see as the future for the architecture profession? (Continued)

❯ The future of the architecture profession in American culture should be to educate the public to have a critical eye for architecture and to critique, through the making of architecture, the status of our society with a vision of human and cultural progress as its driving force.

Margaret DeLeeuw, Marketing Director, Celli-Flynn Brennan Architects & Planners

❯ Sustainable design principles have been around for ages but "green" design is seeping into mainstream culture. Architects need to think about how their creations will affect our environment years from today. In the future, more focus should be given to infusing character into the dull, mass produced buildings of today. Architecture should tell a story about the client or place. human and cultural progress as its driving force.

Marisa Gomez, Bachelor of Science Candidate, University of Maryland

❯ The profession will broaden beyond traditional building. More diverse and better-trained architects with the advantages of the technical age will allow the profession to catapult way beyond building.

Christopher J. Gribbs, Associate AIA, Senior Director, Convention, The American Institute of Architects

❯ I believe the short-term future for architects may be challenging as we battle over control of the design and construction process with contractors and design/builders. The next several years will be critical in determining what entity should orchestrate the building process. We see moves toward eliminating the architect from leading the design team. In the long-term, hopefully architects will regain the respect and recognition as the linchpin of the process and be sought after and regarded as such.

Kathy Denise Dixon, AIA, NOMA, Associate Principal, Arel Architects, Inc.

❯ Students, faculty, and professionals must keep up with technological and globalization changes as best they can, yet keep sight of the fact that their projects must not only serve but also enhance the lives of the people who use them.

Kathryn H. Anthony, Ph.D., Professor, University of Illinois at Urbana-Champaign

❯ I see the profession as a collection of individuals or very small firms—"free-agents" if you will. The exquisite selection and collaboration of these individuals will become the key determinant in the project's success.

Amy Yurko, AIA, Founder/Director, BrainSpaces

❯ The future of the profession is a better understanding of what architecture actually is.

Jennifer Jaramillo, Architectural Intern, Dekker/Perich/Sabatini, LLC

❯ As architects, we must acknowledge our connectivity to others; we must know that what we see is often not the entire truth. We must venture beyond our comfortable boundaries into the reality of others.

Kathryn T. Prigmore, FAIA, Senior Project Manager, HDR Architecture, Inc.

❯ As building information models become standard in architecture practice, architects will reestablish themselves as the master builder coordinating the whole process from design to construction to post-occupancy. Research will continue to gain value in the profession and in society as evidence points to the importance of good design. This will further elevate the role of the architect and provide them with another set of tools. This newly recognized expertise will lead to opportunities for leadership in our communities, in the environment, and in public policy.

Margaret R. Tarampi, Associate AIA, Doctor of Philosophy Candidate, University of Utah

❯ The profession of architecture has changed over its history. Architects were historically involved in every aspect of the design and construction of buildings, but that process has been lost. I believe the idea of the master builder will continue to dissolve, resulting in many specialties in the future. Architecture will comprise thousands of areas of expertise.

Lisa A. Swan, Residential Designer, Design Forward

❯ The future of architecture will see a more integrated process of design with designers from many disciplines collaborating together in a virtual environment. A profession seeking more efficient methods to deliver their designs into the field; architects, engineers, and builders work in a more team-oriented structure; the architect serves as the leader of the team. New software and processes will give architects more time to design. Sustainability remains a force that forces the continued reevaluation the way that buildings are assembled . . . design has value in all situations and business models . . .

Education and practice grow closer and the current curriculums evolve to address the real needs of young practitioners. Leadership and business skills are also taught in addition to the traditional design-oriented courses. Education focuses more on entry into the profession, providing a holistic picture of what it takes to become a successful practitioner. Professional organizations form more strategic alliances to celebrate along with landscape architects and designers of all types . . . without compromising the health, safety, and welfare issues of protecting the public. Architects mentor

and share the knowledge more comprehensively. Architects become more entrepreneurial and develop other businesses that are tangent to their core design businesses.

Catherine McNeel Florreich, Associate AIA, Architectural Intern, Eley Guild Hardy Architects PA

❯ We are generating knowledge and information at an astonishing rate, beyond what we as individuals can possibly comprehend and it is ever increasing. Specific subject-matter experts will become more and more critical to our ability to execute great design. There will be many more opportunities for architects, should we decide to embrace them.

Architects need more and more to demonstrate excellent leadership skills to successfully navigate the team dynamics and different ideas if they are to maintain any reasonable ability to manage a project. But at the same time they need to be open to new ideas and know how to incorporate them when appropriate.

Robert D. Fox, AIA, IIDA, Principal, FOX Architects

❯ Architecture will continue to be one of the most exciting and important professions. Architects will collaborate with other design professionals to improve our built and virtual environments. They will become more sensitive to elements of sustainable design as stewards of natural resources. They will create enriching places for our increasingly global community.

Diane Blair Black, AIA, Vice-President, RTKL Associates, Inc.

What do you see as the future for the architecture profession? (Continued)

❭ The profession needs to return to its roots of providing master builder services that encompass knowledge of finance, politics, planning, and the techniques and strategies used for obtaining information and directing actions that include and influence those arenas. One resulting benefit that will come from this expansion of responsibilities is the legitimate increase in fees to be received for the work. Creating a better quality of life for the client and the community is another benefit that can be realized. There are areas of expertise that are clearly the responsibility of the profession to develop and take control over. Sustainability and environmental design, community development, security issues and their impact on accessibility, inclusion of all parties involved in a design project who will be using and maintaining the project (really a leadership issue during the design phase), and understanding and incorporating all the building components and their life cycle costs through BIM technology are but a few of the expanding professional responsibilities falling on the modern day professional architect's shoulders.

Ambassador Richard N. Swett (r), FAIA, President, Swett Associates, Inc.

Otaniemi Technical University, Otaniemi, Finland. Architect: Alvar Aalto. PHOTOGRAPHER: TED SHELTON, AIA.

❯ Architects are becoming increasingly specialized, which is not necessarily good for the profession as a whole.

Lynsey Jane Gemmell, AIA, Project Manager/Associate, Holabird & Root

❯ Green architecture and development will continue to be significant in architecture's future. As this shift takes place, architecture will likely become more context specific as location plays a large part in determining how a building must be adapted to its environment. In the future this will hopefully cause architectural enclaves to emerge and many communities will develop unique architectural characters that respond to their individual environments.

Allison Wilson, Bachelor of Science Graduate, University of Maryland

❯ As the future continues to become more technology-driven, architects will have to constantly learn about new technologies for both design and construction in order to adapt to the changing landscape and to serve their clients' growing needs. Architects will play a larger role in helping solve many of the society's current imperfections. Whether they are helping provide shelter for all, building more earth-friendly structures, or designing more integrated and efficient cities, architects will need to use more of their expertise for the common good.

David R. Groff, Master of Architecture Candidate, Virginia Tech–Washington Alexandria Architecture Center

❯ Architects will be active leaders in their communities, active leaders in the environment and on issues of sustainability, and active leaders in evidence-based design. The profession will welcome all of those that pursue it—that is, become increasingly diverse and culturally rich. Architects do more than design buildings; they build communities. The profession will embrace those individuals who pursue alternative careers, who find themselves on the client side of the table, or who seek to represent architects and communities through public pursuits. The profession will evolve as architects retake more responsibility in the building process and as technologies such as BIM emerge.

Shannon Kraus, AIA, MBA, Vice-President, HKS Architects

❯ The profession is in a precarious position. Through a continued avoidance of political, economic, and social engagement we have collectively failed to take advantage of myriad opportunities to reassume our position as a socially-relevant profession. The 9/11 attacks, Iowa floods, and Hurricanes Katrina, Rita, and Ike have all come and gone without any demonstrable leadership from American architects. The rebuilding of the World Trade Center alone provided an opportunity to bring people together but was overcomplicated by money, power, and ego.

If our profession can gain comfort with these knowledge sets, place a premium on leadership, and create a milieu where knowledge sharing is facilitated within the profession the future is bright. Anything short of this will leave the nation's 100,000 architects internally competitive, isolated, and irrelevant.

Wayne A. Mortensen, Associate AIA, NASW, Project Manager/Urban Designer, H3 Studio; Lecturer, Washington University

What do you see as the future for the architecture profession? (Continued)

❯ In the last 30 years, the architect's role has shifted farther from artist and craftsman to manager of the process of project delivery. This new identity will continue to solidify. Clients are seldom individuals anymore but rather committees that must be led through a complex process. Moreover, jurisdictional approvals and public hearings expose our designs to individuals without formal architectural training or a financial investment in the project's success. The traditional phases of schematic design, design development, and contract documents are being blurred into one phase of design/documentation. The advent of digital drafting has put the design and documentation processes in constant flux; drawings have become databases that are constantly altered, updated, revised, refined, and transmitted to a host of groups, including clients, lenders, marketing consultants, municipalities, consultants, and vendors. Architects have become the arbiters of a fast-moving and complex documentation exercise. No matter what changes accrue to their role, however, architects will continue to provide aesthetic oversight, technical experience, and legal knowledge to the building process. They will always serve as the conscience of the built environment.

W. Stephen Saunders, AIA, Principal, Eckenhoff Saunders Architects Inc.

NOTES

1. Green Building Certification Institute. (2009). Retrieved January 19, 2009, from http://www.gbci.org.
2. *Integrated Project Delivery: A Guide* (2007). Washington, DC: AIA.
3. Cramer, James P and Simpson, Scott (2007). *The Next Architect: A New Twist on the Future of Design*. Norcross, GA: Greenway Communications.

APPENDIX A

The Resources of an Architect

The following are professional associations, recommended reading, and websites that may be of assistance in your quest to become an architect. In all cases, you should contact them for further information. Many of the associations have state or local chapters that may also be helpful.

COLLATERAL ORGANIZATIONS

These first five associations (AIA, AIAS, ACSA, NAAB, and NCARB) are commonly known as the *collateral organizations* and represent the primary players with the profession—architects, students, educators, the accrediting agency, and the state registration boards.

The American Institute of Architects (AIA)

1735 New York Ave., N.W.
Washington, DC 20006
(202) 626-7300
www.aia.org

Comprising over 83,000 members in almost 300 local and state chapters, the American Institute of Architects (AIA) is the largest association for the architectural profession; its mission is to promote and advance the profession and the living standards of people through their built environment.

American Institute of Architecture Students (AIAS)

1735 New York Ave., N.W.
Washington, DC 20006
(202) 626-7472
www.aias.org

The mission of the AIAS is to promote excellence in architectural education, training, and practice; to foster an appreciation of architecture and related disciplines; to enrich communities in a spirit of collaboration; and to organize architecture students and combine their efforts to advance the art and science of architecture.

Association of Collegiate Schools of Architecture (ACSA)

1735 New York Ave., N.W.
Washington, DC 20006
(202) 785-2324
www.acsa-arch.org

The Association of Collegiate Schools of Architecture (ACSA) is the membership organization that represents the over 100 U.S. and Canadian schools offering accredited professional degree programs in architecture; its mission is to advance architectural education through support of member schools, their faculty, and students.

National Architectural Accrediting Board (NAAB)

1735 New York Ave., N.W.
Washington, DC 20006-5292
(202) 783-2007
www.naab.org

The National Architectural Accrediting Board (NAAB) is the sole agency authorized to accredit U.S. professional degree programs in architecture. While graduation from a NAAB-accredited program does not ensure registration, the accrediting process is intended to verify that each accredited program substantially meets those standards that, as a whole, constitute an appropriate education for an architect.

National Council of Architectural Registration Boards (NCARB)
1801 K St., Ste. 700-K
Washington, DC 20006
(202) 783-6500
www.ncarb.org

The National Council of Architectural Registration Boards (NCARB) is the organization of the 55 states, territorial, and district registration boards that license architects, and the preparer of the Architect Registration Examination and the certification process that facilities reciprocity of individual licenses between jurisdictions.

ARCHITECTURE-RELATED ASSOCIATIONS

Alpha Rho Chi
www.alpharhochi.org

Alpha Rho Chi (APX) is the national professional coeducational fraternity established to encourage closer fellowship and a greater interest in the study of architecture and the allied arts.

American Architectural Foundation (AAF)
1735 New York Ave., NW
Washington, DC 20006
(202) 626-7500
www.archfoundation.org

The American Architectural Foundation (AAF) educates individuals and communities about the power of architecture to transform lives and improve the places where we live, learn, work, and play. Through our outreach programs, grants, scholarships, and educational resources, the AAF inspires people to become thoughtful and engaged stewards of the built environment.

American Indian Council of Architects And Engineers
P.O. Box 15096
Portland, OR 97215
(503) 684-5680
www.aicae.org

The American Indian Council of Architects and Engineers advances the role of Native American professional engineers, architects, and design professionals in practice and encourages them to advance their professional skills and to pursue careers as professional engineers, architects, and design professionals.

American Society of Architectural Illustrators (ASAI)
3301 North Garden Lane
Avondale, AZ 85392
(623) 433-8782
www.asai.org

The American Society of Architectural Illustrators (ASAI), is a nonprofit international professional organization of architectural illustrators, whose goals are to foster communication among architectural illustrators, to raise the standards of architectural illustration, and to acquaint the public with the importance of such drawing as integral to the practice of architecture.

American Society of Golf Course Architects
125 N. Executive Dr., Ste. 106
Brookfield, WI 53005
(262) 786-5960
www.asgca.org

The American Society of Golf Course Architects is composed of leading golf course designers in the United States and Canada actively involved in the design of new courses and the renovation of older courses.

Arquitectos
The Society of Hispanic Professional Architects
P.O. Box 3353
Chicago, IL 60654
www.arquitectoschicago.org

Arquitectos is an architectural organization whose mission is to unite architects to promote professional development, economic development, mentorship, and community assistance, and to further enrich the architectural profession through different cultural views and practices.

Asian American Architects And Engineers Association
11301 W. Olympic Blvd., #387
Los Angeles, CA 90064
(213) 896-9270
www.aaaesc.com

The Asian American Architects and Engineers Association (AAa/e) is committed to providing a platform for empowering professionals working in the built environment in personal and professional growth, business development and networking, and leadership in our community.

The Association for Computer-Aided Design in Architecture
www.acadia.org

Formed in the early 1980s, the purpose of ACADIA is to facilitate communication and critical thinking regarding the use of computers in architecture, planning, and building science. A particular focus is education and the software, hardware, and pedagogy involved in education.

Association of University Architects
www.auaweb.net

This special group of architectural professionals is focused on the development and enhancement of our university campuses. University architects plan for the future and carefully build and renovate facilities for current needs.

Congress for the New Urbanism (CNU)
The Marquette Building
140 S. Dearborn St., Suite 310
Chicago, IL 60603
(312) 551-7300
www.cnu.org

The Congress for the New Urbanism (CNU) is the leading organization promoting walkable, neighborhood-based development as an alternative to sprawl.

National Organization of Minority Architects (NOMA)
c/o School of Architecture & Design
College of Engineering, Architecture & Computer Sciences
Howard University
2366 6th Street, NW - Room 100
Washington, DC 20059
(202) 686.2780
www.noma.net

The NOMA, which thrives only when voluntary members contribute their time and resources, has as its mission the building of a strong national organization, strong chapters, and strong members for the purpose of minimizing the effect of racism in our profession.

Royal Architectural Institute of Canada
55 Murray Street, Suite 330
Ottawa, Ontario K1N 5M3
Canada
(613) 241-3600
www.raic.org

Established in 1907, the Royal Architectural Institute of Canada is a voluntary national association representing more than 3,600 architects, and faculty and graduates of accredited Canadian Schools of Architecture, from every region of the country.

Society of American Registered Architects (SARA)
305 E. 46th Street
New York, NY 10017-3058
(888) 385-7272
www.sara-national.org

The Society of American Registered Architects (SARA) was founded in 1956 as a professional society that includes the participation of all architects, regardless of their roles in the architectural community. The SARA follows the Golden Rule and supports the concept of profitable professionalism for its members.

Tau Sigma Delta

www.tausigmadelta.org

Tau Sigma Delta provides a national collegiate honor society open to students of all American colleges and universities wherein an accredited program of Architecture, Landscape Architecture, or Allied Arts is established. The Society derives its Greek letter name from the first letter of each of the words of its motto, Technitai Sophoikai Dexioti: Tau, Sigma, and Delta. The motto means "Craftsmen, skilled and trained."

Union of International Architects

33 avenue du Maine
75755 Paris cedex 15 France
33 (1) 45 24 36 88
www.uia-architectes.org

The Union of International Architects (UIA) is an international nongovernmental organization founded in Lausanne in 1948 to unite architects from all nations throughout the world, regardless of nationality, race, religion, or architectural school of thought, within the federations of their national associations. The UIA represents over a million architects throughout the world through national architectural associations that form the 92 UIA Member Sections.

United States Green Building Council

1800 Massachusetts Avenue NW, Suite 300
Washington, DC 20036
(800) 795-1747
www.usgbc.org

The U.S. Green Building Council (USGBC) is a nonprofit organization committed to expanding sustainable building practices whose mission is to transform the way buildings and communities are designed, built, and operated, enabling an environmentally and socially responsible, healthy, and prosperous environment that improves the quality of life.

ASSOCIATIONS—RELATED CAREERS

Architectural History

Society of Architectural Historians

1365 N. Astor St.
Chicago, IL 60610-2144
(312) 573-1365
www.sah.org

Founded in 1940, the Society of Architectural Historians (SAH) is an international not-for-profit membership organization that promotes the study and preservation of the built environment worldwide.

Construction

American Council for Construction Education

1717 North Loop 1604 East, Suite 320
San Antonio, TX 78232-1570
(210) 495-6161
www.acce-hq.org

The mission of the American Council for Construction Education (ACCE) is to be a leading global advocate of high-quality construction education programs, and to promote, support, and accredit quality construction education programs.

Associated Schools of Construction

General Business Office Mailing Address
PO Box 1312
Ft. Collins, CO 80522
(970) 222-4459
www.ascweb.org

The Associated Schools of Construction is a professional association for the development and advancement of construction education, where the sharing of ideas and knowledge inspires, guides, and promotes excellence in curricula, teaching, research, and service.

Construction Management Association of America

7926 Jones Branch Drive, Suite 800
McLean, VA 22102
(703) 356-2622
www.cmaanet.org

The mission of the Construction Management Association of America (CMAA) is "to promote professionalism and excellence in the management of the construction process." The CMAA is leading the growth and acceptance of construction management as a professional discipline that can add significant value to the entire construction process, from conception to ongoing operation.

Construction Specifications Institute (CSI)

99 Canal Center Plaza, Suite 300
Alexandria, VA 22314-1791
(800) 689-2900
www.csinet.org

The CSI is a national association dedicated to creating standards and formats to improve construction documents and project delivery.

National Association of Women in Construction (NAWIC)

327 S. Adams St.
Fort Worth, TX 76104
(800) 552-3506
www.nawic.org

Founded in 1955, the NAWIC is dedicated to enhancing the success of women in the construction industry by building educations, careers, futures, and lives.

Design (Graphic, Industrial, Furniture, Lighting)

American Design Council

164 Fifth Ave.
New York, NY 10010
(212) 807-1990
www.americandesigncouncil.org

The American Design Council is an alliance of individual professional associations interested in advancing a shared agenda to promote effective design. The Council enables a unified message on the value of the design process and the contribution designers make to corporate objectives, a comprehensive program for communicating this message to business, and a plan for individual and collective pursuit of these objectives.

American Institute of Graphic Arts (AIGA)

164 Fifth Avenue
New York, NY 10010
(212) 807-1990
www.aiga.org

The AIGA, the professional association for design, is the place design professionals turn to first to exchange ideas and information, participate in critical analysis and research, and advance education and ethical practice.

American Society of Furniture Designers (ASFD)

144 Woodland Dr.
New London, NC 28127
(910) 576-1273
www.asfd.com

Founded in 1981, the ASFD is the only international nonprofit professional organization dedicated to advancing, improving, and supporting the profession of furniture design and its positive impact in the marketplace.

Focus on Design

300 D Street, SW Suite 222
Washington, DC 20024
(301) 218-8428
www.focusondesign.org

Focus on Design evolved from the collaboration of several design organizations whose vision is to create a more socially conscious and culturally sensitive design community, to expand the horizons and influences of the designer, to explore new directions in design, and to introduce cutting-edge ideas and technologies into the design profession.

Industrial Designers Society of America (IDSA)

45195 Business Ct., Ste. 250
Dulles, VA 20166
(703) 707-6000
www.idsa.org

The Industrial Designers Society of America (IDSA) is the voice of the industrial design profession, advancing the quality and positive impact of design.

International Association of Lighting Designers

Merchandise Mart, Suite 9-104
Chicago, IL 60654
(312) 527-3677
www.iald.org

Founded in 1969 and based in Chicago, Illinois, the IALD promotes the visible success of its members in practicing lighting design.

Society for Environmental Graphic Design (SEGD)

1000 Vermont Ave., Suite 400
Washington, DC 20005
(202) 638-5555
www.segd.org

The SEGD is the global community of people who work at the intersection of communication design and the built environment. Environmental Graphic Design embraces many design disciplines including graphic, architectural, interior, landscape, and industrial design, all concerned with the visual aspects of wayfinding, communicating identity and information, and shaping the idea of place.

Historic Preservation

Heritage Documentation Programs

National Park Service
Department of the Interior
1201 Eye Street, NW (2270) Seventh Floor
Washington, DC 20005
(202) 354-2135
www.nps.gov/history/hdp

The Heritage Documentation Programs (HDP), part of the National Park Service, administers HABS (Historic American Buildings Survey), the federal government's oldest preservation program, and companion programs HAER (Historic American Engineering Record), HALS (Historic American Landscapes Survey), and CRGIS (Cultural Resources Geographic Information Systems).

National Council for Preservation Education

www.ncpe.us

The National Council for Preservation Education (NCPE) encourages and assists in the development and improvement of historic preservation education programs and endeavors in the United States and elsewhere.

National Trust for Historic Preservation

1785 Massachusetts Avenue, NW
Washington, DC 20036
(202) 588-6000
www.nationaltrust.org

The National Trust for Historic Preservation is a privately funded nonprofit organization that provides leadership, education, and advocacy to save America's diverse historic places and revitalize our communities.

Interior Design

American Society of Interior Designers (ASID)

608 Massachusetts Ave., N.E.,
Washington, DC 20002-6006
(202) 546-3480
www.asid.org

The American Society of Interior Designers (ASID) is a nonprofit professional society representing the interests of interior designers and the interior design community.

Council for Interior Design Accreditation

206 Grandville Ave., Ste. 350
Grand Rapids, MI 49503
(616) 458-0400
www.accredit-id.org

The Council for Interior Design Accreditation ensures a high level of quality in interior design education through three primary activities: (1) set standards for postsecondary interior design education, (2) evaluate and accredit college and university interior design programs, and (3) facilitate outreach and collaboration with all stakeholders in the interior design community.

International Interior Design Association

222 Merchandise Mart Plaza, Ste. 567
Chicago, IL 60654
(888) 799-4432
www.iida.org

The International Interior Design Association (IIDA) is committed to enhancing the quality of life through excellence in interior design and advancing interior design through knowledge.

Planning/Landscape Architecture

American Planning Association (APA)

1776 Massachusetts Ave., NW, Ste. 400
Washington, DC 20036-1904
(202) 872-0611
www.planning.org

The American Planning Association (APA) brings together thousands of people—practicing planners, citizens, elected officials—committed to making great communities happen. The APA is a nonprofit public interest and research organization committed to urban, suburban, regional, and rural planning. The APA and its professional institute, the American Institute of Certified Planners, advance the art and science of planning to meet the needs of people and society.

American Society of Landscape Architects

636 Eye Street, NW
Washington, DC 20001-3736
(202) 898-2444
www.asla.org

Founded in 1899, the American Society of Landscape Architects is the national professional association representing landscape architects. The ASLA promotes the landscape architecture profession and advances the practice through advocacy, education, communication, and fellowship.

Association of Collegiate Schools of Planning

www.acsp.org

The Association of Collegiate Schools of Planning (ACSP) is a consortium of university-based programs offering credentials in urban and regional planning. Acting together, the ACSP member school faculty are able to express their shared commitments to understanding the dynamics of urban and regional development, enhancing planning practices, and improving the education of both novice and experienced planners.

Council of Landscape Architectural Registration Boards

144 Church Street, NW Suite 201
Vienna, VA 22180
(703) 319-8380
www.clarb.org

The Council of Landscape Architectural Registration Boards (CLARB) is dedicated to ensuring that all individuals who affect the natural and built environment through the practice of landscape architecture are sufficiently qualified to do so.

Landscape Architecture Foundation
818 18th Street NW, Suite 810
Washington, DC 20006
(202) 331-7070
www.laprofession.org

The mission of the Landscape Architecture Foundation is to support the preservation, improvement, and enhancement of the environment.

Technical/Engineering

Accreditation Board for Engineering and Technology, Inc. (ABET)
111 Market Place, Suite 1050
Baltimore, MD 21202-4012
(410) 347-7700
www.abet.org

The ABET provides world leadership in assuring quality and stimulating innovation in applied science, computing, engineering, and technology education. The ABET serves the public through the promotion and advancement of education in applied science, computing, engineering, and technology.

Acoustical Society of America (ASA)
335 East 45th St.
New York, NY 10017
(202) 661-9404
asa.aip.org

The premier international scientific society in acoustics, dedicated to increasing and diffusing the knowledge of acoustics and its practical applications.

American Association of Engineering Societies (AAES)
6522 Meadowridge Rd., Ste 101
Elkridge, MD 21075
(202) 296-2237
www.aaes.org

Multidisciplinary organization of engineering societies dedicated to advancing the knowledge, understanding, and practice of engineering. AAES member societies represent the mainstream of U.S. engineering, more than one million engineers in industry, government, and academia.

American Society of Civil Engineers (ASCE)
1801 Alexander Bell Drive
Reston, VA 20191
(800) 548-2723
www.asce.org

The mission of the ASCE is to provide essential value to members, their careers, its partners, and the public by developing leadership, advancing technology, advocating lifelong learning, and promoting the profession of civil engineering.

Architectural Engineering Institute (AEI)
1801 Alexander Bell Drive
Reston, VA 20191
(800) 548-2723
www.aeinstitute.org

A division of the ASCE, the mission of the Architectural Engineering Institute is to serve the building community by promoting an integrated, multidisciplinary approach to planning, design, construction and operation of buildings and by encouraging excellence in practice, education and research of architectural engineering.

National Society of Professional Engineers (NSPE)
1420 King Street
Alexandria, VA 22314
(703) 684-2800
www.nspe.org

In partnership with the State Societies, the NSPE is the organization of licensed Professional Engineers (PEs) and Engineer Interns (EIs). Through education, licensure advocacy, leadership training, multidisciplinary networking, and outreach, the NSPE enhances the image of its members and their ability to ethically and professionally practice engineering.

Society of Building Science Educators
www.sbse.org

The Society of Building Science Educators is an association of university educators in architecture and related disciplines who support excellence in the teaching of environmental science and building technologies.

INSTITUTIONS DEDICATED TO ARCHITECTURE

ACE Mentor Program
400 Main Street, Suite 600
Stamford, CT 06901
(203) 323-8550
www.acementor.org

The ACE (Architecture, Construction, Engineering) Mentor Program was founded by the principals of leading design and construction firms, to introduce high school students to career opportunities in the industry.

Architecture & Design Education Network (A+DEN)
www.adenweb.org

Founded by the American Architectural Foundation (AAF) and the Chicago Architecture Foundation (CAF), the Architecture + Design Education Network (A+DEN) is a collaborative association of like-minded organizations in the fields of architecture and design, committed to promoting innovative architecture and design education for teachers and students in grades K–12.

Chicago Architecture Foundation (CAF)
224 S. Michigan Ave.
Chicago, IL 60604
(312) 922-3432
www.architecture.org

The Chicago Architecture Foundation (CAF) is dedicated to advancing public interest and education in architecture and related design. Because no art other than architecture so vividly expresses what Chicago is and where it is going, the CAF educates the public to expect the highest standards from Chicago's built environment.

CUBE: Center for Understanding the Built Environment
5328 W. 67th St.
Prairie Village, Kansas 66208-1408
(913) 262-0691
www.cubekc.org

The Center for Understanding the Built Environment (CUBE) brings together educators with community partners to effect change, which will lead to a high-quality built and natural environment, one and interdependent.

Graham Foundation for Advanced Studies in the Fine Arts
4 West Burton Place
Chicago, IL 60610-1416
(312) 787-4071
www.grahamfoundation.org

The mission of the Graham Foundation is to nurture and enrich an informed and creative public dialogue concerning architecture and the built environment.

Learning by Design in Massachusetts
c/o The Boston Society of Architects
52 Broad St.
Boston, MA 02019
www.architects.org/LBD

A core element of the Boston Society of Architects' K–12 design education and design awareness program, Learning by Design gives children the opportunity to express their ideas about their built and natural environments.

National Building Museum
401 F St., N.W.
Washington, DC 20001
(202) 272-2448
www.nbm.org

Created by an act of Congress, the National Building Museum is the only institution uniquely dedicated to exploring the what, who, how, and why of American building. The National Building Museum seeks to broaden public understanding and appreciation of our building heritage by providing people with a variety of skills needed to better understand and shape the built environment.

COMMUNITY SERVICE

AmeriCorps
1201 New York Avenue, NW
Washington, DC 20525
(202) 606-5000
www.americorps.org

AmeriCorps is a network of national service programs that engage more than 50,000 Americans each year in intensive service to meet critical needs in education, public safety, health, and the environment.

Architects, Designers, and Planners for Social Responsibility
P.O. Box 9126
Berkeley, CA 94709
(510) 845-1000
www.adpsr.org

The Architects/Designers/Planners for Social Responsibility (ADPSR) works for peace, environmental protection, ecological building, social justice, and the development of healthy communities.

Architects without Borders
295 Neva Street
Sebastopol, CA 95472
www.awb.iohome.net

Architects without Borders is a nongovernmental, not-for-profit, volunteer humanitarian relief organization.

Architecture for Humanity
848 Folsom, Suite 201
San Francisco, CA 94107-1173
(415) 963-3511
www.architectureforhumanity.org

Architecture for Humanity promotes architectural and design solutions to global, social, and humanitarian crises. Through competitions, workshops, educational forums, partnerships with aid organizations, and other activities, Architecture for Humanity creates opportunities for architects and designers from around the world to help communities in need.

Association for Community Design (ACD)
P.O. Box 712308
Los Angeles, CA 90071
www.communitydesign.org

Established in 1977, the Association for Community Design (ACD) is a network of individuals, organizations, and institutions committed to increasing the capacity of planning and design professions to better serve communities. The ACD serves and supports practitioners, educators, and organizations engaged in community-based design and planning.

Design Corps
2243 The Circle
Raleigh, NC 27608
(919) 828-0048
www.designcorps.org

Founded in 1991, Design Corps is a private nonprofit that was created to coordinate design services that help create responsive affordable housing. Respect for those housed, the local communities and cultures involved are encouraged. Motto: Design for the 98% Without Architects.

Habitat For Humanity International
121 Habitat St.
Americus, GA 31709-3498
(229) 924-6935
www.habitat.org

Habitat for Humanity International is a nonprofit Christian housing ministry that works to build or renovate homes for the inadequately sheltered in the United States and in 20 countries around the world.

The Mad Housers, Inc.
534 Permalume Place
Atlanta, GA 30318
(404) 806-6233
www.madhousers.org

The Mad Housers, Inc., is an Atlanta-based nonprofit corporation engaged in charitable work, research, and education. Their primary endeavor is building temporary, emergency shelters for homeless individuals and families regardless of race, creed, national origin, gender, religion, age, family status, sexual orientation, and the like.

Peace Corps
Paul D. Coverdell Peace Corps Headquarters
1111 20th Street, NW
Washington, DC 20526
(800) 424-8580
www.peacecorps.gov

Established in 1961 by President John F. Kennedy, the Peace Corps has shared with the world America's most precious resource—its people. Peace Corps volunteers serve in 72 countries in Africa, Asia, the Caribbean, Central and South America, Europe, and the Middle East. Collaborating with local community members, volunteers work in areas like education, youth outreach and community development, the environment, and information technology.

Public Architecture
1211 Folsom St., 4th Flr.
San Francisco, CA 94102
(415) 861-8200
www.publicarchitecture.org

Established in 2002, Public Architecture is a nonprofit organization that identifies and solves practical problems of human interaction in the built environment. It acts as a catalyst for public discourse through education, advocacy, and the design of public spaces and amenities.

RECOMMENDED READING

ACSA. (Ed.). (2009). *Guide to Architecture Schools* (8th ed.). Washington, DC: Association of Collegiate Schools of Architecture. ISBN 0-935-50269-5.

Compiled approximately every five years by the Association of Collegiate Schools of Architecture (ACSA), the *Guide to Architecture Schools* provides a valuable resource for individuals seeking to pursue an architectural education. Its primary content is a compilation of two-page descriptions of the over 100 universities offering accredited degree programs in architecture. In addition, the resource contains an introduction outlining the history of architectural education, high school preparation, selecting a school, architectural practice, and accreditation.

AIAS. (Ed.). (2002). *The Redesign of the Studio Culture*. Washington, DC: American Institute of Architecture Students.

The result of a AIAS Task Force, this report examines the issue of studio culture and lists goals to embrace in creating change for architectural education.

Anthony, Kathryn. (2001). *Designing for Diversity: Gender, Race, and Ethnicity in the Architectural Profession*. Champaign, IL: University of Illinois Press. ISBN 0-252-02641-1.

This landmark book offers insight into the issue of diversity as it relates to the profession of architecture. As one reviewer stated, "a must read."

Anthony, Kathryn. (1991). *Design Juries on Trial: The Renaissance of the Design Studio*. New York: Van Nostrand Reinhold. ISBN 0-442-00235-1.

Design Juries on Trial unlocks the door to the mysterious design jury system—exposing its hidden agendas and helping you overcome intimidation, confrontation, and frustration. It explains how to improve the success rate of submissions to juries—whether in academic settings, for competitions, and awards programs, or for professional accounts.

Architecture for Humanity. (2006). *Design Like You Give a Damn: Architectural Responses to Humanitarian Crises*. New York, NY: Metropolis Books. ISBN 1-933-04525-6.

Design Like You Give a Damn is a compendium of innovative projects from around the world that demonstrate the power of design to improve lives. The first book to bring the best of humanitarian architecture and design to the printed page, *Design Like You Give a Damn* offers a history of the movement toward socially conscious design and showcases more than 80 contemporary solutions to such urgent needs as basic shelter, healthcare, education, and access to clean water, energy, and sanitation.

Bell, Bryan. (2003). *Good Deeds, Good Design: Community Service Through Architecture*. Princeton: Princeton Architectural Press. ISBN 1-568-98391-3.

Good Deeds, Good Design presents the best new thoughts and practices in this emerging movement toward an architecture that serves a broader population. In this book, architecture firms, community design centers, design-build programs, and service-based organizations offer their plans for buildings for the other 98 percent.

Bell, Bryan and Wakeford, Katie (eds.). (2008). *Expanding Architecture: Design as Activism*. New York: Metropolis Books. ISBN 1-933-04578-7.

Expanding Architecture presents a new generation of creative design carried out in the service of the greater public and the greater good. Questioning how design can improve daily lives, editors Bryan Bell and Katie Wakeford map an emerging geography of architectural activism—or "public-interest architecture"—that might function akin to public-interest law or medicine by expanding architecture's all too often elite client base.

Boyer, Ernest L. and Mitgang, Lee D. (1996). *Building Community: A New Future for Architecture Education and Practice*. Princeton, NJ: The Carnegie Foundation for the Advancement of Teaching. ISBN 0-931-05059-6.

Commissioned by the five collateral organizations involved with the architecture profession, this independent study focused on architectural education and practice; its conclusion developed seven essential goals or designs for renewal.

Camenson, Blythe. (2008). *Careers in Architecture*. New York: McGraw-Hill. ISBN 0-978-0-07-154556-3.

Part of the VGM Career Books, *Careers in Architecture* provides you with insight on the variety of positions within the architecture field—residential, commercial, and institutional architecture; historic preservation; landscape architecture; engineering; urban and regional planning; and more.

Ching, Francis D. K. (2007). *Architecture: Form, Space & Order*. Hoboken, NJ: John Wiley & Sons. ISBN 0-471-28616-8.

This classic visual reference helps both students and practicing architects understand the basic vocabulary of architectural design by examining how form and space are ordered in the built environment. Using his trademark meticulous drawing, Professor Ching shows the relationship between fundamental elements of architecture through the ages and across cultural boundaries.

Cramer, James P. and Simpson, Scott. (2007). *The Next Architect: A New Twist on the Future of Design*. Norcross, GA: Greenway Communications. ISBN 0-975-56548-6.

The Next Architect takes a fresh look at our fast-evolving profession, starting with the proposition that everyone is an architect, both enabled and empowered to help shape tomorrow's world. Tomorrow's successful practitioners must be adept at collaborative design techniques and comfortable working at warp speed. This book challenges the next generation of design professionals to make full use of their talents to build a better, healthier, and more prosperous world.

Crowe, Norman and Laseau, Paul (1984). *Visual Notes for Architects and Designers*. New York: Van Nostrand Reinhold Co. ISBN 0-442-29334-8.

As stated on the back cover, the authors examine the relationship between note taking, visualization, and creativity. They provide practical guidance on visual acuity, visual literacy, and graphic analysis.

Cuff, Dana. (1991). *Architecture: The Story of Practice*. Boston, MA: MIT Press. ISBN 0-262-53112-7.

In this book, Cuff delves into the architect's everyday work world to uncover an intricate social art of design. The result is a new portrait of the profession that sheds light on what it means to become an architect, how design problems are construed and resolved, how clients and architects negotiate, and how design excellence is achieved.

Earley, Sandra Leibowitz. (2005). *Ecological Design and Building Schools*. Oakland, CA: New Village Press. ISBN 0-976 60541-4.

The only directory of its kind in North America, this comprehensive guide features an annotated listing of schools and educational centers offering programs in ecological architecture and construction. Included also is a 10-year overview of sustainable design education, tables comparing school programs, and listings of instructors, green building organizations, selected textbooks, and publicly available curricula.

Frederick, Matthew. (2007). *101 Things I Learned in Architecture School*. Cambridge, MA: The MIT Press. ISBN 978-0-262-06266-4.

As stated on the book jacket, this is a book that students of architecture will want to keep in the studio and in their backpacks; it provides a much-needed primer in architectural literacy.

Ginsberg, Beth. (2004). *The ECO Guide to Careers that Make a Difference: Environmental Work for a Sustainable World*. Washington, DC: Island Press. ISBN 1-55963-967-9.

This publication provides an overview of career choices and opportunities and identi-

fies development employment trends as the environmental community looks forward to the pressing needs of the twenty-first century.

Kostof, Sprio (ed.). (1977). *The Architect*. New York: Oxford University Press. ISBN 0-195-04044-9.

A collection of essays by historians and architects, *The Architect* explores and surveys the profession of architecture from its beginnings in ancient Egypt to the modern day.

Lewis, R. K. (1998). *Architect? A Candid Guide to the Profession*. Boston, MA: MIT Press. ISBN 0-262-12110-7.

Using three sections: (1) "To Be or Not To Be . . . an Architect," (2) "Becoming an Architect," and (3) "Being an Architect," the author provides an inside look at the profession, its educational process, and weighing the pros and cons of becoming an architect. Written by Roger K. Lewis, a professor of architecture at the University of Maryland, the book is excellent reading for an aspiring architect.

Linton, Harold. (2004). *Portfolio Design*. New York, NY: W. W. Norton & Company, Inc. ISBN 0-393-73095-6.

More than any other, this book provides critical information on creating, preparing and producing a portfolio, an element necessary for architecture students in applying to graduate programs or seeking employment.

Mann, Thorbjoern. (2004). *Time Management for Architects and Designers: Challenge and Remedies*. New York: W. W. Norton & Company. ISBN 0-393-73133-2.

Addresses the special time management issues that confront designers. It offers students and professionals guidance in recognizing and understanding these problems and developing effective strategies for overcoming them.

Marjanovic, Igor, Ruedi Ray, Katerina, and Lokko, Lesley Naa Norle. (2003). *The Portfolio: An Architecture Student's Handbook.* Oxford, England: Architectural Press. ISBN 0-7506-5764-2.

Gives practical advice for the creation of the portfolio covering issues of size, storage, layout, and order. Further, it guides the student through the various forms a portfolio can take: the electronic portfolio, the academic portfolio, and the professional portfolio, suggesting different approaches and different media to use in order to create the strongest portfolio possible.

Marjanovic, Igor, Ruedi Ray, Katerina, and Tankard, Jane. (2005). *Practical Experience: An Architecture Student's Guide to Internship and the Year Out.* Oxford, England: Architectural Press. ISBN 0-7506-6206-9.

In order to give you a real insight into professional experience, this guide includes real-life case studies from students who have been through the experience and from practices that have taken them on. It guides you through the steps of finding a placement, outlines the norms and expectations for internship in different countries, and discusses codes of office behavior and professional ethics.

Masengarb, Jennifer and Rehbien, Krisann. (2007). *The Architecture Handbook: A Student Guide to Understanding Buildings.* Chicago, IL: Chicago Architecture Foundation. ISBN 0-962-05627-8.

Focuses on the design and construction of residential architecture. Through hands-on activities, *The Architecture Handbook* teaches both the fundamentals of architectural design and technical drawing. Students also build knowledge and gain skills through group design projects, sketching, model making, mapping, research, critical thinking, problem solving, and class presentations.

NAAB (2009). *2009 NAAB Conditions.* Washington, DC: NAAB.

Written for faculty and students of professional degree programs in architecture, the *Conditions* informs the reader about the conditions including student performance criteria—required for a program to maintain accreditation. The criteria are the areas every student must demonstrate who graduates from an accredited architecture program. The criteria define the minimum requirements for your professional education in architecture (downloadable from www.naab.org).

O'Gorman, James F. (1998). *ABC of Architecture.* Philadelphia, PA: University of Pennsylvania Press. ISBN 0-812-21631-8.

ABC of Architecture is an accessible, nontechnical text on the first steps to understanding architectural structure, history, and criticism. Author James F. O'Gorman moves seamlessly from a discussion of the most basic inspiration for architecture (the need for shelter from the elements) to an exploration of space, system, and material, and, finally, to an examination of the language and history of architecture.

Parnell, Rosie and Sara, Rachel (2007). *The Crit: An Architecture Student's Handbook.* Oxford, England: Architectural Press. ISBN 0-7506-8225-6.

This fully updated edition includes advice and suggestions for tutors on how to model a crit around a broad range of learning styles to ensure that the process is constructive and beneficial for all architecture and design scholars.

Piper, R. (2006). *Opportunities in Architectural Careers.* Lincolnwood, IL: VGM Career Horizons. ISBN 0-07-145868-9.

Part of the extensive "Opportunities in" series by VGM Career Horizons, *Opportunities in Architectural Careers* aims to assist the reader to learn more about the purpose of architecture in today's environment, understand what an architect does, and grasp the many career opportunities in architecture. The book accomplishes its purpose through five chapters, (1) Our Physical Environment, (2) The Professional Architect, (3) The Architect's Practice, (4) Education for Architecture, and (5) Architectural Resources. Targeted at high school students, the book provides a good picture of the architecture profession and the tasks of an architect.

Pressman, Andy. (1993). *Architecture 101: A Guide to the Design Studio*. New York: John Wiley & Sons. ISBN 0-471-57318-3.

Introduces students to the design studio and helps them to develop a process by which they can complete design projects. Covering every practical element of this central experience, from setting up that first day to landing that first job, this important work features contributions from some of the most distinguished names in architecture.

Rasmussen, Steen Eiler. (1959). *Experiencing Architecture*. Cambridge, MA: MIT Press. ISBN 0-262-68002-5.

Profusely illustrated with fine instances of architectural experimentation through the centuries, this classic manages to convey the intellectual excitement of superb design.

Slafer, Anna and Cahill, Kevin. (1995). *Why Design? Activities and projects from the National Building Museum*, Washington, DC: National Building Museum. ISBN 1-55652-249-5.

Projects cover a range of design themes: buildings, landscapes, nature, products, and communications. Grades 6–12.

Swett, FAIA, Richard N. (2005). *Leadership by Design: Creating an Architecture of Trust*. Atlanta, GA: Greenway Communications. ISBN: 0-9755654-0-0.

Leadership by Design investigates the unique civic leadership strengths of the architecture profession. Drawing upon the compelling history of the profession, both past and present, as well as from his own singular experience as the only architect to serve in Congress during the twentieth century, Swett has produced an insightful volume that is both inspiring and instructive.

Thorne-Thomsen, Kathleen. (1994). *Frank Lloyd Wright for Kids: His Life And Ideas, 21 Activities*. Chicago, IL: Chicago Review Press. ISBN 1-556-52207-X.

Both a biography and an activity book, *Frank Lloyd Wright for Kids* is about a boy growing up on an American farm, a boy who works hard and sees structures and harmonies in the landscape around him. It is the story of a young man becoming a great architect as he uses his love of nature's colors and shapes in his unique designs. Delightful activities enable kids to understand and appreciate the ideas presented in his biography. Grades 4–8.

WEBSITES

These websites are directly related to the topic of this book and are current at the time of publication. You can explore the many other architecture-related websites as well.

ARCHCareers.org —
www.archcareers.org

ARCHCareers.org is an interactive guide to careers in architecture designed to assist you in becoming an architect! It assists you in learning more about and understanding the process of becoming an architect—(1) education, (2) experience, and (3) exam.

ARCHCareers Blog —
archcareers.blogspot.com

A companion to ARCHCareers.org, Dr. Architecture maintains this blog on architectural education and the process of becoming an architect. Questions posed are answered and resources are highlighted.

Archinect —
www.archinect.com

The goal of Archinect is to make architecture more connected and open-minded, and bring together designers from around the world to introduce new ideas from all disciplines.

Archiplanet –
www.archiplanet.org/wiki/Main_Page

Archiplanet is a community-constructed collection for all the buildings, building users, and building creators on planet Earth.

Architectural Record —
archrecord.construction.com

Architecturalrecord.com supplements the monthly magazine with expanded multimedia project stories, in-depth interviews with giants of architecture, daily news updates, weekly book reviews, green architecture stories, and archival material, as well as links to people and products and access to online continuing education credit registration.

ArchNewsNow —
www.archnewsnow.com

ArchNewsNow.com delivers the most comprehensive coverage of national and international news, projects, products, and events in the world of architecture and design.

ARCHSchools –
www.archschools.org

A companion website to the Guide to Architecture Schools compiled by the Association of Collegiate Schools of Architecture (ACSA), ARCHSchools provides a valuable resource for individuals seeking to pursue an architectural education. It provides the opportunity to search architecture programs and review descriptions on over 100 universities offering accredited degree programs in architecture.

ArchVoices —
www.archvoices.org

ArchVoices is an independent, nonprofit organization and think tank on architectural education, internship, and licensure. It exists to foster a culture of communication through the collection and dissemination of information and research.

Design Careers and Education Guide —
ucda.com/careers.lasso

Thinking about an education or career in design? Browse this guide to help you decide which specialty(ies) you are most interested in pursuing. Each specialty has a general description, education and career perspectives.

Design Disciplines, Whole Building Design Guide —
www.wbdg.org/design/design_disciplines.php

A branch of the Whole Building Design Guide, Design Discipline assists in understanding how building design disciplines are organized and practiced. Disciplines included: Architecture, Architectural Programming, Fire Protection Engineering, Interior Design, Landscape Architecture, Planning, and Structural Engineering.

DesignIntelligence —
www.di.net

DesignIntelligence contains a wealth of timely articles, original research, and essential industry news. The organization also publishes an annual review called "America's Best Architecture and Design Schools."

Directory of African-American Architects —
blackarch.uc.edu

The *Directory of African-American Architects* is maintained as a public service to promote an awareness of whom African American architects are and where they are located.

Emerging Professional's Companion (EPC) —
www.epcompanion.org

Launched in 2004, the EPC is an online internship resource for emerging professionals. Primarily intended as a means for interns to supplement and bolster their knowledge as soon-to-be-licensed architects and to earn IDP credit, the EPC can also be used by students to gain exposure to practice issues while still in school, or even as an accompaniment to co-op or part-time employment before they graduate.

Great Buildings Collection —
www.greatbuildings.com

Great Buildings is the leading architecture reference site on the web. This gateway to architecture around the world and across history documents a thousand buildings and hundreds of leading architects with photographic images and architectural drawings, integrated maps and timelines, 3D building models, commentaries, bibliographies, web links, and more, for famous designers and structures of all kinds.

InsideArch —
www.insidearch.org

The primary goal of InsideArch is to gather quantitative and qualitative information about the work, culture, and employee experience at architecture firms, to synthesize and present that information in a meaningful, valuable format so as to empower interns and architects to make career decisions more beneficial to themselves and the profession as a whole.

International Archive of Women in Architecture —
spec.lib.vt.edu/IAWA

The purpose of the International Archive of Women in Architecture is to document the history of women's involvement in architecture by collecting, preserving, storing, and making available to researchers the professional papers of women architects, landscape architects, designers, architectural historians and critics, and urban planners, as well as the records of women's architectural organizations from around the world.

Mentorship: A Journey in Collaborative Learning —
www.aia.org/professionals/mentors

Developed by the AIA, this resource provides insight into mentoring in the profession of architecture. It is for aspiring architects, educators, and practitioners of all experience levels who wish to discover the possibilities in a mentoring relationship.

Portfolio Design —
www.portfoliodesign.com

A companion to the ever popular publication by the same name, *Portfolio Design,* the website includes essential information on the digital and multimedia direction of portfolios today. Portfolio Design shows you how to assemble a portfolio that will display your talents and qualifications to the best advantage.

APPENDIX B

Accredited Architecture Programs in the United States and Canada

This list is up to date as of the publication date. For an up-to-date list, contact NAAB: www.naab.org.

ALABAMA

Auburn University
College of Architecture, Design and Construction
School of Architecture
Auburn University, AL
www.cadc.auburn.edu/soa
B.Arch.

Tuskegee University
College of Engineering, Architecture and Physical
 Sciences
Department of Architecture
Tuskegee, AL
www.tuskegee.edu/ceaps
B.Arch.

ALASKA

None

ARIZONA

Arizona State University
College of Architecture + Environmental Design
 School of Architecture and Landscape
 Architecture
Tempe, AZ
design.asu.edu
M.Arch.

**Arizona, University of College of Architecture and
Landscape Architecture**
School of Architecture
Tuscon, AZ
www.architecture.arizona.edu
B.Arch.

Frank Lloyd Wright School of Architecture
Scottsdale, AZ
www.taliesin.edu
M.Arch.

ARKANSAS

Arkansas, University of
School of Architecture
Fayetteville, AR
architecture.uark.edu
B.Arch.

CALIFORNIA

Academy of Art University
School of Architecture
San Francisco, CA
www.academyart.edu/architecture-school
M.Arch.

California at Berkeley, University of
College of Environmental Design
Department of Architecture
Berkeley, CA
arch.ced.berkeley.edu
M.Arch.

California at Los Angeles, University of (UCLA)
Department of Architecture and Urban Design
Los Angeles, CA
www.aud.ucla.edu
M.Arch.

California College of the Arts
School of Architecture
San Francisco, CA
www.cca.edu
B.Arch.; M.Arch.

California State Polytechnic University–Pomona
College of Environmental Design
Department of Architecture
Pomona, CA
www.csupomona.edu/~arc
B.Arch.; M.Arch.

California State Polytechnic University–San Luis Obispo
College of Architecture and Environmental Design
Architecture Department
San Luis Obispo, CA
www.arch.calpoly.edu
B.Arch.

New School of Architecture & Design
Architecture
San Diego, CA
www.newschoolarch.edu
B.Arch.; M.Arch.

Southern California Institute of Architecture (SCI-ARC)
Los Angeles, CA
www.sciarc.edu
B.Arch.; M.Arch.

Southern California, University of
School of Architecture
Los Angeles, CA
arch.usc.edu
B.Arch.; M.Arch.

Woodbury University
School of Architecture and Design
Burbank, CA
www.woodbury.edu
B.Arch.

COLORADO

Colorado at Denver, University of
College of Architecture and Planning
Denver, CO
www.cudenver.edu/aandp
M.Arch.

CONNECTICUT

Hartford, University of
College of Engineering, Technology, and Architecture
Department of Architecture
uhaweb.hartford.edu/architect
M.Arch.

Yale University
School of Architecture
New Haven, CT
www.architecture.yale.edu
M.Arch.

DELAWARE

None

DISTRICT OF COLUMBIA

The Catholic University of America
School of Architecture and Planning
Washington, DC
architecture.cua.edu
M.Arch.

Howard University
College of Engineering, Architecture, and Computer
    Science
School of Architecture and Planning
Washington, DC
www.howard.edu/ceacs/departments/architecture
B.Arch.

FLORIDA

Florida A&M University
School of Architecture
Tallahassee, FL
www.famusoa.net
B.Arch.; M.Arch.

Florida Atlantic University
College of Architecture, Urban and Public Affairs
School of Architecture
Ft Lauderdale, FL
www.fau.edu/arch
B.Arch.

Florida International University
College of Architecture + The Arts
School of Architecture
Miami, FL
soa.fiu.edu
M.Arch.

Florida, University of
College of Design, Construction and Planning
School of Architecture
Gainesville, FL
www.arch.ufl.edu
M.Arch.

Miami, University of
School of Architecture
Coral Gables, FL
www.arc.miami.edu
B.Arch.; M.Arch.

South Florida, University of
School of Architecture and Community Design
Tampa, FL
www.arch.usf.edu
M.Arch.

GEORGIA

Georgia Institute of Technology
College of Architecture
Architecture Program
Atlanta, GA
www.coa.gatech.edu/arch
M.Arch.

Savannah College of Arts and Design
Department of Architecture
Savannah, GA
www.scad.edu/architecture
M.Arch.

Southern Polytechnic State University
College of Architecture, Civil Engineering
    Technology and Construction
School of Architecture
Marietta, GA
architecture.spsu.edu
B.Arch.

HAWAII

Hawaii at Manoa, University of
School of Architecture
Honolulu, HI
www.arch.hawaii.edu
D.Arch.

IDAHO

Idaho, University of
College of Art and Architecture
Department of Architecture and Interior Design
Moscow, ID
www.caa.uidaho.edu/arch
M.Arch.

ILLINOIS

Illinois at Chicago, University of
College of Architecture and the Arts
School of Architecture
Chicago, IL
www.arch.uic.edu
M.Arch.

Illinois at Urbana-Champaign, University of
College of Fine and Applied Arts
School of Architecture
Champaign, IL
www.arch.uiuc.edu
M.Arch.

Illinois Institute of Technology
College of Architecture
Chicago, IL
www.iit.arch.edu
B.Arch.; M.Arch.

Judson University
School of Art, Design, and Architecture
Department of Architecture
Elgin, IL
www.judson-il.edu
M.Arch.

The School of the Art Institute of Chicago
Department of Architecture, Interior Design, and
    Designed Objects
Chicago, IL
www.saic.edu/degrees_resources/departments/
    aiado
M.Arch.–Candidate

Southern Illinois University Carbondale
College of Applied Sciences and Arts
School of Architecture
Carbondale, IL
www.siuc.edu/~arc_id
M.Arch.–Candidate

INDIANA

Ball State University
College of Architecture and Planning
Department of Architecture
Muncie, IN
www.bsu.edu/architecture
M.Arch.

Notre Dame, University of
School of Architecture
Notre Dame, IN
www.architecture.nd.edu
B.Arch.; M.Arch.

IOWA

Iowa State University
College of Design
Department of Architecture
Ames, IA
www.arch.iastate.edu
B.Arch.; M.Arch.

KANSAS

Kansas State University
College of Architecture, Planning, and Design
Department of Architecture
Manhattan, KS
www.capd.ksu.edu/arch
M.Arch.

Kansas, University of
School of Architecture and Urban Planning
Architecture Program
Lawrence, KS
www.saup.ku.edu
M.Arch.

KENTUCKY

Kentucky, University of
College of Design
School of Architecture
Lexington, KY
www.uky.edu/Design
M.Arch.

LOUISIANA

Louisiana at Lafayette, University of
College of the Arts
School of Architecture and Design
Lafayette, LA
soad.louisiana.edu
M.Arch.

Louisiana State University
College of Art and Design
School of Architecture
Baton Rouge, LA
www.design.lsu.edu/architecture.htm
B.Arch.; M.Arch.

Louisiana Tech University
College of Liberal Arts
School of Architecture
Ruston, LA
www.arch.latech.edu
M.Arch.

Southern University and A&M College
School of Architecture
Baton Rouge, LA
www.susa.subr.edu
B.Arch.

Tulane University
School of Architecture
New Orleans, LA
architecture.tulane.edu
M.Arch.

MAINE

None

MARYLAND

Maryland, University of
School of Architecture, Planning and Preservation
Architecture Program
College Park, MD
www.arch.umd.edu/architecture
M.Arch.

Morgan State University
Institute of Architecture and Planning
Baltimore, MD
www.morgan.edu/academics/IAP/index.html
M.Arch.

MASSACHUSETTS

Boston Architectural College
School of Architecture
Boston, MA
www.the-bac.edu
B.Arch.; M.Arch.

Harvard University
Graduate School of Design
Department of Architecture
Cambridge, MA
www.gsd.harvard.edu
M.Arch.

Massachusetts Amherst, University of
Department of Art, Architecture and Art History
Architecture + Design Program
Amherst, MA
www.umass.edu/architecture
M.Arch.

Massachusetts College of Art
Department of Art/Art History
Boston, MA
www.massart.edu
M.Arch.–Candidate

Massachusetts Institute of Technology
School of Architecture and Planning
Department of Architecture
Cambridge, MA
architecture.mit.edu
M.Arch.

Northeastern University
College of Arts and Sciences
School of Architecture
Boston, MA
www.architecture.neu.edu
M.Arch.

Wentworth Institute of Technology
Department of Architecture
Boston, MA
www.wit.edu/arch
M.Arch.

MICHIGAN

Andrews University
School of Architecture
Berrien Springs, MI
www.andrews.edu/arch
M.Arch.

Detroit Mercy, University of
School of Architecture
Detroit, MI
www.arch.udmercy.edu
M.Arch.

Lawrence Technological University
College of Architecture and Design
Department of Architecture
Southfield, MI
ltu.edu/architecture_and_design
M.Arch.

Michigan, University of
Taubman College of Architecture and Urban Planning
Ann Arbor, MI
www.tcaup.umich.edu/arch
M.Arch.

MINNESOTA

Minnesota, University of
College of Design
School of Architecture
Minneapolis, MN
arch.cdes.umn.edu
M.Arch.

MISSISSIPPI

Mississippi State University
College of Architecture, Art, and Design
School of Architecture
Mississippi State, MS
www.caad.msstate.edu/sarc
B.Arch.

MISSOURI

Drury College
Hammons School of Architecture
Springfield, MO
www.drury.edu
B.Arch.

Washington University in St. Louis
Sam Fox School of Design and Visual Arts
College of Architecture
St. Louis, MO
www.arch.wustl.edu
M.Arch.

MONTANA

Montana State University
College of Arts and Architecture
School of Architecture
Bozeman, MT
www.arch.montana.edu
M.Arch.

NEBRASKA

Nebraska-Lincoln, University of
College of Architecture
Department of Architecture
Lincoln, NE
architecture.unl.edu/programs/arch/
M.Arch.

NEVADA

Nevada-Las Vegas, University of
College of Fine Arts
School of Architecture
Las Vegas, NV
architecture.unlv.edu
M.Arch.

NEW HAMPSHIRE

None

NEW JERSEY

New Jersey Institute of Technology
School of Architecture
Newark, NJ
architecture.njit.edu
B.Arch.; M.Arch.

Princeton University
School of Architecture
Princeton, NJ
soa.princeton.edu
M.Arch.

NEW MEXICO

New Mexico, University of
School of Architecture and Planning
Architecture Program
Albuquerque, NM
saap.unm.edu
M.Arch.

NEW YORK

City College of The City University of New York
School of Architecture, Urban Design, and
    Landscape Architecture
Architecture Program
New York, NY
www1.ccny.cuny.edu/prospective/architecture
B.Arch.; M.Arch.

Columbia University
Graduate School of Architecture, Planning and
    Preservation
New York, NY
www.arch.columbia.edu
M.Arch.

The Cooper Union
Irwin S. Chanin School of Architecture
New York, NY
www.cooper.edu
B.Arch.

Cornell University
College of Architecture, Art, and Planning
Department of Architecture
Ithaca, NY
www.aap.cornell.edu/arch
B.Arch.; M.Arch.–Candidate

New York Institute of Technology
School of Architecture and Design
Old Westbury, NY
iris.nyit.edu/architecture
B.Arch.

Parsons School of Design
School of Constructed Environments
Department of Architecture, Interior Design, and
    Lighting
New York, NY
www2.parsons.edu/architecture
M.Arch.

Pratt Institute
School of Architecture
Brooklyn, NY
www.pratt.edu/arch
B.Arch.; M.Arch.

Rensselaer Polytechnic Institute
School of Architecture
Troy, NY
www.arch.rpi.edu
B.Arch.; M.Arch.

State University of New York at Buffalo
School of Architecture and Planning
Department of Architecture
Buffalo, NY
www.ap.buffalo.edu/architecture
M.Arch.

Syracuse University
School of Architecture
Syracuse, NY
soa.syr.edu
B.Arch.; M.Arch.

NORTH CAROLINA

North Carolina at Charlotte, University of
College of Arts + Architecture
School of Architecture
Charlotte, NC
www.coa.uncc.edu
B.Arch.; M.Arch.

North Carolina State University
College of Design
School of Architecture
Raleigh, NC
ncsudesign.org
B.Arch.; M.Arch.

NORTH DAKOTA

North Dakota State University
College of Engineering and Architecture
Department of Architecture and Landscape
    Architecture
Fargo, ND
ala.ndsu.edu
M.Arch.

OHIO

Cincinnati, University of
College of Design, Architecture, Art, and Planning
School of Architecture and Interior Design
Cincinnati, OH
www.daap.uc.edu/said
M.Arch.

Kent State University
College of Architecture and Environmental Design
Architecture Program
Kent, OH
www.saed.kent.edu
M.Arch.

Miami University
School of Fine Arts
Department of Architecture and Interior Design
Oxford, OH
www.muohio.edu/architecture
M.Arch.

Ohio State University
Austin E. Knowlton School of Architecture
Columbus, OH
knowlton.osu.edu
M.Arch.

OKLAHOMA

Oklahoma State University
College of Engineering, Architecture and
    Technology
School of Architecture
Stillwater, OK
architecture.ceat.okstate.edu
B.Arch.

Oklahoma, University of
College of Architecture
Division of Architecture
Norman, OK
arch.ou.edu
B.Arch.; M.Arch.

OREGON

Oregon, University of
School of Architecture and Allied Arts
Department of Architecture
Eugene, OR
architecture.uoregon.edu
B.Arch.; M.Arch.

Portland State University
School of Fine and Performing Arts
Department of Architecture
Portland, OR
www.pdx.edu/architecture
M.Arch.–Candidate

PENNSYLVANIA

Carnegie Mellon University
School of Fine Arts
School of Architecture
Pittsburgh, PA
www.arc.cmu.edu
B.Arch.

Drexel University
Antoinette Westphal College Media Arts and Design
Department of Architecture and Interiors
Philadelphia, PA
www.drexel.edu/westphal/architecture
B.Arch.

Pennsylvania State University
College of Arts and Architecture
School of Architecture and Landscape Architecture
Department of Architecture
University Park, PA
www.arch.psu.edu
B.Arch.

Pennsylvania, University of
School of Design
Department of Architecture
Philadelphia, PA
www.upenn.edu/gsfa/arch
M.Arch.

Philadelphia University
School of Architecture
Philadelphia, PA
www.philau.edu/schools/add
B.Arch.

Temple University
Tyler School of Art
Architecture Program
Philadelphia, PA
www.temple.edu/architecture
B.Arch.; M.Arch.

PUERTO RICO

Polytechnic University of Puerto Rico
The New School of Architecture
San Juan, PR
www.pupr.edu/arqpoli/homepage.htm
B.Arch.

Puerto Rico, Universidad de
Escuela de Arquitectura
San Juan, PR
archweb.uprrp.edu
M.Arch.

RHODE ISLAND

Rhode Island School of Design
Architecture + Design
Department of Architecture
Providence, RI
www.risd.edu
B.Arch.; M.Arch.

Roger Williams University
School of Architecture, Art, and Historic Preservation
Bristol, RI
www.rwu.edu/academics/schools/saahp
M.Arch.

SOUTH CAROLINA

Clemson University
College of Architecture, Arts and Humanities
School of Architecture
Clemson, SC
virtual.clemson.edu/caah/architecture
M.Arch.

SOUTH DAKOTA

None

TENNESSEE

Memphis, University of
Department of Architecture
Memphis, TN
architecture.memphis.edu
M.Arch. – Candidate

Tennessee-Knoxville, University of
College of Architecture and Design
School of Architecture
Knoxville, TN
www.arch.utk.edu
B.Arch.; M.Arch.

TEXAS

Houston, University of
Gerald D. Hines College of Architecture
Houston, TX
www.arch.uh.edu
B.Arch.; M.Arch.

Prairie View A&M University
School of Architecture
Prairie View, TX
www.pvamu.edu
M.Arch.

Rice University
School of Architecture
Houston, TX
www.arch.rice.edu
B.Arch.; M.Arch.

Texas A&M University
College of Architecture
Department of Architecture
College Station, TX
archone.tamu.edu/college
M.Arch.

Texas at Arlington, University of
School of Architecture
Architecture Program
Arlington, TX
www.uta.edu/architecture
M.Arch.

Texas at Austin, University of
School of Architecture
Austin, TX
soa.utexas.edu
B.Arch.; M.Arch.

Texas at San Antonio, University of
College of Architecture
Architecture Program
San Antonio, TX
www.utsa.edu/architecture
M.Arch.

Texas Tech University
College of Architecture
Lubbock, TX
www.arch.ttu.edu/architecture
M.Arch.

UTAH

Utah, University of
College of Architecture and Planning
School of Architecture
Salt Lake City, UT
www.arch.utah.edu
M.Arch.

VIRGINIA

Hampton University
School of Engineering and Technology
Department of Architecture
Hampton, VA
www.hamptonu.edu/academics/schools/
   engineering
M.Arch.

Virginia Tech
College of Architecture and Urban Studies
School of Architecture + Design
Blacksburg, VA
www.archdesign.vt.edu
B.Arch.; M.Arch.

Virginia, University of
School of Architecture
Charlottesville, VA
www.arch.virginia.edu/architecture
M.Arch.

VERMONT

Norwich University
School of Architecture and Art
Northfield, VT
www.norwich.edu
M.Arch.

WASHINGTON

Washington, University of
College of Architecture and Urban Planning
Department of Architecture
Seattle, WA
www.arch.washington.edu
M.Arch.

Washington State University
College of Architecture and Engineering
School of Architecture and Construction
   Management
Pullman, WA
www.arch.wsu.edu
M.Arch.

WEST VIRGINIA

None

WISCONSIN

Wisconsin-Milwaukee, University of
School of Architecture and Urban Planning
Department of Architecture
Milwaukee, WI
www.uwm.edu/SARUP//architecture
M.Arch.

WYOMING

None

INTERNATIONAL

American University of Sharjah
School of Architecture and Design
P.O. Box 26666
Sharjah UAE
www.aus.edu/arcdes/arc/index.php
B.Arch.–Candidate

CANADA

This list is up to date as of the publication date. For an up-to-date list, contact CACB-CCCA: www.cacb-ccca.ca.

British Columbia, University of
School of Architecture + Landscape Architecture
Vancouver, British Columbia
www.arch.ubc.ca
M.Arch.

Calgary, University of
Faculty of Environmental Design
Calgary, Alberta
www.ucalgary.ca/evds
M.Arch.

Carleton University
The Azrieli School of Architecture and Urbanism
Ottawa, Ontario
www.arch.carleton.ca
M.Arch.

Dalhousie University
Faculty of Architecture and Planning
Halifax, Nova Scotia
www.dal.ca/architecture
M.Arch.

Laval Université
School of Architecture
Quebec, Quebec
www.arc.ulaval.ca
M.Arch.

Manitoba, University of
Faculty of Architecture
Winnipeg, Manitoba
umanitoba.ca/faculties/architecture
M.Arch.

McGill University
School of Architecture
Montreal, Quebec
www.mcgill.ca/arch
M.Arch.

Montreal, Université de
School of Architecture
Montreal, Quebec
www.arc.umontreal.ca
M.Arch.

Toronto, University of
John H. Daniels Faculty of Architecture, Landscape and Design
Toronto, Ontario
www.daniels.utoronto.ca
M.Arch.

Waterloo, University of
School of Architecture
Waterloo, Ontario
www.architecture.uwaterloo.ca
M.Arch.

APPENDIX C
Career Profiles

This list is up to date as of the publication date. For an up-to-date list, contact NAAB: www.naab.org.

Kathryn H. Anthony, Ph.D.
Professor
School of Architecture
Department of Landscape Architecture
Gender and Women's Studies Program
University of Illinois at Urbana-Champaign
Champaign, Illinois

F. Michael Ayles, AIA
Principal, Business Development
Antinozzi Associates
Bridgeport, Connecticut

Robert M. Beckley, FAIA
Professor and Dean Emeritus
Taubman College of Architecture and Urban Planning
University of Michigan
Ann Arbor, Michigan

Joseph Bilello, Ph.D., AIA
Professor and Former Dean
College of Architecture and Planning
Ball State University
Muncie, Indiana

Diane Blair Black, AIA
Vice-President
RTKL Associates Inc.
Baltimore, Maryland

H. Alan Brangman, AIA
University Architect
Georgetown University
Washington, DC

William J. Carpenter, Ph.D., FAIA
Associate Professor
School of Architecture, Civil Engineering Technology and Construction
Southern Polytechnic State University
Marietta, Georgia

President
Lightroom
Decatur, Georgia

Barbara Crisp
Principal
bcrisp llc
Tempe, Arizona

Margaret W. DeLeeuw
Marketing Director
Celli-Flynn Brennan Architects & Planners
Pittsburgh, Pennsylvania

Kathy Denise Dixon, AIA, NOMA
Associate Principal
Arel Architects, Inc.
Clinton, Maryland

Catherine McNeel Florreich, Associate AIA
Architectural Intern
Eley Guild Hardy Architects PA
Jackson, Mississippi

Thomas Fowler, IV, AIA
Professor and Director, Collaborative Integrative-
Interdisciplinary Digital-Design Studio (CIDS),
College of Architecture and Environmental Design
California Polytechnic State University–San Luis
Obispo, California

Robert D. Fox, AIA, IIDA
Principal
FOX Architects
McLean, Virginia/Washington, DC

Douglas Garofalo, FAIA
Professor
School of Architecture
University of Illinois–Chicago
Chicago, Illinois

President, Garofalo Architects, Inc.
Chicago, Illinois

Lynsey Jane Gemmell, AIA
Project Manager/Associate
Holabird & Root
Chicago, Illinois

Marisa Gomez
Bachelor of Science Candidate
Maryland, University of
College Park, Maryland

Christopher J. Gribbs, Associate AIA
Senior Director, Convention
The American Institute of Architects
Washington, DC

David R. Groff
Master of Architecture Candidate
Virginia Tech–Washington Alexandria Architecture
Center
Alexandria, Virginia

Michelle Hunter
Project Architect/Project Manager
Mark Gould Architect
New York, New York

Jennifer Jaramillo
Architectural Intern
Dekker/Perich/Sabatini, LLC
Albuquerque, New Mexico

Ahkilah Z. Johnson
Chief of Staff Investment Services
Cherokee Investment Partners
East Rutherford, New Jersey

Carolyn G. Jones, AIA
Director
Callison
Seattle, Washington

Elizabeth Kalin
Architectural Intern
Studio Gang Architects
Chicago, Illinois

Grace H. Kim, AIA
Principal and Cofounder
Schemata Workshop, Inc.
Seattle, Washington

Nathan Kipnis, AIA
Principal
Nathan Kipnis Architects, Inc.
Evanston, Illinois

Shannon Kraus, AIA, MBA
Vice-President
HKS Architects
Dallas, Texas

Mary Kay Lanzillotta, FAIA
Partner
Hartman-Cox Architects
Washington, DC

Jessica L. Leonard, Associate AIA, LEED AP
Campus Planner/Intern Architect
Ayers Saint Gross Architects and Planners
Baltimore, Maryland

Clark E. Llewellyn, AIA, NCARB
Dean
School of Architecture
University of Hawaii at Manoa
Honolulu, Hawaii

Courtney Miller-Bellairs
Assistant Director/Senior Lecturer
Architecture Program, University of Maryland
College Park, Maryland

Wayne A. Mortenson, Associate AIA, NASW
Project Manager/Urban Designer
H3 Studio
St. Louis, Missouri

Lecturer
Washington University
St. Louis, Missouri

John W. Myefski, AIA
Principal
Myefski Cook Architects, Inc.
Glencoe, Illinois

Patricia Saldana Natke, AIA
Principal and President
Urban Works, Ltd.
Chicago, Illinois

Casius Pealer, J.D.
Assistant General Counsel (Real Estate)
District of Columbia Housing Authority
Washington, DC

Kathryn T. Prigmore, FAIA
Senior Project Manager
HDR Architecture Inc.
Alexandria, Virginia

Tamara Redburn, AIA, LEED AP
Project Architect
Fleming Associates Architects, P.C.
Memphis, Tennessee

Robert D. Roubik, AIA, LEED AP
Project Architect
Antunovich Associates Architects and Planners
Chicago, Illinois

Elva Rubio
Executive Vice President, Creative Director
Bruce Mau Designs
Chicago, Illinois

W. Stephen Saunders, AIA
Principal
Eckenhoff Saunders Architects, Inc.
Chicago, Illinois

Edward J. Shannon, AIA
Director of Design
Benvenuti & Stein Design, LLC
Winnetka, Illinois

Lynn N. Simon, AIA, LEED AP
President
Simon & Associates, Inc.
San Francisco, California

Lisa A. Swan
Residential Designer
Design Forward
Pasadena, California

Ambassador Richard N. Swett (r), FAIA
President
Swett Associates, Inc.
Concord, New Hampshire

Margaret R. Tarampi, Associate AIA
Doctor of Philosophy Candidate
University of Utah
Salt Lake City, Utah

Eric Taylor, Associate AIA
Photographer
Taylor Design & Photography, Inc.
Fairfax Station, Virginia

Randall J. Tharp, R.A.
Senior Vice-President
A. Epstein and Sons International, Inc.
Chicago, Illinois

Lois Thibault, R.A.
Coordinator of Research
U.S. Architectural and Transportation Barriers Compliance Board (Access Board)
Washington, DC

Max Underwood, AIA
Professor of Architecture
School of Architecture and Landscape Architecture
Herberger Institute for Design and the Arts
Arizona State University
Tempe, Arizona

Allison Wilson
Bachelor of Science Graduate
University of Maryland
College Park, Maryland

Amy Yurko, AIA
Founder/Director
BrainSpaces
Chicago, Illinois

Brad Zuger
Architectural Designer
Shanghai MADA S.P.A.M.
Shanghai, P. R. China

INDEX